THE GROWTH
OF
AMERICA
1878–1928

by
Clarence B. Carson

D1565929

Other Books
by
Clarence B. Carson

The Fateful Turn
The American Tradition
The Flight from Reality
The War on the Poor
Throttling the Railroads
The Rebirth of Liberty
The World in the Grip of an Idea
Organized Against Whom? The
    Labor Union in America
The Colonial Experience
The Beginning of the Republic
The Sections and the Civil War

A Basic History of the United States—Book IV

THE GROWTH OF AMERICA 1878–1928

by
Clarence B. Carson

Beth A. Hoffman
Editorial Consultant

American Textbook Committee
P.O. Box 8
Wadley, Alabama 36276

Grateful acknowledgment is hereby made to Dover Publications for permission to use an extensive number of portraits from *Dictionary of American Portraits*, edited by Hayward and Blanche Cirker and published by Dover Publications, Inc.

Sixth Printing, January 1991

Contents

Chapter 1

Introduction

The main theme of this book is the growth and development of the United States: the filling out of the country by the settlement of the West, the subduing of the Western Indians, the building of the transcontinental railroads and the linking of the parts of the country to one another by a network of railroads, the development of nationwide businesses, the growth of the corporate mode of organizing the production and distribution of goods, the large-scale influx of immigrants, the rise of the city to a prominent place in America, and the development of large financial institutions. During the years from the 1870s through the 1920s, the United States also assumed an increasingly influential role in international affairs. Within little more than a century of coming into being, the United States had grown from a few colonies remote from the centers of world trade and power in Europe into an industrial and agricultural colossus. Both American agricultural and industrial products were competing for their share of world markets.

On the world scene, Great Britain was the leading naval and commercial power in the 19th century. From the 1820s onward Britain ceased to be a threat to the United States and became instead a great influence for freedom in the world. The British began to abandon mercantilistic policies in the 1820s, and by the 1850s were wholeheartedly committed to free trade. Britain's parliamentary government and constitutional monarchy served as a model for country after country in Europe, and was being imitated in other places in the world as well. Broadly speaking, the 19th century was the great age of expanding freedom, and quite often Britain was in the forefront. Population increased rapidly in many lands, but the prosperity which resulted from the spread of free trade and less restricted enterprise was more widespread than ever. Many things undoubtedly contributed to British pre-eminence, but the central one is the liberty to manage their own affairs which the people enjoyed. An English historian has noted that

> Until August 1914 a sensible law-abiding Englishman could pass through life and hardly notice the existence of the state, beyond the post office and the policeman. He could live where he liked and as he liked. He had no official number or identity card. He could travel abroad or leave his country forever without a passport of any sort of official permission. He could exchange his money for any other currency without restriction or limit. He could buy goods from any country in the world on the same terms as he bought goods at

1

home. . . . An Englishman could enlist, if he chose, in the regular army, the navy, or the territorials. He could also ignore, if he chose, the demands of national defense. Substantial householders were occasionally called on for jury service. Otherwise, only those helped the state who wished to do so. The Englishman paid taxes on a modest scale. . . .[1]

British commerical supremacy had a worthy competitor in the United States by or before the end of the 19th century. And British parliamentary government and constitutional monarchy was challenged by the republican government and presidential system of the United States as a political system to be imitated by those seeking free institutions. Indeed, republican government as practiced in the United States had so far proved its worth that opposition to it by monarchists was no longer of any great significance. America, too, was a land of extensive freedom, individual liberty, and prosperity. The superiority of both systems as they limited government and freed men was widely acclaimed.

The material prosperity of the latter part of the 19th century provided the framework within which the Idea of Progress gained sway over the minds of many in Europe, and especially in the United States. The Idea of Progress refers primarily to the belief that things are getting better generally and, more broadly, that improvement with the passage of time is a virtual law of the universe. Much evidence appeared to support this belief in the latter part of the 19th century, particularly on the material side. New discoveries and inventions abounded; sanitation and health facilities were clearly improving; population was increasing, perhaps as never before in history; and people generally had the means for producing and had a greater variety of goods available than ever before. Indeed, this variety and abundance continued to increase into the 20th century, but before long other sorts of development began to cast doubt upon the universality of progress.

The Idea of Progress was not new to the 19th century. It had been around since the 17th century, at the latest, and more and more people championed it in the 18th century. Modern thinkers even ceased to believe that even the ancient Greeks were their superiors. The Idea of Progress was mightily bolstered by the material improvements and expansion of information in the 19th century, and by the 20th century was widely accepted by people generally. At its simplest level, it translated into the view that the latest is the best, or, as the French publicist of the 1920s, Emil Coué, put it "Every day in every way, we are getting better and better." By the 1920s, too, American automobile makers were taking advantages of the popular idea and bringing out new models annually, each year's model presumably an improvement over that of the preceding year. More deeply, the Idea of Progress got intellectual support from the idea of evolution which gained sway in the 19th century. This was especially the case with the Darwinian conception of the survival of the fittest. If the fittest survive in the struggle for survival, it would appear to tend to make some sort of progress inevitable. In any case, the Idea of Progress enjoyed great vogue in the midst of the growth and expansion of America in the late 19th and early 20th century.

Granted that the theme of growth is the dominant one in this book, however, there are a good many important subthemes that emerge as well. New currents of ideas were emerging which would eventually challenge the dominent developments. Even as governments were being restricted and free men were demonstrating what they could do, the foundations of this order were coming under attack and a new outlook was coming to the fore. If, as is sometimes claimed, the ideas of one century are applied in the next, then it should not surprise us that there were new currents in the 19th century that would sweep all before them in many lands in the 20th century. There is abundant evidence that this was the case. Moreover, new developments cast doubt on the progressive course of history. The 20th century was hardly underway before much of the world was locked in a titanic conflict which we call World War I. In its wake came a new despotism: totalitarian governments with all power concentrated in a central government, governments which used modern devices to spread the tentacles of power more deeply into the lives of people than had been the case in the past. The hallmarks of the 20th century have been unleashed government power, total war, concentration camps, vast propaganda efforts and brainwashing by those in power, and government efforts to control everything both within and outside their borders. Another face of these developments has been government-engendered terrorism, both on their own peoples and those in other lands.

Indeed, the seeds of such practices were sown in the 19th century. It is not too much to say that 19th century thinkers sowed the wind, and the 20th century has reaped the whirlwind. Looked at in one way, evolutionary theories gave great impetus to the Idea of Progress. But from another angle, they tended to undercut the very foundations of individual liberty, limited government, and the bases of freedom and responsibility. The theory of natural law was abandoned by some thinkers, and with it the natural rights on which individual rights were based in the United States. (That does not necessarily mean that people ceased to believe in rights, but they tended to attribute them to other sources than nature and nature's God—usually government.)

A great wave of materialism swept through intellectual circles, and, supported by evolutionary theories, thinkers began to conceive of natural law as an active force rather than as neutral laws imbedded in the nature of the universe. Above all, evolutionary hypotheses were used in an attempt to explain the origin of life and of man without requiring or having a creative and providential God. On this view, man arose from nature and was wholly a natural being, not a special being created by God to have dominion over the earth. Naturalistic explanations of all sorts of things became commonplace, a point that will be developed in its place.

The full impact of these hypotheses and theories were not felt in the 19th century. For one thing, those who advanced these theories did not have the power to impose their ideas on people usually. For another, those thinkers greatly influenced by these ideas, or who originated them, were by no means in agreement as to their significance or how they were to be applied. The materialistic and evolutionary ideas were interpreted by some as meaning that man was caught in the grip of natural forces which determined his conduct. He was powerless, in this view, to alter the course of development. On the other hand, some thought that in a universe without God man could do all things. The central belief to come out of this attitude was the belief that men working together could build a utopia. Indeed, utopianism undergirds many of the social and political beliefs of the 20th century.

The main point here, however, is that the seeds of the 20th century developments are to be found in the intellectual currents of the 19th century. The fruits of these seeds have often been such things as the massive uses of governmental power, uses based on naturalism, revolution, evolution, and a host of particular theories either for forcing men into the current of "progress" or remaking him. In the two decades before World War I, both Republican and Democratic parties, or at least their leaders, were shifting toward the belief in much more concentration of power in the federal government and its use more extensively. World War I was a fertile ground for those interested in ways to extend and totalize government power. The Bolshevik Revolution in Russia, getting underway just before World War I came to a close, was the brainchild of Karl Marx who lived in the 19th century. Very shortly, another totalitarian state had been formed in Italy, and in another decade Hitler was bringing his Nazi dictatorship to Germany. Totalitarianism was on the march, and it was being widely touted as the wave of the future.

During the period covered by this book, the United States was usually on the periphery of these undercurrents of ideas and developments. In significant ways, America was set apart from Europe. Americans were less cynical than Europeans, did not suffer so much from World War I, were more optimistic, and less inclined to turn to extreme measures or adopt radical ideas. The instabilities of central and eastern Europe, as well as France, were not present in the United States, and it was these instabilities that paved the way for totalitarian solutions. Americans generally were still very much under the sway of the belief that they were progressing and would continue to progress under their constitutional system, nor did they waver much from this belief until after 1928. Indeed, rarely, if ever before had Americans enjoyed such widespread and expansive prosperity as in the

1920s. And all about them were new inventions and devices which heralded progress: the radio, electric refrigerators, automobiles, motion pictures, and a great bounty of other goods. Americans generally were more disposed to insulate themselves from Europe than to copy the dismal political systems taking hold there.

Even so, America was not shut off from the currents of ideas and movements which had produced these developments in Europe. On the contrary, many of them had begun to have an impact in America even before the 1920s. Thus, while the growth and development of America is the overarching theme of this book, the undercurrent of ideas and movement which would erode the foundations will occupy our attention as well. Nor should it be forgotten that while change is more dramatic and often occupies the center of the stage, much changes very slowly, if at all.

Chapter 2
Economic Growth

To make a ton of steel one and a half tons of iron stone has to be mined, transported by a rail a hundred miles to the lakes, carried by boat hundreds of miles, transferred to cars, transported by rail one hundred and fifty miles to Pittsburgh. . . . How then could steel be manufactured and sold without loss at three pounds for two cents? This, I confess, seemed to me incredible . . . but it was so.

—Andrew Carnegie

Modern society has created a class of artificial beings who bid fair soon to be the masters of their creator. . . . Everywhere. . . , they illustrate the truth of the old maxim of the common law, that corporations have no souls. . . . The system of corporate life and corporate power . . . tends always to development—always to consolidation—it is ever grasping new powers. . . .

—Charles Francis Adams

No percentage of the profits of the Standard Oil Company came from advantages given by railroads at any time. . . . The advantages to the Standard from low freight rates consisted solely in the increased volume of its business arising from the low prices of its products.

—John D. Rockefeller

Chronology

1852—Invention of the elevator.

1856—Bessemer process of making steel introduced.

1859—Oil discovered in Pennsylvania.

1864—Pullman sleeping car constructed.

1867—Practical typewriter developed.

1869—First transcontinental railroad completed.

1872—Improved air brake built.

1874—Invention of electrically powered street car.

1875—Tariff Act.

1876—Battle of Little Bighorn.

1878—Bland-Allison Act.

1879—Edison invents incandescent light bulb.

1881—Standard Oil Trust formed.

Generally speaking, politics did not occupy the center of the stage very often from the middle of the 1870s to the mid-1890s. Of the Presidents during these years, only one—Grover Cleveland—served two terms, and none of them captured the imagination of the American people very strongly. Nor did any great debates in Congress galvanize the American people. This should not be taken to mean that these were not lively days in America; they were indeed. But politics was not in the ascendant, which is rarely hardly to be lamented.

Rather than politicians, it was an age of inventors, entrepreneurs, speculators, daring investors, and builders—of Thomas A. Edison, John D. Rockefeller, Andrew Carnegie, James J. Hill, Leland Stanford, Jim Fisk, George Pullman, and P. T. Barnum. It was an age of growth, of the growth of the cities, of the filling out of the West, of the development of great businesses, and industrial expansion. It was such economic expansion as had never before occurred in America, if it had anywhere. America moved from whale oil to kerosene to electricity for lighting, from the use of wood and iron to steel in construction, from the horsedrawn carriage to the electrically propelled street car for city transportation, and shifted from a predominantly rural toward an urbanized country.

Much of this change occurred swiftly; the old was replaced by the new nearly as soon as the technology was available. Often, the changes were propulsively introduced, growth occurred by leaps and bounds, and plans were executed almost as quickly as they were conceived. The pace of change was sometimes so quick that recent improvements were outmoded before they could be exploited. The telegraph lines had hardly been strung before they were being outdated by the telephone. Steam power had hardly reached full utilization before it began to be replaced with electricity, and hard on the heels of this came the internal combustion engine fired with gasoline. The swiftness of changes in technology were on a scale that never occurred before in history.

The development of the railroads illustrates both the great growth and the swiftness of so much of the change. As recently as 1840, say, some had feared that the human could not withstand exposure to such speeds as 30 miles per hour. In 1893, a New York Central locomotive traveled at the speed of 120 miles per hour! The following figures indicate the rapidity of the railroad building: the rail mileage in the country in 1866 was approximately 37,000 miles; by 1880, it had grown to 93,000, and by 1890 to 163,500 miles. Mileage continued to increase until in 1910 it stood at over 250,000 miles, and except for the Rocky Mountains there were few places in the country more than a few miles from a railroad track. As building feats, the transcontinental railroads were among the wonders of the world. James J. Hill built his Great Northern route through the Rockies in less time than it would take nowadays to get the approval of governmental bodies for such a project. Technological changes came swiftly to aid railroading: the telegraph to make the use of single track lines by numerous trains practical; cheap steel which could withstand the battering of heavy trains; the air brake which made it possible to stop long trains within short distances.

None of the growth was more dramatic than that of the railroads, but there was much that paralleled it or followed in its wake. Before telling of these, however, it will be helpful to examine the conditions within which this growth and development occurred.

James J. Hill (1838–1916)

Photograph by Pach Brothers

Hill was a railroad builder and magnate. He was born in Ontario province in Canada, but eventually settled in St. Paul, Minnesota. He began work in a village store at the age of 14 and eventually got involved in transportation as a clerk in a steamboat company. His earliest interest was in river transportation between Minnesota and Canada, but his future lay with the railroad, as did that of the country. He joined with other investors to buy the St. Paul and Pacific railroad, a company operating in Minnesota, and this road became the nucleus for his vast Great Northern system. The Great Northern reached from Lake Superior to the Puget Sound on the Pacific, was a landmark for free enterprise in transcontinental railroad building because he received no government aid, and was remarkably successful for such undertakings. Hill was known as the "Empire Builder" of the Northwest for his contribution to railroad building in that region.

Conditions of Growth and Development

Some historians have attempted to explain the economic growth of the latter part of the 19th century as being the result of the stimulation provided initially by the Civil War. They usually emphasize the great demand by the Union Army for goods during the war and the expansion by manufacturers to fill it. In the course of doing this, some large businesses emerged, meatpacking, for example, and some entrepreneurs accumulated fortunes. In 1865, Senator John Sherman of Ohio wrote his brother, General William T. Sherman, "The truth is," he said, "the close of the war with our resources unimpaired gives an elevation, a scope to the leading capitalists, far higher than anything ever undertaken before. They talk of millions as confidently as formerly of thousands."[2] One history text, for example, says: "In the economic history of the United States the Civil War was extremely important . . . In the North it speeded the Industrial Revolution and the development of capitalism by the prosperity which it brought to industry."[3]

On the other hand, there is considerable evidence that the Civil War may have actually retarded some industrial development. Economic growth in general and the development of manufacturing in particular was well underway before the Civil War. The general statistics indicate that growth was not nearly so great in the decade 1860–1869 as it had been for the past two decades.[4] Moreover, war is generally an economically wasteful undertaking, and certainly the Civil War was highly destructive. That is not to say that war demand did not stimulate some enterprises and bring profit to their investors. Surely, it did. Other industries, however, were probably retarded. But the Southern economy was devastated by the war and Reconstruction; any gains in the North were offset by these. During the late sixties and early seventies agricultural production in the South was far below what it had been before the war. The destruction of cotton gins, factories, and other equipment, such as that of railroads, left the South in much worse condition at the end of the war than at the beginning. Moreover, the capital investment in slaves was wiped out by the uncompensated abolition of slavery. The South was a capital-poor region for the remainder of the century.

Even so, there were developments during the Civil War that did give impetus to some kinds of economic growth, particularly to manufacturing and transportation. The Republican Party, which dominated the government, was favorably disposed to promoting manufacturing, transportation, and the settlement of the lands west of the Mississippi. Domestic manufacturing was promoted by the protective tariff, which was not only raised to high levels during the war but also was kept high (with brief reductions from time to time) for the rest of the 19th century. So far as the tariff was successful, it tended to reduce the importation of manufactured goods and make it much easier for American manufacturers to compete with those that did come in. In general, the protective tariff benefited manufacturing, but not farming, trade, or sea transport. There was little world competition in the domestic market for farm goods produced in quantity in America. Moreover, farmers, and other consumers, were hurt by the tariff to the extent that they had to pay higher prices for manufactured goods. Since the protective tariff tended to discourage foreign trade, it also reduced the foreign market for American farm products.

The federal government promoted the development of transportation as well as manufacturing. It did this mainly by providing grants and subsidies, or loans, in the building of the railroads. Large acreages of land were granted by the federal government for the building of railroads in the West. The largest grants were made to such transcontinental roads as the Union Pacific and Central Pacific. Generally, the government granted unoccupied land on either side of the projected lines, in alternate sections. That is, the government kept one section and granted one to the railroad alternately. That way, as the value of the land appreciated (rose), the government could benefit by the rise in price due to the building of the railroads. The federal government also secured loans to aid in the building of some of the railroads, permitted the railroads to exercise the right of eminent domain to acquire privately owned lands, and extended the privilege of cutting timber on government lands for construction purposes. The main period of these grants of land and loans was from the mid-1860s to the early 1870s. For a time, then, the federal government promoted the building of railroads vigorously, mainly in the West.

Both federal and state governments promoted the concentration of wealth and its deployment in business enterprises in a variety of ways. The federal government facilitated the private concentration of wealth in several ways, especially during the Civil War. One was in the way it went into debt to finance the war. The federal government issued a large number of Greenbacks (paper money) which it caused to circulate as money by making them legal tender for most purposes. These Greenbacks declined in value in relation to gold or other specie. Second, government bonds were sold, and the interest on them was payable in specie. It was possible, then, to buy the bonds with Greenbacks, which were worth much less than their face value, draw interest in gold, and possibly have them redeemed later in much more valuable money. Thus, bondholders might be enriched.

The other major means by which the federal government aided concentration of wealth was by the national banking system set up in 1864. Banks by receiving deposits are by their nature devices for concentrating wealth. As they make business loans and investments they also foster various kinds of enterprises. The National Bank Act, and supplementary legislation, gave the national banks a monopoly of the issuance of paper money currency, since notes (paper money) issued by state banks were subjected to a 10 per cent tax. On the other hand, the national banks were used by the federal government as devices for obtaining loans. National banks were required to back their paper money issues with government bonds equal in value to the bank notes issued. This national currency was supposed to be issued throughout the United States on the basis of population, but actually it was concentrated in New England and the northeastern states more generally. Thus, monetary holdings tended to be concentrated in those areas where industrialization was being most vigorously pushed.

States facilitated the concentration of wealth for business enterprises particularly by authorizing limited liability corporations. The business corporation came into being as a device for concentrating wealth to provide capital for various undertakings. The corporation promotes such concentration by offering limited liability to investors in organizations which have a corporate charter. Limited liability makes investment less hazardous than it would otherwise be. Ordinarily, the owner of a business is individually liable (legally responsible) both for all the debts of the business and for any injury done to others in the conduct of the business. These liabilities also usually extend to each member of a partnership. By contrast, investors in a corporation are commonly liable only for the actual amount of their investment and, unless they serve the corporation in a managerial capacity, have no direct liability for injury done to others in the conduct of the business. Moreover, ownership consists in shares in the corporation, which shareholders may sell at will. Organized stock exchanges, such as the New York Stock Exchange, provide a ready market for such buying and selling. Thus, the limited liability corporation encourages investment and the concentration of capital because the owners need not concern themselves with the running of the business, are not liable as investors beyond the amount of their investment, and can usually dispose of their shares as they choose.

The limited liability corporation was authorized by states in the early years of the Republic as a special privilege to investors to encourage them to invest in companies engaged in some project, such as bridge or road building, which governments supposed to be needed for the public benefit. They were usually authorized by special acts of state legislatures, and limited liability was such an asset for those seeking capital that it was sought as a special privilege and advantage. The Jacksonians attacked it as a special privilege, and legislatures in the 1840s and 1850s began to pass general incorporation laws, making it possible to incorporate simply by filing the necessary papers with the appropriate state authorities. When that change had been made, incorporation ceased to be a special privilege, but retained its advantages over other forms of organization. So it was that the states made available a device for the concentration and deployment of wealth in business enterprise. Incorporation was ever more widely used after the Civil War.

In a variety of ways, then, governments gave positive encouragement to enterprises after the Civil War, especially in manufacturing and transportation, but also in the settlement of the West. These government actions provided a part of the framework of this Age of Enterprise, as it has been called, but not all. America was also free of most restraints on productive activity; there were few government regulations to be complied with, except in banking. With the abolition of slavery, all the inhabitants of the country were usually free to dispose of their labor as they would and to get the rewards from it. As the zeal to make over the South lessened, property was generally secure, and by the 1880s the Federal courts signified their intent to protect the property of corporations as well as individuals against intrusions which violated the Fourteenth Amendment.

There was yet another factor in the economic growth of the United States during this period. It could be called the spirit of enterprise: the drive to build, to make companies grow, to succeed, to get ahead. Undergirding this spirit was the belief that this was a land of opportunity, that if a man would apply himself diligently he stood a good chance of getting ahead, prospering, even becoming wealthy. Indeed, men did go from poverty to riches sometimes, and there was a literature and a lore, containing both fact and fiction, encouraging efforts to forge ahead. Horace Greeley said, "Young men, I would have you believe that success in life is within the reach of every one who will truly and nobly seek it." Or, as Russell Conwell put it in his popular work, *Acres of Diamonds*: "To secure wealth is an honorable ambition, and is one great test of a person's usefulness to others. . . . I say, get rich, get rich! But get money honestly, or it will be a withering curse." The British writer, Samuel Smiles, whose numerous books were read in America as well as Britain, emphasized the importance of the individual and of individual striving. "'Heaven helps those who help themselves' is a well tried maxim," he said, "embodying in a small compass the results of vast human experience. The spirit of self-help is the root of all genuine growth in the individual; and, exhibited in the lives of many, it constitutes the true source of national vigor and strength. Help from without is often enfeebling in its effects, but help from within invariably invigorates."[5]

Nor should there be any doubt that many Americans took these admonitions to heart. Men built factories, bridged rivers, crossed mountains, brought land under cultivation, and sought in hundreds of ways to improve and better their condition. Some hoped to grasp wealth quickly, of course, and they rushed to those places where gold, silver, or other mineral wealth had been discovered. Others were more plodding in their quest, breaking the sod and irrigating prairie land to make it grow food. But whatever path they followed, either to sustain themselves or to prosper, there should be little doubt that Americans generally were busily trying to help themselves.

On the matter of government involvement, it should be noted that the government actions described above, such as land grants and loans to some railroads, the protective tariff, national banks, issuance of Greenbacks, and others, were, in effect, government intervention in the economy. While they promoted some kinds of economic development, such as rail transportation and manufacturing, they retarded others, such as foreign trade and water transport. Government intervention produces distortions in an economy, makes for uneven and often wasteful development, sets the stage for booms and busts, tends to enrich some and impoverish others. During and immediately after the war, the federal government greatly increased the money supply with Greenbacks and national bank notes. However, as the federal government began to retire its bonds in the 1870s, the banks began also to reduce the bank notes in circulation. In addition, the government began to redeem the Greenbacks. The result was a reduction of the money supply, a deflation, and a depression. Some railroads were in bad shape, too, during this period, attributable in some measure to overbuilding fostered by government. Many of the economic difficulties of these years, which will be reviewed later, can be traced back to these government interventions.

Development of Nationwide Business

A major development in the economic growth in the United States after the Civil War was large nationwide businesses. Prior to the war, most businesses had been relatively small and had catered to local or, at most, regional customers. Indeed, until a decade or so before the war, most goods, except specialty items had been made in the home or on the farm. What set the stage for the major change was inventions and developments in technology. The development of rail transportation, regular and fast mail delivery by trains, and even swifter communication by telegraph, made nationwide businesses feasible. Government promotion of closer national connections gave impetus to national businesses. The national banks provided a more convenient, though less stable, national currency than had coins or precious metals. And certainly, the national bank notes provided a better national medium of exchange than did the notes of state banks. The concentrations of wealth achieved by using the corporate device provided the financial structure of many of these large businesses.

The railroads were among the largest of large businesses themselves. With their hundreds, and sometimes thousands, of miles of track, numerous locomotives, boxcars, switching equipment, passenger cars, stations and freight depots, and reserves of wood and coal for fuel, they often represented huge capital investments. The larger systems were often forged from many short lines. For example, Commodore Cornelius Vanderbilt put together the New York Central system reaching from New York City to Chicago from shorter lines. James J. Hill, who extended the Great Northern from Minnesota to the Pacific, without benefit of government grants or loans, began by linking small lines in Minnesota before thrusting across the Rockies with his road. However, no single rail system was ever nationwide on its own rails. Those that were called transcontinentals extended only from the Midwest or mid-South to the Pacific—the Union Pacific from Omaha and Kansas City to the Pacific, the Northern Pacific and Great Northern from Minneapolis to the Pacific, the Santa Fe from Chicago to the Pacific, and so on. Even so, the railroad did provide a national transportation system by the 1880s. The main lines had standard width tracks, and boxcars were exchanged from railroad to railroad so as to make it possible to ship goods across the continent without unloading and reloading shipments.

Some of the railroad spawned industries did, however, become nationwide in scope under single companies. George Pullman constructed a workable sleeping car in 1864. Three years later he organized the Pullman Palace Car Company and was soon manufacturing luxury railway cars. Instead of selling them to the railroads, however, he leased them, and before long his sleeping cars were being pulled by passenger trains throughout the United States.

The telegraph was very essential to railroading almost from the beginning. By the use of it, railroads could make effective use of their tracks by keeping up with the progress of trains and scheduling them. Western Union had emerged by the time of the Civil War as the leading telegraph company; it had been formed by combining more than fifty small companies. The company grew rapidly in the 1870s by absorbing other telegraph companies as well as extending its own lines as new railroads were built. In 1878, Western Union had 76,955 miles covered by lines, and in 1881 it absorbed its two largest competitors. In 1883 Western Union transmitted forty million messages over 400,000 miles of wire. There was still some competition, but the company was doing business all across the nation.

The rapid growth and expansion of railroads in the latter part of the 19th century spurred the explosive growth of the steel industry. Until the time of the Civil War, steel had been used primarily for the making of cutlery and fine tools. It had been much too expensive and difficult to make for ordinary uses. That changed rather quickly after 1857, when Henry Bessemer in England devised an inexpensive process for refining steel. While his process is better known, a few years earlier an American, William ("Pig Iron") Kelly, had patented a process for the conversion of pig iron to steel. These rival claims were resolved, or compromised, in 1866, and thereafter steel making burgeoned in the United States. In 1865, for example, only a few thousand tons of steel were produced. In 1875, 375,000 tons were produced, and by 1879 production had risen to 929,000 tons. While steel was produced in many places, Pittsburgh, because of its proximity to the coal field and its location on the rivers, became the leader in steel production. Andrew Carnegie was the leading steelmaker there.

Steel, because of its greater flexibility and durability, quickly replaced iron for rails and much of the rolling stock of the railroads. Thus, for the remainder of the century and in the early years of the 20th century, railroads provided an almost insatiable market for steel. But there were other markets

Andrew Carnegie
(1835–1919)

Carnegie was born in Scotland, came with his family to the United States as a boy, and settled in western Pennsylvania. His was truly the story of a man who went from poverty to great wealth. He started as a bobbin boy in a cotton mill, became a telegraph operator, served as secretary to a manager of the Pennsylvania Railroad, and eventually became superintendent of a division of it. He purchased some oil-rich land during the Civil War and afterward established an iron works. The demand for steel rails provided the opportunity for his meteoric rise, and he expanded his business around Pittsburgh until it was the largest steel company in the United States. Carnegie sold his steel business in 1901 to United States Steel and retired as one of the wealthiest men in the world. Thereafter, he devoted himself to his numerous philanthropies, by which he attempted to help those who were intent on improving and helping themselves. Among the best known benefactions are: Carnegie libraries, Carnegie Tech (now Carnegie-Mellon University), and Tuskegee Institute.

as well. It was not long before bridges, farm equipment, and numerous other implements were being made mainly of steel. Moreover, structural steel made it possible to build multistoried buildings for the first time in history. That, and the invention of the elevator by Elisha Otis in 1852, made the skyscraper both possible and practical.

A meat-packing industry, centered in Chicago and Kansas City, emerged as a large-scale industry after the Civil War, and was soon shipping its products across the nation. It rested upon the location of large-scale cattle growing in the Western plains, the expansion of the railroad toward the places where they were grown, the invention of refrigeration, and the vigor of strong men who organized the preparing of meat and shipping it to the markets. Philip D. Armour went into meat packing in Milwaukee during the war, but contracts to provide meat for the Union Army soon led him to expand the business to Chicago and Kansas City. In the early days of the

Philip D. Armour (1832–1901)

Armour was a merchant, a leader in the meat-packing industry, and a philanthropist. He was born in New York, was educated at an academy, and worked for several years on his father's farm. He went to California in the 1850s to seek his fortune, but came back to the Midwest when he did not succeed, and there he did make a fortune in the meat-packing industry. Armour went into that business with a partner in Milwaukee during the Civil War. Chicago, however, was a better location, and after the war he founded his own company, Armour and Company, there. The company continued to grow over the years and to be a leader in the field.

war, Nelson Morris went into meat-packing in Chicago at the age of 22, and by the end of the war he had become a leading packer. Gustavus Swift had been in the meat-packing business in New England, but by 1875 he realized that Chicago provided a much better location, and he built a plant there. He began the practice of shipping fully dressed beef from Chicago to the East in refrigerator cars. So it was that these midwestern centers began to provide meat for more and more of the country.

But perhaps the best example of a mushrooming industry which swiftly became national in the sales of its products was oil. Colonel E. L. Drake brought in oil from a well he sunk near Titusville, Pennsylvania in 1859. In 1864, the district around it produced over two million barrels of oil, and in the following years it became a nationwide and a worldwide business, providing not only oil for the lamps of America but also oil for the lamps of China. Kerosene for lamps and lanterns was the most immediately valuable product of oil. Oil lamps were in use before 1860, but they had been most commonly lit by whale oil. Lubricants, too, were important early as byproducts of oil. The increasing use of machinery made good lubricants a necessity, and those made from petroleum were generally best and least expensive. Oil was initially shipped from wellheads to refineries in barrels, but before long tank cars replaced these, and pipe lines were also being built.

Perhaps the most spectacular story in oil was the rise of John D.

Rockefeller to leadership in the industry and Standard Oil to dominance. This story, too, should help shed some light on how some of the difficulties of operating large businesses were overcome, to the extent that they were. A large business does have some advantages over a small one. It can often benefit from what are called economies of scale, i. e., the savings that can result from producing a large number of some item, savings that can be augmented by division of labor and specialization. But there are disadvantages, too, to large businesses in competition with small ones, especially if the large business engages in far flung operations. How can such operations be supervised so as to make them as effective as a small business either operated or managed in person by the owner? The problem had not been so pressing in America before 1840, say. Most businesses were small and could be easily overseen by the owner. Indeed, most of them were located in a single building or buildings adjacent to one another. But with the establishment of the railroad systems, particularly, all that changed quickly. The supervision of a railroad involved trains operating over hundreds of miles, stations at considerable distance from the home office, repair shops located here and there, and so on. Large businesses distributing products over a wide area posed similar problems of effective control over workers.

At any rate, John D. Rockefeller was undoubtedly an organizational genius who, if he did not overcome the central problems of a large organization, certainly managed one so as to make it highly profitable. In general, Rockefeller took full advantage of the large size of his organization and imparted vigor to it with attention to detail in the performance of his employees. Rockefeller did not start out with a large organization, of course, but he forged one. He went into refining with a partner in Cleveland in 1865. Refining of oil was centered in Cleveland, and refining was the crucial activity for dominating the oil industry, but the chances are good that if Rockefeller had started by making axle grease for wagon wheels he would have eventually dominated the industry. It was a matter of tenacious drive. He soon brought in another large investor and began acquiring other refineries in the area. With this base, Rockefeller spearheaded the organization of a major corporation, Standard Oil Company of Ohio, in 1870. At that point, he headed the largest company in the largest refining center in the country. But he was far from being satisfied. He took the lead in forming the South Improvement Company, a giant combine, which he hoped to wield so as to get such privileges from the railroads in shipping rates that he could smother the competition. The association was short-lived, but Rockefeller did succeed in getting favorable shipping rates and forged ahead to control major facilities in Pittsburgh, Philadelphia, and other eastern cities. When competitors tried to avoid the railroads by building pipelines, he usually succeeded in buying the pipelines. It is estimated that by 1878 Standard Oil and its varied associated companies controlled 90 per cent or more of the oil

John D. Rockefeller (1839–1937)

Courtesy Library of Congress

Rockefeller was an entrepreneur, an oil magnate, and a financial genius. He was born in New York, moved to Cleveland, and was educated in public school. He went to work as an assistant bookkeeper, for which he was paid initially about $16 per month. During the Civil War he invested his small savings in a fledgling oil refining business, and within a few years he dominated refining in Cleveland. Rockefeller was a master of forming combinations with other oil companies and using the leverage to get better rail rates so as to increase their share of the business. He was one of the first to organize a nationwide distribution business under centralized control. When he retired in 1911, he was reckoned to be the richest man in America, with a fortune estimated at more than $1 billion. The rest of his long life he devoted mainly to philanthropic activities, and it is estimated that at the time of his death he had given away over one-half billion dollars.

refining capacity in the United States, and through their extensive marketing facilities, dominated the petroleum industry.

Rockefeller was not convinced, however, that the assortment of companies in many states by which the dominance had been achieved could be centrally directed and controlled. Standard Oil Company was incorporated in Ohio, and was not authorized to own property or do business directly in other states. A national corporation would have served his need, but no such charter was available to him. In the absence of that, the men around Rockefeller devised what was called a Standard Oil Trust, first put in operation in 1879, then much more effectively reorganized in 1882. The trust was formed by turning the controlling shares in the various companies in several states over to trustees. That way unified control and direction could be exercised over the whole. The Trust had no standing at law, but the various companies comprising it did within their respective states.

Although other companies did nationwide business, Rockefeller and Standard Oil led the way in forming an organization to operate nationally. When the trust came under fire and charges of monopoly were raised, a new possibility opened up for centralized control over operations in many states. The state of New Jersey offered incorporation with few restraints as to the territorial extent of the operation or the holding of stock in other corporations. Standard Oil eventually became a New Jersey corporation, as did many others.

Many kinds of goods were produced in manufacturing and milling centers around the country and sold throughout the nation in the years after the Civil War. Flour milling was concentrated in Minneapolis, shoe manufacturing in New England, ready made clothing in New York City, McCormick's reapers and farm implements in Chicago, the brewing of beer in Milwaukee and St. Louis, and cigarette and tobacco manufacturing in North Carolina and Virginia. The control over and integration of large businesses was aided by such inventions as the typewriter, adding machine (1872), and calculator (1884); by swift communications made virtually instantaneous with the telegraph and telephone; and by high-rise office buildings.

As the writer of a book on social studies published in 1886 said: "The change that is being wrought in all our methods of industry, and trade and commerce, by the discoveries and inventions of our century, is wholly without parallel in history, and staggers the imagination of the boldest believer in progress. Steam, electricity and the other astonishing factors that are now for the first time introduced into the service of man, are revolutionizing the world of business."[6]

The Growth of Cities

From time immemorial, such cities as existed were primarily trade and shipping centers. The larger cities were usually port cities with access to the ocean. Cities have continued to be trading and shipping centers, of course, but they took on added economic dimensions with the development of the railroad and large-scale manufacturing. They became themselves manufacturing as well as distribution centers. Extensive railroads opened up vast hinterlands as markets for goods and sources of supply. Neither natural barriers nor season of the year interrupted continual and widespread trade. Cities continued to be located near bodies of water or on navigable streams as a rule, but except for foreign commerce that was increasingly a relic of their history rather than the necessity of water either for transportation or to power machinery. Increasingly, steam replaced the water wheel, and in the 1880s electricity was beginning to replace steam.

Cities grew with increasing rapidity after the Civil War. This was true for many of the older port cities of the East, where New York City increased in population from somewhat over a million in 1860 to nearly 2 million by 1880 and to just under 3½ million by 1900. Boston had 177,840 in 1860, 326,839 in 1880, and 560,892 in 1900. But midwestern cities burgeoned in this period as well, and grew at an even more rapid rate than those of the

East. Chicago had only 109,200 in 1860, but it had grown to over one-half million in 1880, and had become a metropolis of 1,698,575 in 1900. Minneapolis almost quadrupled in size from 1880 to 1900, and Cleveland grew from 43,000 in 1860 to 560,000 in 1910. The South lagged far behind the other two regions in the growth of cities; the only large city in the deep South as late as 1900 was New Orleans. Even there, however, cities were taking shape: Birmingham, which did not exist in 1860, had reached a size of 38,415 by 1900, and was only on the threshold of its greatest growth.

The land of farmers which Thomas Jefferson had envisioned as ideal was changing rapidly in the latter part of the 19th century. While the United States was not nearly so urbanized as it would become in the course of the 20th century, the city was undoubtedly making an impact. At some point in size, a city tends to become distinct in character from the countryside, its inhabitants a breed apart, conscious of their difference from and confident of their superiority to the country ''hick'' or rural ''hayseed.'' This was especially so before the automobile and radio/movies/television tended to homogenize city and country in many ways. The census figures, however, are somewhat misleading about the distinction between urban and rural, since they count any town of 2,500 or more as urban. On that basis, 21 per cent of the population of the United States was urban in 1860, 39.9 per cent in 1900, and 51.4 per cent in 1920. In fact, a town of 15-20,000, which is primarily a trading center for the surrounding rural area may be hardly urban at all, in the usual senses. On the other hand, a factory town of several thousand people, and these were fairly common in the latter part of the 19th century, may be neither much akin to the surrounding rural area nor citylike. But whatever the dividing line should be, there should be no doubt that the growth of large cities signified important changes in the face of America.

Moreover, many of the larger cities were quite different from the older America, made much more so by the polyglot character of their populations. The cities drew much population, of course, from the children and descendants of the farmers who had predominated earlier. But increasingly, in the last decades of the 19th century and the first decade or so of the 20th century wave after wave of immigrants poured into the United States. Some of these, particularly Germans and Scandinavians, frequently settled on farms, usually in the upper Midwest. Those who came from southern and eastern Europe—Italians, Poles, Russians, Jews, etc.—however, settled mainly in cities, at first in such port cities on the East coast as Boston and New York, and then in the industrial cities of the Midwest. There, they often formed enclaves within the cities, each speaking their native language, clinging to their customs, preserving ancient dietary habits, and only gradually becoming Americanized. A city such as Chicago, for example, differed not only from rural America because of its size, but also because of the diversity of people and the differences in their ways and habits from most of those who lived in the country.

Above all, though, American cities were great commercial centers, not separated from rural America but joined to it with ribbons of steel over which trains ran to transport passengers and cargo to and fro. The cities were centers of manufacturing, of finance, of insurance, of trade, of printing and publishing, seats of government, and headquarters for numerous organizations. If they sometimes grew too rapidly, if people poured into them before they could be well housed, employed, or serviced, their spasmodic growth reflected what was happening in America at large during these years.

The Filling Out of the West

While nationwide businesses were being forged and cities were becoming metropolises in the East and Midwest, the agricultural domain was being greatly expanded and the farther West was being populated. The change occurring west of the Mississippi and east of the Pacific coastal states can be suggested by the growth of population and the admission of new states. The population of Kansas, which was 107,000 in 1860, had grown to 1,428,000 in 1890; Nebraska increased from 28,000 to 1,062,000 in the same period; Colorado from 39,000 to 413,000 from 1870 to 1890; and Montana from 20,000 to 142,000. Nevada was admitted to statehood in 1864, Nebraska in 1867, and Colorado in 1876. In 1889, four states—North and South Dakota, Montana, and Washington—were admitted to the Union, followed by Wyoming and Idaho in 1890, and Utah in 1896.

The period from about 1870 to 1890 is often referred to as the Last Frontier in the West. It was an era much celebrated in saga, legend, and lore: the era of the mining camps in the mountain territories, of the cowboy, roundup, cattle drive, and cattle kingdom on the High Plains, of the coming of the railroads and the slaughter of the buffalo, of the last Indian wars and the defeat of such fierce tribes as the Arapahoe, Sioux, and Commanche, and of lawlessness and lawmen, of "Billy the Kid," Frank and Jesse James, the Younger Brothers, "Wild Bill" Hickock, and "Doc" Holliday. In 1890, the census bureau reported that a frontier line no longer existed in America, and in 1893, historian Frederick Jackson Turner delivered a paper before the American Historical Association in which he declared that "the frontier has gone, and with its going has closed the first period of American history."

The land west of the Mississippi is hardly a geographically homogenous region. Indeed, there is only one such extensive region in the United States, that of the Mississippi Valley. But the West is even more diverse than any other portion of America: containing the highest mountains, lowest valleys, the driest and some of the wettest areas. Most of the West is semi-arid (10 to 20 inches of rainfall annually), and much of it has few trees, but the tallest trees and some of the most impressive forests can be found on the Pacific side of the Rockies. There are three fairly distinct geographical areas in the

West: the Great Plains extending upward on plateaus toward the mountains, the Rocky Mountains, and the Pacific coastal region.

The settlement of the country west of the Mississippi did not proceed along a line from east to west as it had generally done east of the Mississippi. It had been widely believed that the plains to the west of the Mississippi constituted "the Great American Desert" until well past the middle of the 19th century. Thus, the first extensive settlements were in Oregon in the 1840s, and a few years later in California. The Mormons, of course, had found a refuge in Utah, and before long they were making the "desert" bloom. In the 1850s, settlers did press into Kansas, Nebraska, and Minnesota, and they had already moved into eastern Texas, Arkansas, and Missouri west of the Mississippi. But beyond these, settlements in the High Plains and Rocky mountain regions were episodic and highly scattered until the 1870s and 1880s. These areas did not attract people with a European background, who were used to much more rainfall, trees, and gentler sloping hills and mountains. The High Plains were windswept, treeless, foraged by great herds of buffalo, and portions of them were patrolled by fierce Indian tribes. Without wood for fires, as building material, for fences, and many of the amenities of living, how could people survive? If anything, the mountains were even less inviting.

Even so, settlers were drawn into the High Plains and to portions of the mountains. The transcontinental railroads opened up some of the lands, providing transport for goods produced and bringing the necessities for people coping with unaccustomed surroundings. Those railroads receiving land grants were eager to sell the land as well as attract settlers who would be their customers. Thus, they advertised the land and the opportunities both in the United States and in Europe. Government land policies also made homesteading easier, and the terms were made more generous over the years. The Homestead Act of 1862 had made it possible for a settler to acquire as much as 160 acres of land by paying a small fee and improving and living on it for 5 years. Actually, however, 160 acres was often not enough to provide a livelihood for a family where grazing and grain growing were the main commercial possibilities. Congress acted twice in the 1870s to increase allotments. The Timber Culture Act of 1873 made an additional 160 acres of land available to farmers who would plant 40 acres of it in trees. The Desert Land Act of 1877 provided for the sale of a section of 640 acres at $1.25 per acre to those who would irrigate a portion of the land within three years. Even larger acquisitions from government owned land were made possible a little later where lands were not suitable for farming.

The buffalo herds were virtually exterminated between 1870 and the early 1880s. The coming of the railroads sealed the fate of the American bison. They could not coexist with railroads, to say nothing of ranchers and farmers. The buffalos moved in great herds back and forth over a vast region stretching from Canada to the Gulf of Mexico, and when they were on the move they would trample underfoot railroad tracks or anything in their path. By 1870, they were under concerted attack by hunters. The commercial value of the buffalo was their skins, which were in great demand for a few years in the making of buffalo robes. Regular hunting parties of four were formed, consisting of one shooter, two skinners, and a person to stretch and hang the skins. When a herd was located, a man could shoot as fast as he could load and sight, and for as long as he could hold out. William F. (Buffalo Bill) Cody first gained national fame for his tenacity in shooting buffalo. It is estimated that from 1870–1874, nearly 4 million buffalo were killed, mostly by professional hunters. There were, perhaps, 15 million buffalo west of the Mississippi following the Civil War; by the mid-1880s, the animal was all but extinct.

The Indians fared somewhat better than the buffalo, but for a while the issue was in doubt for some tribes. The United States Cavalry was the main instrument for subduing the Indians. Some tribes, such as the five civilized tribes—Cherokee, Choctaw, Chickasaw, Creek and Seminole—which had removed to Oklahoma Territory, had long since adopted settled ways. In a similar fashion, the Navaho and Pueblo Indians were farmers and herders and not warlike. On the other hand, some of the plains tribes were migratory

William F. Cody (1846–1917)

Courtesy New York Historical Society

Cody helped to glamorize and popularize the Wild West with his spectacular road show on the subject, a show which toured in Europe as well as in America. He was born in Iowa and became a rider for the Pony Express when he was around fourteen years of age. A year or so later he became a scout in the army when the Pony Express was discontinued because of the completion of a telegraph line to the West Coast. Cody joined the Kansas cavalry in 1863 and served with it until the end of the war. After the war, he made a contract with a railroad to provide buffalo meat to their construction employees, and it was in this connection that he became known as Buffalo Bill. Later, he served once again in the army and was involved in the Indian wars. His lasting fame came from his Wild West Show, but he was an authentic representative of the Last Frontier.

Geronimo
(circa 1829–1901)

Geronimo was a chief of a maverick band of Apaches who continued hostilities against the whites after the main body of the tribe had made peace. He was born in Arizona and grew up to be an Apache brave. Geronimo's band terrorized settlers in New Mexico and Arizona during the years 1875–1885. When he came to terms with the United States in 1886, it signaled the end of open warfare by the Indians. He requested to be sent to Florida, but when that did not work out, he was removed to Indian Territory (Oklahoma) where he remained for the rest of his life.

hunters and quite warlike. The killing of buffalo removed the main source of their food and clothing, and when the United States tried to limit their range to reservations they rebelled and went on the warpath. Among the more famous of the chiefs and leaders were Sitting Bull, a Sioux medicine man; Cochise of the Apaches; Black Kettle of the Commanches; and Geronimo, who led a rebellious Apache tribe.

The conflict between the Cavalry and Indian tribes was occasional, episodic, and, in the long run, one-sided. The Cavalry was well organized, disciplined, and, as soon as the railroads expanded over the West, mobile and well supplied. By contrast, Indian tribes could rarely muster any considerable force for any time, and they could hardly survive for long in opposition to the United States. The Indian uprisings usually ended in defeat for the Indians. A notable exception was the confrontation of Colonel George A. Custer with the Sioux, led by Chief Crazy Horse, at the Battle of the Little Bighorn in Montana. Both Custer and his men were slaughtered, but they were outnumbered approximately 10 to 1. But the victory changed nothing; the Indian army soon disintegrated and was rounded up by the Cavalry. Perhaps the usual outcome is better illustrated by the fate of Chief Joseph and a small band of Nez Percé Indians who attempted to flee to Canada. They were caught just short of their goal and sent back to the reservation. Chief Joseph delivered himself of this poignant speech on the occasion:

I am tired of fighting. Our chiefs are killed. The old men are all dead. It is the young who say yes or no. . . . It is cold and we have no blankets. The little children are freezing to death. My people, some of them, have run away to the hills and have no blankets, no food. . . . Hear me, my chiefs, I am tired. My heart is sick and sad. From where the sun now stands I will fight no more forever.[7]

The Apaches held out the longest, but with the capture of Geronimo in 1886 their resistance was finally broken. The wars with the Indians were over.

Long before this, however, white settlers had begun to go on to the High Plains and into the mountains to claim portions of that territory. The first wave upon the plains were the cattlemen. In the years following the Civil War there was an increasing demand for beef, especially in the growing cities of the Midwest and the East. The Great Plains, with its open ranges on which summer grass grew naturally, provided an excellent place for growing cattle. The Mexicans had started a cattle culture, particularly in Texas, and the Texans built upon it as the demand for beef accelerated. Cattle ranches were established first in the Southwest, and from there extended northward in the 1870s and 1880s. The cattle were grown usually on open range, rounded up and branded, and those suited for market were driven long distances to a railhead, most commonly in Kansas. They could be fattened along the way, and despite the long trip, often weighed more at the end than the beginning. At the railhead, they were sold, loaded on cattle cars, and shipped to markets in the East.

Ranching on the open range did not last in most places for very long. Often, ranchers had legal claim on very little of the land over which their cattle roamed. Homesteaders—often called squatters and nesters by the ranchers—began staking out claims to land. Not only did these claims break up grazing grounds but they also made large movements of cattle, as in cattle drives, quite difficult. Farmers no more wanted cattle being driven across their fields than they would have wanted buffalo roaming over them. Sheep herders moved in, too, and cattle will not graze after sheep. Also, in 1874 Joseph Glidden began marketing barbed wire, which both solved the problem of fencing in country where wood rails were in short supply and brought an end to ranching on unowned land.

Discoveries of gold and other precious metals drew people into the mountain region. Word of the discovery of gold anywhere drew a motley throng of prospectors and adventurers into the area. Thousands would set out for the locale as soon as they received reports of the find. In 1858, gold was discovered in the mountainous Pike's Peak region of Colorado. Within a year of the discovery, upwards of 50,000 people had arrived at the site. It turned out, however, that while there was gold in "them thar hills," there was little that could be obtained except by professional mining and extracting processes. Some, nonetheless, settled in the region and provided a nucleus for permanent settlements, though many drifted away when they were thwarted in their search for quick riches. Meanwhile, a new strike had been made in Nevada where, it turned out, the silver (in the Comstock Lode) was much more extensive and available in such quantities that it was more important than gold. In short order, a town had been constructed, Virginia City, and Carson City, a small trading post, became a populous town almost over night. "This country," Mark Twain wrote in 1861, "is fabulously rich in gold, silver, copper, lead, coal, iron, quicksilver, marble, granite, chalk, plaster of Paris, thieves, murderers, desperadoes, ladies, children, lawyers, Christians, Indians, Chinamen, Spaniards, gamblers, sharpers, coyotes, poets, preachers, and jackass rabbits."[8] Gold discoveries were made in the following years in Idaho, Montana, Washington, and the Dakotas, and people rushed in to take advantage of whatever opportunities they could find. Individual prospectors, however, rarely struck it rich; the long-term task of developing large mines usually fell to well-financed companies. Often, too, the boom towns were short-lived, and a goodly number of them became ghost towns when the accessible minerals, if any, had been mined. Even so, the populations of the mountain states grew steadily in most instances after its onset with mining camps.

Some historians in the 20th century have made much ado about the impact of the frontier on the formation of American character and ways. Some people have even ascribed a lawlessness, which they attribute to Americans, to the frontier habits of vigilante "justice" and lynch law. It is true, of course, that along the frontier in sparsely inhabited regions, communities were sometimes beset with gangs of outlaws, that people were more apt than in settled communities to act for themselves in avenging wrongs (real or imagined), and that the niceties of the law were not always carefully observed. Most likely, the West had more than its share of criminals, since people who were accused of crimes in the East did sometimes take refuge there. Moreover, the lawless do tend to congregate where enforcers of the law are scarce. Although stories of those years have entertained people in the 20th century, the lawlessness was not so remarkable after all. What was more remarkable was how quickly law and order and regular government came to western communities. Beyond that, the influence of the frontier on Americans was of less account than the impact of Western Civilization and established American institutions and ways upon the West. The West was tamed, state, county, and city governments were established, and the customs and traditions transplanted from Europe and modified in eastern America did generally prevail. Churches were built in short order; libraries, schools, and colleges were founded; and an ancient culture set its seal on a new portion of the earth. Except for that begun by the Spanish in some locales, much of this was accomplished within a generation. None of this is meant to deny that the West had a distinct flavor all its own or that the frontier may have left some deposits of its own and even have influenced the older America. In a broader perspective, however, these were minor variations in the grand saga of the Americanization of the West.

The New South

The story of economic growth would hardly be complete without some account of the South that emerged after the battering of the Civil War and the disruption of Reconstruction. It has sometimes been called the New South, especially because of the growth of manufacturing there, but it was, in any case, a different South after defeat on the battlefield, after the abolition of slavery, after the scourge of radical attempts to change it, and after it tentatively rejoined the rest of the nation.

The first thing to point out about the different South which emerged after Reconstruction is that it was still a predominantly agricultural region well into the 20th century. "In 1910 only 15 per cent of Southerners gainfully employed were engaged in manufacturing. . . . As late as 1930, 67 per cent of the people of the South Atlantic states and 72 per cent of those of the east South Central states were rural; the comparative figure for the United States as a whole was 44 per cent."[9] Farm production was severely curtailed and disrupted by the disorders of war and Reconstruction, as well as by the freeing of the slaves. Indeed, the production of rice in South Carolina never fully recovered and was eventually abandoned. It had depended heavily, almost exclusively, upon slave labor. But by the late 1870s generally the production of most major crops had reached pre-Civil War levels and was soon greatly exceeding them. In 1879, the production of cotton surpassed what had been before the war; nearly 5½ million bales were produced. By 1899, the production of cotton had risen to nearly 8½ million bales. Tobacco followed a similar pattern: Production sharply decreased during and after the war, recovered by the end of the 1870s, and almost doubled the prewar figure by 1900. Other crops generally proceeded apace, though the South was now greatly outstripped in grain growing by the Midwest, and the South became a major producer of fruit and vegetables for the northern market in the last decades of the century.

The major agricultural change occurred in the way labor was organized for farm production. It might be supposed that when the slaves were freed they would continue to work on the plantations and be paid wages. Although some Blacks did work for wages, at least occasionally, it was the exception rather than the rule. Most did not want to continue relations that smacked so much of servitude, if not actual slavery. Many hoped that there would be a great land redistribution and that each family would get forty acres and a mule, a notion born of deep longings and vague references by Republican politicians at the end of the war. It did not happen, in any case. Despite all the difficulties of planters after the war, there was no great land redistribution. Some plantations were sold, but there was no noticeable decrease in land holdings in the ensuing years. Most whites could not have afforded to pay wages after the war, nor did many of them believe that Blacks would make effective wage workers (with the old slave disciplinary system gone and the Black Codes disallowed) if they could have paid them.

Instead, what developed was an extensive rental system. Most Blacks who farmed, as well as a considerable number of whites over the years, became tenant farmers The most common arrangement, especially for Blacks, who had little or no capital equipment and rarely acquired any, was "sharecropping." It was called sharecropping because the crops were usually divided equally between landlord and tenant when they were harvested. The landlord usually provided the land, a dwelling place and barns for the tenant, and most, if not all, the equipment for farming. The tenant and his family provided the labor. They might divide equally the cost of seed and fertilizer. Where tenants could provide their own equipment and horses, they might contract for a larger share of the crop.

Even under these arrangements, tenants (and sometimes landlords as well) needed credit to buy food and supplies while growing the crops. Merchants provided the credit under the crop lien system. The tenant pledged—gave a lien—on his portion of the money crop—usually cotton or tobacco—and received credit up to some specified amount. When the crop was harvested, the creditor had the first claim upon it. It sometimes happened that the crop did not suffice to pay off the debt, and the tenant might go deeper in debt from year to year. It was not unusual for the tenant and his family to live better during the crop-growing season, as long as his credit lasted, than at any other time of the year. It should be noted, too, that the crop lien system added to the normal pressures to plant more of the land to the money crop and give it the most careful attention. This led eventually to much greater production of money crops than many people could profitably grow and sell.

There was a way out of this crop lien system and perpetual indebtedness, always in theory, and sometimes in practice. It was to save from the past harvest for the next year's crop. Beyond that, a tenant could increase the portion of the crop he kept by providing his own equipment. Best of all, he might acquire his own land to farm. By all accounts, few Blacks were ever able to accomplish this kind of emancipation (and few enough whites, once they had become tenant farmers). The sharecropper and crop lien system did enable Blacks to have greater independence than they had known under the earlier system and provided an opportunity for them to assume full responsibility for themselves and manage their own affairs. But most of them never sufficiently mastered the skills of thrift and saving to become completely independent.

Even though the South did not turn to manufacturing and other industrial activities on anything like the scale of the North and Midwest, Southerners were making strides in that direction before the end of the 19th century. Aside from the fact that the South had historically been more closely tied to agricultural pursuits than other regions, there was very little excess capital in the South after the Civil War. Northerners did invest in the completion and rebuilding of the railroads in the South, but they were much less enthusiastic about fostering manufacturing. Thus, it was only in the closing decades of the century that considerable expansion of manufacturing did take place.

This push to bring manufacturing to the South became a crusade for some leaders during these years. It was, they believed, the one hope for the South to regain something of its former position in the American sun. The Raleigh *News and Observer* said, "The South should make money, build up its waste places, and thus force from the North that recognition of our worth and dignity of character to which that people will always be blind unless they can see it through the medium of material strength." Referring to the spindles in cotton mills, the Columbus (Georgia) *Inquirer* declared,"These are the weapons peace gave us, and right trusty ones they are.!"[10] Often, leaders of a community pitched in to raise the initial capital to finance a cotton mill for their town.

After 1880, there was a rapid and expanding increase in textile manufacturing in the South. Factories wre mostly built in the piedmont region on the falls of a stream (for water power), and they soon dotted the line stretching from Danville, Virginia to Sylacauga, Alabama. Between 1880 and 1900, the number of mills increased from 161 to 401, and the number of people employed from 16,741 to 97,559. As a rule, only white people were employed in the factories; Blacks were excluded from all but the most menial of tasks. Indeed, there is some evidence that a part of the motive for pushing the building of factories was to provide an avenue of escape for whites from competition for the available land in tenant farming. In any case, the factory was usually a white preserve in the South until after World War II.

The textile industry was not the only one to flourish in the South during these years. The cottonseed oil industry became a major one, with oil mills located all across the South. Not only was the oil pressed from the seed an important food product but also what was left could be sold as feed for cattle and used as fertilizer. Steel was produced in increasing quantities in the Birmingham-Chattanooga region, and coal mining came into its own along the Appalachians from Birmingham through eastern Tennessee and into Kentucky and West Virginia. Furniture making became an important industry, particularly in western North Carolina. Tobacco processing was concentrated in the upper South.

With the development of manufacturing, Southern cities grew as well. Atlanta grew from 37,000 to 65,000 between 1880 and 1900 as the major distribution center for the Southeast. Richmond and Chattanooga were almost boom cities, and Durham, North Carolina was a thriving center for tobacco manufacturers. Textile factories, however, contributed less to the growth of cities than might be supposed, because they were often located in villages separate from any incorporated town.

Thus, the South was changing in the direction of the rest of the country with the development of industry and the growth of cities, though somewhat more slowly.

Chapter 3
Naturalistic Outlook

The main conclusion arrived at in this work . . . is that man is descended from less highly-organized form. . . . We thus learn that man is descended from a hairy quadruped, furnished with a tail and pointed ears, probably arboreal [a tree dweller] in its habits. . . , as would the common and still more ancient progenitors of the Old and New World monkeys. . . . I would as soon be descended from that heroic little monkey. . . , or from that old baboon. . . , as from a savage. . . .
—Charles Darwin, 1871

The Greatest modern event—that God is dead . . . —has now begun to cast its first shadows over Europe. . . . In fact, we philosophers and "free spirits" feel ourselves irradiated as by a new rosy dawn by the report that "the old God is dead"; our hearts overflow with gratitude, astonishment, presentiment and expectation. At last the horizon seems once more unobstructed. . . .
—Friedrich Nietzsche, 1882

The great stream of time and earthly things will sweep on just the same in spite of us. . . . It is only in imagination that we stand by and look at and criticize it and plan to change it. Every one of us is a child of his age and cannot get out of it. He is in the stream and is swept along with it. Therefore the tide will not be changed by us. It will swallow up both us and our experiments.
—William Graham Sumner, 1894

Chronology

1830—Publication of Comte's *Positive Philosophy* begins.

1830–33—Publication of Lyell's *Principles of Geology*.

1851—Publication of Spencer's *Social Statics*.

1859—Publication of Darwin's *Origin of the Species*.

1863—Publication of Huxley's *Man's Place in Nature*.

1871—Publication of Darwin's *Descent of Man*.

1883—Publication of Sumner's *What Social Classes Owe to Each Other.*

1884—Publication of Carnegie's *Triumphant Democracy.*

1900—Publication of Dreiser's *Sister Carrie.*

1903—Publication of London's *Call of the Wild.*

A new wave of ideas swept over America in the latter part of the 19th century. They were not entirely new ideas—there are few enough of those, in any case—, but many of them were certainly given new twists. The one idea which entranced, gripped, and served as a kind of illumination for, many intellectuals was the idea of evolution. Not simply biological evolution—though that was central—but evolution applied in every direction, for many thinkers came to see everything through evolutionary lenses, so to speak. Undoubtedly, some thinkers were questing for a natural explanation for the world and all that in it is, and evolutionary ideas and theories appeared to provide an answer for them.

Once again, the formulations of these ideas were done mostly in Western Europe and were taken up in America afterward. Not only were these ideas naturalistic in character but they were also generally opposed to supernatural and older philosophical and metaphysical ideas. Science, or *scientism*, was replacing philosophy, man replacing God at the center in men's minds, and history replacing metaphysics. Romanticism, by exalting feeling and insight, tended to downgrade reason. As reasoned philosophy lost its disciplinary hold on thinking, thinkers turned more and more to explanations with a single idea at the base (ideology). This tendency was further reinforced by the increasingly monistic character of thought. Monism is the belief that there is only a single level of reality, that it is material or physical, for example. This is in contrast with earlier views of reality that it is dual or multiple, i. e., physical and metaphysical or material, mental, and spiritual. Thus, philosophers had usually provided much more complex explanations of reality. But with the breakdown in philosophy and the tendency toward monism, such systems of thought as appeared were often based upon a single idea.

The 19th century has sometimes been referred to as an Age of Ideology. Certainly, many ideas and doctrines were brought forth in Europe in that century, and some of them have had a powerful impact on the world in the 20th century. An ideology may be defined as a system or doctrine based on a single root idea. They quite often have an "ism" suffix, as in social*ism*, though it has become so common to use this suffix on words that they do not always signify an ideology. The appearance of some of these "isms" is indicated by this description in an European history: "So far as is known the word 'liberalism' first appeared in the English language in 1819, 'radicalism' in 1820, 'socialism' in 1832, 'conservatism' in 1835. The 1830's first saw 'individualism,' 'constitutionalism,' 'humanitarianism,' and 'monarch-ism.' 'Nationalism' and 'communism' date from the 1840's. Not until the 1850's did the English-speaking world use the word 'capitalism'. . . ." Such words and systems continued to pour forth in the ensuing years, such words as "Darwinism" and "Marxism." And, as the historians say, "Without the 'isms' created in the thirty-odd years after the Peace of Vienna it is impossible to understand or even talk about the history of the world. . . ."[11]

From the mid-19th century onward there was, if anything, more of an ideological bent to the thought systems that were brought forth. Moreover, the idea of evolution became a galvanizing agent for a variety of ideologies, giving them a thrust and vigor they did not have before that.

Theories of Evolution

Evolution was in the intellectual wind for most of the 19th century. This was so while the idea of biological evolution was still only a quaint theory which some person here or there had advanced. Romanticism provided the setting by shifting the focus of thought from the enduring features of things (their natures) toward that in which they were unique, different, and individual. It emphasized change and growth. Undoubtedly, too, such developments as rapid population growth and increasing technological change reinforced the sense of a prevalent growth and change. In any case, thinkers began casting about for explanations of change, seeking for the laws of development and change, and even for methods of predicting the course of changes to come.

The German philosopher G. W. F. Hegel developed a full-fledged theory of how change takes place. The method is called the dialectic. Change, Hegel held, results from the ideas that men hold. These change dialectically, that is, out of the contest between two conflicting ideas. First, there is the thesis (the proposition, idea, or theory), then its opposite, the antithesis. Out of the contest over these, there comes the synthesis, the resolution of these opposing views which contains elements of both of them. The synthesis, in turn, becomes a new thesis, and the process goes on and on, not around in a circle, however, but upward in progressive improvement. Hegel was the major German philosopher of the first half of the 19th century, and, when German philosophy became an influence on America in the second half, he had followers in this country.

The French sociologist Auguste Comte set forth a scheme that attempted to explain the development of mind and society through three successive stages. The first stage he called theological, when thinkers explained things in terms of religion. The second stage was metaphysical, when explanations were in terms of abstractions, and the third—final and highest—stage was the scientific, by which he seems to have meant mainly the factual stage. The scientific stage he also referred to as the Positive stage, and, in connection with it, he set forth what might be loosely called a religion of Positivism. It might better be called a religion of the worship of humanity, or humanis, to use one of his words, for he said: "Towards Humanity, who is for us the only true Great Being, we, the conscious elements of whom she is composed, shall henceforth direct every aspect of our life, individual and collective. Our thoughts will be devoted to the knowledge of Humanity, our affections to her love, our actions to her service."[12] Although these ideas were important ingredients in the New (secular) Humanism which arose, the central point here is that he was explaining change in terms of successive stages of development.

But it was Herbert Spencer, the English synthetic philosopher of the mid-19th century, who set forth a scheme of universal evolution for the English speaking world. Everything is undergoing change, Spencer held,

Herbert Spencer (1820–1903)

Spencer was the leading philosopher of evolution in the English language. He was born in Derby, England, the son of an English schoolmaster. He did not get a university education, but rather usually depended upon private study and conversations with men of learning to get the information he used in his voluminous writings. As a young man, he worked for nearly a decade as a railroad engineer before he began his literary career. Spencer conceived the idea of synthesizing—drawing together in a harmonious whole—all knowledge under the themes of evolution and progress. During the years 1850–1900, he produced his massive synthetic philosophy, not so much a compendium of all learning as a fitting of what he knew into the framework of evolutionary theory. He knew Darwin, Huxley, and the other leaders in evolutionary thought, but he gave a much broader and more comprehensive turn to evolution than anyone else. His writings were quite popular during his lifetime, but his influence declined in his waning years.

not simply random change, but change which is moving in the direction of fulfillment and perfection. All this was supposed to be occurring according to the law of change and progress. He described the mode of the change in this way: "Evolution . . . is a change from a less coherent to a more coherent form. This is the universal process through which sensible existences, individually and as a whole, pass during the ascending halves of their histories."[13] The end toward which this "universal process" moves, according to Spencer, is progress:

> Progress, therefore, is not an accident, but a necessity. Instead of civilization being artificial, it is a part of nature; all of a piece with the development of the embryo or the unfolding of a flower. The modifications mankind have undergone, and are still undergoing, result from a law underlying the whole organic creation; and provided the human race continues . . . , those modifications must end in completeness. . . .[14]

Spencer focused entirely upon the changing, ignoring the enduring and reducing the eternal to a remote Unknowable. Even so, his works enjoyed a wider circulation and greater popularity than had those of any thinker of his depth before him. He wrote many volumes, and the sales of his books in America from the early 1860s to 1903 amounted to 368,755 copies. Henry Holt, the publisher, said, "Probably no other philosopher ever had such a vogue as Spencer had from 1870 to 1890."[15] At least one general theory of evolution had been thoroughly publicized.

Biological Evolution

It was Charles Darwin's theory of biological evolution, however, presented in his book, *The Origin of the Species*, which set the intellectual world afire after 1859. Up to that time, "the developmental theory," as it was then called, had not made great headway, though it was widely known. Even Spencer's great vogue came mostly after the publication of *The Origin of the Species*.

Charles Darwin was hardly the first person to propose that species of plants and animals had evolved and new ones emerged in the course of time. Indeed, the idea had been advanced among the ancient Greeks, but was generally rejected during the classic age of Greek thought. It was revived in the late 18th century by French thinkers, most notably by Jean Baptiste Lamarck. Lamarck believed that higher and more complex forms of life had developed from simpler forms by natural processes. He thought this might come about through the inheritance of acquired characteristics. However, this theory was never widely accepted. Charles Darwin's grandfather, Erasmus Darwin, also studied animal life extensively and advanced the idea

Charles Darwin
(1809–1882)

Darwin is famed because of his hypothesis that plants and animals evolve and new species emerge in the course of time. Beyond that, he explained this development in terms of natural selection and set forth a large amount of evidence by which he intended to support his claims. In short, he provided a scientific gloss for the theory or hypothesis of evolution. He was born at Shrewsbury in England, the son of a physician. Charles was sent to Edinburgh to medical school, but when he showed no aptitude for that, he went to Cambridge to study for the clergy. However, he was no more attracted to the ministry than to medicine; instead, he was drawn to the study of plants and animals, and he devoted himself to this from the 1830s onward. After his five-year voyage on the *Beagle* in the 1830s, during which he was able to examine or observe plants and animals, as well as remains of them, in a great variety of climes, he spent the rest of his life studying and writing. He got the first glimmerings of his main thesis in the 1840s, but allowed it to mature for nearly 20 years before going into print. His ideas stirred controversy from that day to this, but his general thesis about species came to be widely accepted.

that all the higher forms of life could have developed from a single simple beginning.

Herbert Spencer, too, put forth the idea that new species arise naturally by way of development, several years before Darwin did. Indeed, Spencer sent Darwin a copy of one of his books dealing with the subject, to which Darwin replied: "Your remarks on the general argument of the so-called development theory seem to me admirable. I am at present preparing an Abstract . . . on the change of the species; but I treat the subject as a naturalist, and not from a general point of view, otherwise, in my opinion, your argument could not have been improved on, and might have been quoted by me with great advantage."[16] Moreover, another Englishman, Alfred Russell Wallace, arrived at virtually the same conclusions as Charles Darwin before *The Origin of the Species* was published. In 1858, he sent a paper to Darwin which explained his theory. Darwin was astounded. "I never saw a more striking coincidence," he wrote Sir Charles Lyell, "if Wallace had my Ms. sketch written out in 1842, he could not have made a better short abstract! Even his terms now stand as heads to my chapters. . . ."[17] Darwin got up a short abstract of his ideas so that they could be presented alongside those of Wallace.

In any case, Darwin's *Origin of the Species* made the great impact for evolution. Indeed, the concept of evolution became more or less synonymous with Darwinism after the publication of his book. Theories of biological evolution had generally been rejected or ignored before Darwin's work was published. Thereafter, it soon became the dominant theory and bade fair to replace all others. Three decades after Darwin's work appeared, Alfred Russell Wallace declared, with not any great exaggeration: "The whole scientific and literary world, even the whole educated public, accepts as a matter of common knowledge, the origin of the species from other allied species by the ordinary process of natural birth." Moreover, he continued, " . . . we claim for Darwin that he is the Newton of natural history, and that . . . Darwin, by his discovery of the law of natural selection . . . [has] not only thrown a flood of light on the process of development of the whole organic world, but also established a firm foundation for all future study of nature."[18] Darwin focused his attention almost from the outset of his studies upon varieties of plants and animals within species. He came to believe that some varieties developed away from the original species over long periods of time until eventually they emerged as a new species. The process of development of superior varieties or breeds had long been well known among animal breeders. They select the hardier specimens, or those with the most desired characteristics, generation after generation, and thus are able to develop distinct breeds (as in horses, cows, and other domestic animals). If this process were carried on long enough, Darwin thought, perhaps tens or hundreds of thousands of years, a new species could emerge. But human selection could hardly account for the process by which species had originated; it had to occur in nature if all plants and animals (including man) had developed in this fashion.

The key Darwin hit upon was *natural selection*. He borrowed the idea of *struggle for survival* from Malthus, and the idea of *survival of the fittest* from Spencer. Darwin noted, as have others, that plants and animals reproduce in prodigious quantities; they multiply much more rapidly than does the means for their survival. In consequence, a struggle for survival goes on in nature, especially among those of the same species. Variations, which become the basis of varieties, enable some to survive while others die out. These "fittest" which survive in the struggle for life develop along paths which may eventually lead to new species, Darwin held. He also believed that *sexual selection* might have played a role, at least among the higher animals. (Thus, if gentlemen do indeed prefer blondes, blonde would presumably become the dominant hair trait.)

If Darwin had contented himself with merely stating his theory, or more correctly, hypothesis, it might have fared little better than others which had preceded it. But he did much more than that. He did present his hypothesis, indeed, gave it first place in the book. He considered it important, too, that he gave much thought to the objections that would be raised and dealt with them at some length. Beyond that, however, and probably much more important for the acceptance of his hypothesis as a valid theory, he summarized a vast amount of material which he submitted as evidence for his case. This gave to the work as a whole the appearance of scientific (or factual) support, something which greatly impressed many of his contemporaries. Indeed, Darwin had been collecting geologic, botanic, and zoological evidence for 25 years before he published the *Origin*. His five-year voyage on the *Beagle* enabled him to collect a vast assortment of information from other places in the world. After returning to England, he spent many more years collecting and studying all sorts of anecdotes, specimens, plants and domestic and wild animals. In his book, he brought this tremendous array of information to bear, or arranged it in such a way that it gave support to, his thesis on natural selection and biological evolution. Darwin had a well-established reputation as a careful observer and faithful reporter before he published his most impressive work. When he assembled this information behind such a broad and comprehensive thesis as biological evolution, he accomplished a *tour de force*. It commanded attention.

Darwin did not leave it entirely to chance, however, that his book would have an impact. Many books are published; few change men's minds to any extent. Not only had he already established a reputation as a naturalist by publishing books and articles, but he also cultivated others in the field to bring them around gradually toward his view for years before he published the *Origin*. He corresponded with and conversed much with Sir Charles Lyell, who was a leader in his field. He corresponded with Asa Gray at Harvard, who became his champion in America. Above all, he had almost persuaded T. H. Huxley before his book appeared, and afterward Huxley became a one-man publicity manager for Darwin's explanation (though he harbored some misgivings about the mutability of the species). Most likely, Huxley was more concerned with seeing to it that a natural explanation get a fair hearing than with Darwin's particular hypothesis, but he served Darwin well nonetheless.

Darwin believed that he had hit upon an explanation, and a grand one at that, for the development of all life forms. He described it this way:

Thus, from the war of nature, from famine and death, the most exalted object which we are capable of conceiving, namely, the production of higher animals, directly follows. There is grandeur in this view of life, with its several powers . . . that . . . from so simple a beginning endless forms most beautiful and most wonderful have been, and are being, evolved.[19]

If there had been any doubt that Darwin believed that man evolved from lower animals, he removed it with the publication of *The Descent of Man* in 1871. In this exceedingly long treatise, Darwin maintained that man had evolved from some ancestor of the ape, or at least that man had common ancestors with these creatures. He attempted to explain how consciousness, conscience, moral sentiments, and man's more or less peculiar features might have evolved. Much attention was devoted to describing attributes in lower animals which bear resemblance to those much more highly developed in man. Ultimately, he maintained, the differences between man and the lower animals are differences of degree, not of kind.

Asa Gray
(1810–1888)

Courtesy Library of Congress, Brady-Handy Collection

Gray was an American botanist and a vigorous advocate of Darwin's ideas in America. He was born in Paris, New York, attended Fairfield Medical School, and devoted himself for the rest of his life to the study of plant life, particularly in the United States. He wrote textbooks on botany as well as published many other books on plants. Gray became professor of natural history at Harvard, where he greatly expanded the facilities for studying plants. Darwin corresponded with Gray in the years before the publication of *The Origin of the Species*, and thus Gray was not only familiar with his evolutionary thesis in advance but also prepared to give it a favorable reception in America. Gray was a particularly valuable ally of Darwin because he was an evangelical Christian, yet argued both for the emergence of new species and for God's design and Providence in the world.

Critique of Darwinian Evolution

Almost from the beginning, the belief in the natural origin of the species—and, more broadly, of the natural development of all things—has been a kind of faith. The faith can be called Darwinism, naturalism, or evolutionism, or something on that order. It is an essential ingredient in the faith that is nowadays often referred to as secular humanism, about which, more later. Evolutionism is held to as a faith, however, not because names have been applied to the believers but because they exhibit an attitude of faith toward it rather than submitting it to logical and evidential tests. To demonstrate that this is the case, it may be helpful to apply some of these tests to it here.

The theory of natural evolution of the species is fraught with difficulties. In the first place, despite the claims made for its scientific validity, it is basically an historical proposition, not scientific in character. That is, it deals with events and developments that are supposed to have taken place in the course of time. Very precisely, it is natural history, not human history, such as we ordinarily encounter. Even so, the rules of evidence that apply in history generally are the ones that basically apply to it. Moreover, the crucial events alleged—namely, that new species emerged naturally—are hypothetical. There are no witnesses to the events, and such evidence as there is that they ever occurred is negative. There is evidence, of sorts, that some species appeared later in time than others, but it is negative, i. e., no remains have been found of particular species in earlier deposits of remains. The absence of evidence does not prove anything. If the crucial events had been proved, then Darwin's explanation might be correctly described as a theory of evolution. As matters have stood, since the crucial events are hypothetical, Darwin's explanation is at best a theory to explain a hypothesis. Darwin's evolutionary hypothesis can be stated this way: *If* new species occurred in the process of natural development, the process *might* have taken place much as Darwin imagined it.

The scientific difficulties with the Darwinian hypothesis are, if anything, even greater than the historical ones. One of the most striking facts in nature is the tenacious persistence of species. A species is most readily distinguished from other species by the fact that males and females within it may mate and produce potent offspring. Simply stated, like begets like, and offspring do likewise in an apparently endless chain. Under man's guidance there has been some breeding across the apparent line between species. The offspring are hybrids, which are either sterile or unpredictable. The classic example of a hybrid is the mule. The mule is the predictable result of breeding a donkey and a horse. But the mule is sterile, i. e., cannot normally produce offspring. Every mule is the end of the line, normally.

Darwin tried to get around these various difficulties by positing the development of new species which diverged farther and farther from the parent species over a vast span of time. In short, the change would occur so gradually that the emergence of a new species would involve only infinitesimal changes over hundreds of years, say. Looked at in this way, there never would be anything which an historian might call an event in the emergence of a new species. That sort of disposes of one problem, but it gave rise to another. Namely, there would need to be numerous gradations of beings in the gaps between species. To get from monkey to man, for example, proof would require evidence of creatures who became more and more manlike and less and less monkeylike. Darwin was quite aware that he did not have these, so to get around the difficulty he posited "missing links," beings which *must* have existed at one time because they are necessary to the proof of his theory. Contrary to what has been widely believed, there is not simply one "missing link" but innumerable ones that would fill in all the gaps between species.

The mountainous evidence accumulated by Darwin provided abundant proofs of the development of varieties, strains, and breeds *within* species. That is, he proved many times over what nobody much doubted in the first place. Domestic plants and animals have long been subject to selective planting and breeding to produce plants and animals with the desired characteristics. It may be, too, that Darwin's (and later accumulations) points to a natural process whereby hardy varieties are developed and sustained. That is, it may be that Darwin contributed to our understanding of an evolution *within* species. But he did not prove the evolution *of* the species, nor establish as fact the method by which it occurred. Those who believe this take it on faith, not because it has been shown to be true. Undoubtedly, those who believe that God created man in His image, that He created the other species and gave man dominion over them, accept this on faith also. The latter are aware of and avow their faith; the former conceal theirs under a scientific gloss.

The Impact of Evolution

Darwinism sent shock waves into all areas of thought, shock waves which have not yet spent themselves. Darwinism was brought forth in a framework in which the idea of evolution as a natural explanation of all sorts of developments was gaining sway. When its claims were accepted, they provided confirmation of evolution in a most vital area.

Both Darwinism and the general idea of evolution had as great an impact upon the United States as upon England, if not greater. The popularity of Spencer has already been noted. His leading disciple in America was William Graham Sumner, but there were many others. The contacts between Darwin and Asa Gray at Harvard have already been noted, and Gray became a leading exponent of Darwin's ideas in the United States. Louis Agassiz, also of Harvard, was a vigorous opponent of Darwin's theories, but the theory of biological evolution gained ground rapidly in this country nonetheless. John Fiske, historian and philosopher, made evolution much more congenial for theists by describing it as being the way God works in the world. Far from being overwhelmed by any notion of man as simply a littler higher animal, Fiske declared that "the whole creation has been groaning and travailing together in order to bring forth that last consummate specimen of God's handiwork, the Human Soul."[20] But if Darwinism was to serve as the basis of philosophy or ideology, which it certainly did, there were other directions in which it could and was pointed.

The most general impact of the idea of evolution was to focus attention on the changing and mutable features of reality and to downgrade or ignore the enduring, the fixed, and the eternal. Indeed, to a thoroughgoing evolutionist it often seemed as if there were no fixed or enduring features to reality. Looked at broadly, all was in a state of flux, alteration, adaptation, and adjustment. Everything seemed to be relative to time and place and to everything else. The idea of *relativism* was given great impetus by Darwinism, and early in the 20th century Albert Einstein made public his general theory of relativity, bringing the whole universe under its rule. Fixed points and enduring laws tended to recede into the background or fade out of mind.

John Fiske
(1842–1901)

Fiske was an American historian, philosopher, and popularizer of evolutionary ideas. He was born in Hartford, Connecticut, educated at Harvard, and trained for the law. He was destined, however, for a literary career, and he became a popular lecturer and writer. Fiske wrote extensively on American colonial history as well as the Revolutionary and Confederation period. In philosophy, Fiske tended to follow the teachings of Spencer, but he cast them within a religious framework, thus making evolutionary ideas much more palatable to Americans generally. The tenor of his ideas and the direction of his thought comes through in the titles of such works as *The Idea of God as Affected by Modern Knowledge, Outline of Cosmic Philosophy,* and *The Destiny of Man, Viewed in the Light of His Origin.*

God was, for Herbert Spencer, the Unknowable, but for many contemporary intellects, He was most apt to be the Unknown. As a youth, Charles Darwin had begun studies which would lead to a career in the church, but he abandoned that for science. In the course of his life, he drifted away from earlier religious beliefs, though he usually took pains to avoid religious controversy. Not so, T. H. Huxley, an agnostic—a word which he invented to indicate that he did not know whether or not there is a God—, for he tangled with the clergy whenever the occasion arose in his career. Adam Sedgwick, a geologist, declared of Darwin's theory of natural selection that it was a "dish of rank materialism cleverly cooked and served up merely to make us independent of a Creator."[21] Undoubtedly, Darwinism caught on because it offered a natural explanation, and, while it might not dispose of the need for some sort of Beginner, if not Creator, it certainly required no more than a most remote God.

Indeed, the German philosopher, Friedrich Nietzsche, proclaimed that God is dead. His meaning, we may suppose, is that the belief in God is no longer supportable. If that were the case, it certainly portended great changes to come, for without God, much would surely be different. But "the event itself is far too great," Nietzsche said, "is far too great . . . for even the report of it to have reached . . . many people . . . , to say nothing of their capacity for knowing what is really involved and what must all collapse, now that this belief has been undermined. . . ." He foresaw a "prolonged excess and continuation of demolition, ruin and overthrow which is now impending. . . ."[22] The whole system of morality would collapse, he thought, and much that had restrained men in times past. "Man has one terrible and fundamental wish," Nietzsche declared; "he desires power, and this impulse, which is called freedom, must be the longest restrained."[23] While Nietzsche professed to greet the coming era without God as a new and "rosy" dawn, he did correctly foresee the destruction that might follow when the will to power was released from restraints and exercised by tyrants, as has been the case in many lands in the 20th century.

Strangely, man without God cannot acquire knowledge. He can acquire reams upon reams of more or less factual information, of course, as men have busied themselves at doing ever more vigorously since the latter part of the 19th century (and devised ever more effective means to spread it), but it does not add up to knowledge or truth. Without God, we lack a first and final premise for knowledge, a Knower in whose information is knowledge, a fixed point from which to proceed to get knowledge. That is the ultimate source of the relativism of this age, of which evolutionist relativism is a reflex. None of this is meant to suggest that men have ceased entirely to believe in God generally since that time. That is hardly the case universally. What has happened, however, is that belief in God has become increasingly unsprung from intellectual endeavor, resulting in deep wounds both to religious belief and to intellectual endeavor.

One other general impact of evolution and Darwinism needs to be discussed before turning to some particular applications of them. The thrust of this revolution in thought was for history to replace philosophy (and theology). To put it another way, the study of virtually everything tended to become a study of its history. (Notable exceptions were chemistry, physics, and mathematics, though there have been strenuous efforts to place mathematics and physics into a relativistic framework, e. g., the "new mathematics.") Thus, philosophy tended to become the history of philosophy, literature the history of literature, political science the history of political development, biology the history of the evolution of plants and animals, theology the history of religions, economics the history of economic institutions, and so on. The focus everywhere tended to be on how things had evolved, whether the subject was animals, monotheism, or government.

The quest was on, too, for the "laws" of historical development or evolution. A major shift occurred in the meaning and significance of natural law, so far as thinkers continued to believe in it at all. At the time of the founding of the United States, people had usually thought of natural law as principles of regularity imbedded in things; they were metaphysical, that is, underlying the physical. These laws were conceived of as the framework within which actions and events occur, potentialities until someone or something had acted. Thus, natural laws determined effects, but were not causes. In the historical framework which had come to prevail in intellectual circles in the latter part of the 19th century, metaphysics had been largely abandoned. Natural laws were now thought of as forces, causes, if you will, which explained the course of development. Natural-law-as-force was the cause of things happening, not the result of human and other behavior. Thus, thinkers spoke of the forces which produced change. The evolution of all things came to be widely thought of as the result of natural forces at work in the world.

Man, too, was in this forceful stream of causation of natural development. It could hardly be otherwise for those who believed in evolution as a natural process and in man as a product of natural evolution. It was an easy step from this to the belief that human behavior was *determined* by these causative forces. The mind and will were not free; they were in a stream of causation which determined them. Thus, thinkers and writers cast about and came up with theories of determinism. Biological determinism lay ready at hand as an explanation for how behavior was determined. Those who emphasized this would focus upon heredity as a primal cause of human behavior and development. After all, heredity must surely be the main causative factor in biological evolution. Ominous racial theories grew out of these beliefs. But environment also was often conceived as playing a large role, and environmentalism was another determinism that gained currency. John B. Watson, an American psychologist, developed a thoroughgoing mechanical view of the role of the environment with his stimulus and response theory. Deterministic theories tended not only to cut away any belief in the freedom of action or choice of man but also any personal responsibility for acts. Probably, the other most prominent determinism was economic determinism. Karl Marx was the most vigorous proponent of this view. He held that control over the instruments of production determined social organization, and that "it is not the consciousness of men that determines their existence, but, on the contrary, their social existence determines their consciousness."[24]

It should be noted, too, that as more and more things came to be viewed historically, what had been thought of as history lost much of its meaning. History becomes largely the story of how things got to be the way they are, plus some attempt to discover trends that would show the way they were going. Some historians boldly proclaimed in the early 20th century that there were no lessons to be learned from history. Historian James Harvey Robinson said:

> It is true that it has long been held that certain lessons could be derived from the past. . . . But there is a growing suspicion . . . that this type of usefulness is purely illusory. . . . Their value rests on the assumption that conditions remain sufficiently uniform to give precedents a perpetual value, while, as a matter of fact, conditions . . . are so rapidly altering that for the most part it would be dangerous indeed to attempt to apply past experience to the solution of current problems.[25]

Harry Elmer Barnes thought the very idea of seeking truth from the past was hilarious. "Not even a Texas Methodist Kleagle," he argued, "would think of taking his car to Moses, Joshua, Luther, or George Washington to have the carburetor adjusted or the valves ground, yet we assure ourselves . . . that we ought to continue to attempt to solve our contemporary problems of society, politics and conduct on the basis of . . . information which in many cases far antedates Moses."[26] If all is indeed changing, as many evolutionists came to believe, if there is only history, the ironic truth seems to be that history does not matter much.

Naturalism in Literature

The 19th century was the age of the novel in literature. Poetry had been revived considerably during the surge of romanticism in the first half of the 19th century, but it succumbed once more to the prosaic character of the times after the Civil War. Walt Whitman lived for many years after the war, but he no longer brought forth thunderous poetry to match his earlier *Leaves of Grass*. Newspapers increased in number and even more impressively in circulation between the Civil War and World War I, but the journalistic mode had not yet come to dominate as a literary form. The essay was an important means of expression, and there were a number of quality magazines of opinion and information, such as *The Atlantic Monthly* and *Harper's*. By the 1890s, popular magazines, such as *Ladies' Home Journal* and *Collier's*, were making an impact with their stories and articles.

But the novel had come into its own as the most important vehicle of literary expression. It focused on the individual, gave scope for the full development of the rise and fall of individuals, in an era when individualism was highly prized as a way of life by Americans. All sorts of novels were published, ranging from romances, to poor-boy-makes-good-in-the-big-city stories of Horatio Alger, to utopian scenarios, to realistic ones which depicted the details of life and living with great exactness. Some of the most enduring of the literature produced during the period is often described as "local color." This refers to short stories and novels mainly which are based on some particular locale in the country and try to capture its particular flavor and character. Edward Eggleston, who wrote about life in the Midwest, explained what moved him to do local color for his region this way: "It used to be a matter of no little jealousy with us . . . that the manners, customs, thoughts, and feelings of New England country people filled so large a place in books, while our life, not less interesting, not less romantic . . . had no place in literature. It was as though we were shut out of society."[27] His best known book was *A Hoosier Schoolmaster*. George Washington Cable wrote stories of Louisiana, Sarah Orne Jewett of New England, and Joel Chandler Harris captured the flavor of Black stories and dialect in Georgia in his account of *Uncle Remus*.

Mark Twain (born Samuel Clemens) was much too versatile in his writings to place him in a single category. He was a humorist, a satirist, a writer of local color, and an accomplished teller of tall tales in the American vein. In *Roughing It*, he described life on the frontier, and *Innocents Abroad* captured the contrast between European and American ways. But he endeared himself to generations, especially of the young, with *The Adventures of Tom Sawyer* and *The Adventures of Huckleberry Finn*. Once read, who can ever forget Tom's attending his own funeral, or beguiling other boys into whitewashing Aunt Polly's fence, or Nigger Jim and Huck on their journey down the Mississippi? Henry James was the studied master of the realistic novel, and William Dean Howells was the leading literary critic of the period.

It is the naturalistic writers, however, that fit most nearly into the theme of this chapter. It might be supposed that naturalism in literature is closely akin to realism, but that is only the case, if at all, in a perverse sort of way. The naturalists tended to conceive of man as a part of nature, devoid of heroism, idealism, and having only a veneer of civilization. "Animalism" might capture the thrust of naturalism better, for naturalistic writers focused on man as a barely tamed animal. They could fully exploit by way of imaginative novels some of the conclusions that seemed to follow from the theory of evolution and Darwinism. Some had read or studied the evolutionists and were quite carried away with the ideas. "To give up Spencer," Jack London had one of his characters say, "would be equivalent to a navigator throwing the compass and chronometer overboard."[28] Theodore Dreiser read Huxley and Spencer, and they had a fateful impact on his writing. Until he had read Huxley, he said, he had at least a lingering belief in Christianity, but afterward he concluded that the Old and New Testaments were "not compendiums of revealed truth but mere records of religious experiences, and very erroneous ones at that. . . ." From Spencer, Dreiser discovered all "I deemed substantial—man's place in nature, his importance in the universe, this too, too, solid earth, man's very identity save as an infinitesimal speck of energy or a 'suspended equation' drawn or blown here and there by larger forces in which he moved quite unconsciously as an atom. . . ."[29]

But wherever they picked up the ideas, whether by reading original evolutionists or getting their ideas second or third hand, the novelists embodied them in the stories of their characters. For Jack London, who wrote such novels as *The Sea Wolf*, *The Call of the Wild*, and *White Fang*, man was to revert at any time to his animal nature:

> Civilization has spread a veneer over the surface of the soft shelled animal known as man. It is a very thin veneer. . . . Starve him, let him miss six meals, and see gape through the veneer the hungry maw of the animal beneath. . . .Touch his silly vanity, which he exalts into high-sounding pride, call him a liar, and behold the red animal in him that makes a hand clutching that is quick like the tensing of a tiger's claw, or an eagle's talon, incarnate with the desire to rip and destroy.[30]

Frank Norris, the author of *The Octopus* and *The Pit* described one of his characters as afflicted by a "foul stream of hereditary evil." The greater emphasis, however, was usually on the role of the environment in shaping men's lives. Stephen Crane, author of *Maggie, A Girl of the Streets*, said that the novel shows "that environment is a tremendous thing and often shapes lives regardlessly."[31] Theodore Dreiser, in a spate of novels from *Sister Carrie* to *An American Tragedy*, depicted characters caught in the grip of forces which they could not withstand or overcome.

Naturalistic novelists could and did give impact to the idea that man's behavior is determined by forces—instinctual, hereditary, environmental, and social—beyond his control. They could give imaginary flesh and blood to a dubious theory. Moreover, if man's behavior is determined in this way, he is not responsible for it or to blame for the consequences of his acts. This was a powerful idea, corrosive both to morality and to traditional ways of apportioning responsibility. It pointed, too, toward the conclusion that the individual acting alone was powerless to deal with life and thus gave impetus to collectivism in the 20th century.

Conservative Darwinism

Professor Richard Hofstadter called his book on the social and economic application of evolutionary ideas *Social Darwinism in America*. The term "Social Darwinism" has been widely used, following his lead, to applications in more than one direction. As historian Eric Goldman has pointed out, it is somewhat less confusing to refer to one application as "Conservative Darwinism." While it is somewhat doubtful that any thoroughgoing application of evolution would be especially conservative, the distinction that he makes is an important one, and will be followed here.

In any case, the initial impact of evolutionary ideas only served to reinforce some of the prevailing ideas, and that could be called conservative. They gave added support to an already widely accepted belief in progress. If the fittest survive in the struggle, then here is a clear case both for believing that the latest is the best and that free competition among individuals is the way to achieve it. Moreover, Spencer and his disciples generally believed in free enterprise and opposed government regulation or intervention in the economy. For example, Spencer said: "Fortunately it is now needless to enforce the doctrine of commercial freedom by any considerations of policy. After making continual attempts to improve upon the laws of trade, from the time of Solon downwards, men are at length beginning to see that such attempts are worse than useless. Political economy has shown us in this matter—what indeed it is its chief mission to show—that our wisest plan is to let things take their own course."[32] More broadly, it could be argued that any attempt to change the course of development by human activity would be to short circuit the benevolent process of progress.

The Spencerian idea of the survival of the fittest (incorporated into Darwin's biological evolution as well) suited well the outlook of many successful businessmen. James J. Hill proclaimed that the "fortunes of railroad companies are determined by the law of the survival of the fittest."[33] John D. Rockefeller seconded these views enthusiastically:

> The growth of a large business is merely a survival of the fittest. . . . [In the process, many small businesses fall by the way. But that, Rockefeller thought, is the way of natural development.] The American beauty rose can be produced in the splendor and fragrance which bring cheer to its beholder only by sacrificing the early buds which grow up around it. This is not an evil tendency in business. It is merely the working out of a law of nature and a law of God.[34]

Andrew Carnegie said that as a result of reading Darwin and Spencer, the "light came as in a flood and all was clear. Not only had I got rid of theology and the supernatural, but I found the truth of evolution." And the truth, he thought, was that in a natural order progress took place onward and onward toward perfection. As for those who found fault with this struggle for survival, he had these words of counsel: "It is here; we cannot evade it; no substitutes for it have been found; and while the law may sometimes be hard for the individual, it is best for the race, because it insures the survival of the fittest."[35] William Graham Sumner put it bluntly when he said: "The millionaires are a product of natural selection, acting on the whole body of men to pick out those who can meet the requirement of certain work to be done. . . ."[36] The above views are sometimes referred to as "rugged individualism."

Most important, this concept of a natural order of the survival of the fittest which produced progress was a weighty argument against any reformist or revolutionary effort to change the political and economic system. Talk of

---

Courtesy Yale University News Bureau

William Graham Sumner (1840–1910)

Sumner became a sociologist and applied the evolutionary view to society in his studies. He was born in New Jersey, grew up in Connecticut, and graduated from Yale. He studied divinity in Europe and became a minister in the Episcopal Church. But he soon took up a different calling, and spent most of his working life as a professor of political and social science at Yale. Sumner was an enthusiastic advocate of Herbert Spencer's *laissez faire* views regarding government and the economy, spread Spencer's sociology, but was not so optimistic as Spencer about future progress toward perfection. Unlike some of the other evolutionists in America, and despite his training for the clergy, he did not interpret evolution in a Christian framework. On the contrary, he emphasized the natural character of society and the forces or laws determining its development. His book entitled *Folkways* was his most original contribution to sociology.

reform, utopian visions, and socialist ideas were widespread in the last two or three decades of the 19th century, as we shall see later. Conservative Darwinism provided a forceful argument against these. Of the people who presented such notions, Sumner said: "These persons, vexed with the intricacies of social problems and revolting against the facts of the social order, take upon themselves the task of inventing a new and better world. They brush away all which troubles us men and create a world free from annoying limitations and conditions—in their imagination."[37] Such visions ignore the stage of civilization and the course of evolution, Sumner thought. Evolution had brought man to the industrial stage, he held; everyone is within this framework and unable to alter it. In Sumner's own vigorous words:

> It controls us all because we are all in it. It creates the conditions of our existence, sets the limits of our social activity, regulates the bonds of our social relations, determines our conceptions of good and evil, suggests our life-philosophy. . . .

In short, "the industrial organization" exercises an "all pervading control over human life."[38] In an even more dramatic mood, Sumner maintained that

> The great stream of time and earthly things will sweep on just the same in spite of us. . . . It is only in imagination that we stand by and look at and criticize it and plan to change it. Every one of us is a child of his age and cannot get out of it. He is in the stream and swept along with it.[39]

Such ideas had a considerable impact. Henry George, a man with a determined reformist bent himself, listened to a friend decry the ills besetting New York City in his day. George asked the man what he proposed to do about it. "Nothing," he replied. "you and I can do nothing at all. . . .Perhaps in four or five thousand years evolution may have carried men beyond this state of things."[40]

Even so, Conservative Darwinism, if that is the right phrase for it, was a shortlived philosophy, so far as much popular following was concerned. There may have some elements of truth in it, but Spencer and Sumner's evolutionary ideas provided highly unstable grounds for the defense of free enterprise, individual liberty, or American institutions. It attempted to ground the defense in a changing rather than an enduring order. Moreover, Sumner's view was so thoroughly deterministic that it did not appear to leave room for any significant human freedom. As for his defense of private property—which he believed was an invaluable institution—he thought that it "may give way at a future time to some other institution which will grow up by imperceptible stages out of the efforts of men to contend successfully with existing evils. . . ."[41] In addition, Sumner repudiated the natural rights doctrine which undergirds the Declaration of Independence and the United States Constitution. "There are," he said, "no rights against Nature except to get out of her whatever we can, which is only the fact of the struggle for existence stated over again."[42]

Reform Darwinism

In any case, reformers did not wait long to claim Darwinism, the idea of evolution, and the idea of progress through gradual development, for their own. The idea of stages of development had been advanced by Saint Simon and Comte, reform-minded men, even before Spencer's or Darwin's ideas had made their impact. In that context, Darwinism has only served to cut the ground from under another very important fixity—that of the species. Reformers wanted to make fundamental changes, and the focus upon change turned out to be grist for their mill.

The American who is most often credited with having shifted the evolutionary argument in the direction of reform was an obscure sociologist by the name of Lester Frank Ward. Ward maintained that a new stage in evolution had been emerging for a long time. What made this stage possible, he claimed, was the appearance and development of the mind of man in the

Courtesy Brown University

Lester Frank Ward (1841–1913)

Ward was a sociologist, a government bureaucrat, and a reform Darwinist. He was born in Illinois, served in the Union army during the Civil War, and graduated from what is now George Washington University. Although he studied law, he did not practice it, but rather became a government worker, first in the Treasury and then as a geological surveyor. He even taught botany for a couple of years at his *alma mater*. But his claim to historical recognition comes from his books on sociology, among which was one appropriately titled *Dynamic Sociology*. It was in these works that he set forth his ideas about mental progress having reached a point that men could direct social development to desirable ends by using the power of government.

course of evolution. (The mind was to be greatly aided now, he thought, by the development of a science of sociology.) It was, Ward said, the "advent with man of the thinking, knowing, foreseeing, calculating, designing, inventing and constructing faculty, which is wanting in lower creatures. . . ." This development repealed "the law of nature and enacted in its stead the psychologic law, or law of mind."[43]

This development having occurred, or so Ward alleged, it had now become possible to take over the development and direction of society. In the past, the development of society had occurred more or less naturally, without any clear line of control or planning. But now it could be taken over and directed. By whom? Undoubtedly, Ward would have nominated sociologists to do the social planning, or "social invention," as he sometimes called it. There should be no doubt, however, that what he had in mind was for government to control the process of social development. He wanted to set about "the improvement of social conditions through cold calculation. . . ." The aim should be not "merely to alleviate present suffering," but "to create conditions under which no suffering can exist."[44] This would be accomplished through legislation. "Legislation," Ward said, "is nothing else but social invention. It is an effort so to control the forces of a state as to secure the greatest benefits to its people."[45] He admitted that governments had usually made a mess with their interventions in the past, but that was due, he thought, to the ignorance of those who made the laws. The science of sociology would change all this:

> Before progressive legislation can become a success, every legislature must become . . . a laboratory of philosophical research into the laws of society and of human nature. No legislator is qualified to propose or vote on measures . . . until he masters all that is known of the science of society. Every true legislator must be a sociologist. . . .[46]

Ward was at least somewhat aware that massive government efforts to alter the ways of people would meet with resistance. This was where "social invention" would come in, he thought. "Social invention consists in making such adjustments as will induce men to act in the manner most advantageous to society." He hoped that most of those who opposed these changes would not "require to have their liberty restricted, since they, too, have wants, and the social inventor should devise means by which such wants shall be spontaneously satisfied through . . . socially beneficial action."[47] The greatest social problem, he declared, was redistribution of goods, and he proposed to solve this problem collectively by the use of government. (Not to put too fine a point on it, he proposed to use the force of government to take goods from those who owned them and distribute them to others.) "This is an exclusively social problem," Ward said, "and can only be solved by social action. It is today the most important of all social problems, because its complete solution would accomplish nothing less than the abolition of poverty and want from society."[48]

The most important point here, however, is that Ward turned the argument of Darwinians against reform and revolution into an evolutionary argument for reform. He began the process by reformers of laying claim to the latest stage of evolution as being favorable to reform, and progressive as well. He did not prove, of course, that such government-initiated reforms as he favored would achieve the results that he sought, or even that some new stage in evolution had taken place. But his position set the stage for the gradualist movement toward socialism in America, and he made it appear that all this would be progressive.

Chapter 4
Radical Ideas and Collectivism

And, unpleasant as it may be to admit it, it is at last becoming evident that the enormous increase in productive power which . . . is going on . . . has no tendency to extirpate poverty or to lighten the burdens of those compelled to toil.
—Henry George, 1879

No man any more has any care for the morrow, either for himself or his children, for the nation guarantees the nurture, education, and comfortable maintenance of every citizen from the cradle to the grave.
—Edward Bellamy, 1888

Wall Street owns the country. . . . The great common people of this country are slaves, and monopoly is the master. . . . We want money, land and transportation . . . , and we want the power to make loans direct from the government. We want the accursed foreclosure system wiped out. . . .
—Mary E. Lease, 1890

Capital possesses one thing which labor does not—ready cash. They will not hesitate to make the best possible use of it. But labor possesses that which capital does not—numbers. They should be made effective.
—James B. Weaver, 1892

Chronology

1867—Karl Marx published first volume of *Das Kapital*.

1871—Organization of the Knights of Labor.

1878—Organization of Greenback-Labor Party.

1884—Organization of British Fabian Society.

1887—National Farmers' Alliance formed.

1888—Publication of *Looking Backward*.

February, 1892—Organization of Populist Party.

August, 1892—Socialist Labor Party nominates Presidential Candidate.

1905—Organization of Industrial Workers of the World.

The middle and latter part of the 19th century presents a great paradox for the student of history. It is not the supposed paradox to which Henry George referred in the title of his book, *Progress and Poverty*. He claimed that the material progress going on had no tendency to relieve poverty. The bulk of the evidence does not support his allegation. The paradox is that in the midst of a century in which great technological and material improvements were going on, as well as scientific, political, and social ones, especially in the United States and Western Europe, there was a rising tide of criticism and attempts to promote drastic changes. It is true, of course, that there were great differences between the wealth and incomes of people, that some were rich while others were poor, that not everyone participated to the same degree or in the same way in the benefits of improvement, and that there were injustices and wrongs, as always, that needed to be righted. The length of the work day and the conditions under which women and children, as well as men, worked in factories, for example, would not appeal to most people nowadays.

But the dominant thing is that conditions were generally improving. Goods were available in greater quantity and variety than ever before, and prices generally declined in the latter part of the 19th century, placing these goods in the reach of more and more people. Ready-made clothing, canned goods, fresh fruit and vegetables, daily newspapers, and the like were ever more widely available. Moreover, steam and electrical power were replacing much human and animal effort in production and transportation. Learning and literacy was increasingly widespread. There were writers who celebrated these developments and attributed them to hard work, to saving, and to investment. No one did so more enthusiastically than Samuel Smiles, an English writer popular in both Britain and America:

> The men who economize by means of labor become the owners of capital which sets other labor in motion. Capital accumulates in their hands, and they employ other laborers to work for them. . . .
>
> The thrifty build houses, warehouses, and mills. They fit manufactories with tools and machines. They build ships and send them to various parts of the world. They put their capital together, and build railroads, harbors, and docks. They open up mines of coal, iron, and copper; and erect pumping-engines to keep them clear of water. They employ laborers to work the mines, and thus give rise to an immense amount of employment.
>
> All this is the result of thrift. It is the result of economizing money, and employing it for beneficial purposes. . . .[49]

There were other writers and speakers, however, who saw the matter quite differently. What Smiles described as providing employment, they called the exploitation of workers. What looked for all the world like spreading prosperity (when surveyed broadly) was described by them as descending poverty and engulfing hardship. What certainly appeared to be the liberation of workers from backbreaking toil by the use of machines, they lamented as enslaving men to machines. Karl Marx declared that along with "this process of transformation" by which increased production had been accomplished "grows the mass of misery, oppression, slavery, degradation, exploitation. . . ."[50] Marx and Friedrich Engels wrote in *The Communist Manifesto* that capitalist production led to overproduction and periodic crises in economies. "And why? Because there is too much civilization, too much means of subsistence, too much industry, too much commerce."[51] The American Henry George proclaimed that "wherever the new forces are anything like fully utilized, large classes are maintained by charity or live on the verge of recourse to it; amid the greatest accumulations of wealth men die of starvation, and puny infants suckle dry breasts. . . ."[52] The Populist Party platform of 1892 argued that "The fruits of the toil of millions are boldly stolen to build up colossal fortunes for a few . . . ; and the possessors of these, in turn, despise the Republic and endanger liberty. From the same prolific womb of governmental injustice we breed the two great classes—tramps and millionaires."[53]

In comparison with what times and what places were these alleged conditions so bad and getting worse? In comparison with the Middle Ages in Europe? Was the factory worker more oppressed than the serf in the Middle Ages? Was his lot worse than that of the Chinese peasant? Were these pauperized Americans alleged by the Populist platform in worse conditions than the tribesmen in deepest Africa? Was the governmental injustice in America greater than that in Ivan the Terrible's Russia? If not—and the answer in the materialistic framework that was being used, is surely no—then by what standards or by what comparison do the allegations have any validity?

The answer to this question brings us to a strange aspect of the modern reformist and revolutionary critics of conditions as they exist. Basically, their criticisms are not made in comparison with the past or those that prevail elsewhere (though they may sometimes refer to these). They are made in terms of their *visions* of what *might be* (or is going to be, some have thought) in the *future*, not what has been in some time or place. Theirs is a vision of an ideal, of something that has never been and is nowhere, that is, of utopia. The reality does not come off very well, of course, in comparison with an ideal or utopia, at least for those who conceive of such things.

These utopian visions were the brainchildren of an increasing number of reformist and revolutionary *intellectuals* in the 19th century. Ironically, such intellectuals—often so bitterly critical of contemporary society—could hardly have found refuge in most past societies. It was only with the increasing freedom and prosperity of the 19th century that they could find means to live and propagate their ideas. Probably, too, it was only in terms of the dramatically improving conditions of that century that others could be drawn into their vision. They were often men who had cut themselves off from their past (emigrés of the mind, if not in fact), from their religion, and were more or less at odds with their own society and culture. Indeed, these attitudes were the hallmark of what has sometimes been denounced as intellectualism. At any rate, their visions have undergirded much that has happened in the 20th century.

These intellectuals often differed with one another about the details of their descriptions, analyses, and visions, and often bitterly opposed one another. Even so, the following characteristics were shared by most of them. First, they were critical of and rejected to greater or lesser extent the economic and social systems that prevailed at the time. Second, they were futuristic in orientation. Their minds tended to focus on the societies that would come in the future; they were reformers and revolutionaries, equipped with a vision for the future. Third, they were collectivists. That is, they believed that the change that they sought must be achieved by collective action. Individuals could not improve their circumstances. They must join with others to effect a social change. Collectivism is the broad term which embraces a variety of socialists, and they were socialists of one stripe or another. Fourth, they generally, though not universally, believed in collective action through the use of government. That is, they usually believed in the use of government power to impose their changes.

With these things in mind, we can turn now to an examination of the rise and spread of these reform and revolutionary ideas. The stage was set for the spread of these ideas in the United States by the tide of immigrants which poured into the United States in the late 19th and early 20th centuries.

The New Immigration

Immigration into the United States declined in the late 1850s and during the Civil War. It picked up again after the war and swelled in the ensuing decades until it peaked just before World War I. In the first two decades after the Civil War most of the immigrants continued to come from northern and western Europe, as they had in the past. Between 1860 to 1890 nearly 85 per cent came from northern and western Europe (plus Canada): from Germany nearly 3 million, from England 1.6 million, from Ireland 1.5 million, from the Scandinavian countries, mainly Sweden and Norway, 1 million, and 930,000 from Canada.

Immigrants from northwestern Europe continued to come to America in considerable numbers until the beginning of World War I, but the tide began to shift to southern and eastern Europe after 1880. The shift was not so great in the first decade. Southern and eastern European immigrants amounted to only 18.3 per cent of the total of immigrants from 1881 to 1890. But they became the dominant grouping of immigrants from 1891 to 1900, constituting nearly 52 per cent. From 1901–1910, their proportion mounted to 72 per cent. They came mostly from Italy, the Austro-Hungarian Empire, and the Russian Empire. To put it another way, they were mostly Slavs, Italians, and Jews.

Over 2 million Italians entered the United States from 1901–1910, and well over a million more in the next four years. They came mainly from southern Italy and Sicily, the least industrial and poorest regions of the country. The population of the country was growing rapidly, and the commercial and agricultural opportunities were not expanding in those regions. The Italian government encouraged the poorer people to leave the country, and they did so in large numbers, coming not only to the United States, but also to some of the South American countries.

The Slavs, too, came in ever increasing numbers after 1900, though they had begun to comprise a sizeable portion of the immigrants during the two decades before that. From 1891–1900 nearly 1,200,000 came into the United States, and over 5 ½ million from 1900 to 1914. They were mostly subject peoples within the Austro-Hungarian and Russian Empires; in the order of their numerical importance, they were Poles, Slovaks, Croatians, Ruthenians, Czechs, Bulgarians, Serbians, Russians, and Dalmatians. Most of these peoples were under imperial governments dominated by the Austro-Hungarians or Russians. They were mostly peasants, many of them no more than a generation removed from serfdom, almost invariably poor, and many of the adults were illiterate.

The other major migration from Eastern Europe to the United States was that of the Jews. Nearly 2 million Jews came into this country between 1881–1915. Predominantly they came from Russian Poland and other parts of the Russian Empire. The rest came mainly from within the Austro-Hungarian Empire. Jews have a long history of being persecuted and of migrating to more favorable circumstances. They left Russia in great numbers after 1881 because of an active policy of discrimination against them and persecution by the government. They were subjected to *pogroms* from time to time, organized efforts, either ignored or fostered by the government, to drive them out of the country or kill them. This treatment by the government of the Czars left bitter memories of the czarist regime in the minds of many of the Jewish immigrants.

In one respect these newer immigrants were similar to many of those who had come earlier. They were seeking greater opportunities to improve themselves materially, to participate in government, and to practice their beliefs without persecution. They were different in significant ways as well, which is why they have been referred to as "new" immigrants. Their languages differed from those of most of the older immigrants, which had been predominantly Anglo-Germanic. The Italians were closest to the older stock in language, since theirs is a Romance language, derived from Latin and akin to French and Spanish. The Slavic languages are much more remote from English, and the difference is aggravated in that many of them are written with a different alphabet. Most of the new immigrants were Roman Catholic or Eastern Orthodox in religion. The Irish, too, had been mostly Catholics, but otherwise the earlier immigrants had been preponderantly Protestant. The Jews were the most distinct in religion of all major immigrations until the past decade or so, since they are not Christians, and their rituals and practices, more ancient in origin, are quite distinct. The differences between Christians and Jews were further accentuated to the extent that Jews clung to the orthodox Hebrew religion, wore distinctive dress, observed their dietary prescriptions, and celebrated the ancient Sabbath on Saturday. It is part of their heritage that they are the chosen people of God. The Hebrew faiths do not usually welcome or seek converts from among Christians, and tend to resist intermarriage with or assimilation into the Christian culture.

The new immigrants differed from most of the older immigrants, too, in that they usually settled in cities. The Germans and Scandinavians who came in large numbers in the 1870s and 1880s moved mainly into the rural areas of the upper Midwest. By contrast, the new immigrants settled almost exclusively in the towns and above all in the cities. The Irish had earlier shown this penchant for city life, had settled in large numbers in New York City, Boston, and other eastern cities, and became politically prominent, if not always dominant. They were now joined in these cities by Italians, Slavs, and Jews (as well as immigrants from many other lands: Greeks, Magyars, French Canadians, and so on) in the eastern cities and in the Midwest especially. By 1910, nearly half the immigrant population in the United States was concentrated in four states: New York, Massachusetts, Pennsylvania, and Illinois. The Slavs concentrated particularly in such heavy industries as coal mining, steelmaking, meat-packing, and railroad building. There were large concentrations of them in the mining regions of Pennsylvania and the Midwest. Italians were most notably located in manufacturing centers, but many of them also worked in heavy industries. Jews flocked in great numbers into the clothing manufacturing districts of New York City.

Chicago grew to be a huge and bustling city in the latter part of the 19th century as a focal point of immigrant settlement. The foreign-born inhabitants of that city in 1890 came close to outnumbering the whole population of a decade earlier. A writer in the 1890s pointed out that "only two cities in the German Empire, Berlin and Hamburg, have a greater German population than Chicago; only two in Sweden, Stockholm and Göteborg, have more Swedes; and only two in Norway, Christiania and Bergen, more Norwegians."[54] But the new immigrants, too, were pouring into Chicago. As Schlesinger says, "The sweatshops in the garment industry were recruited largely from Bohemians and Russian Jews; the rough unskilled jobs in the building trades fell chiefly to the Irish and Italians; while the business of peddling became a specialty of Jews."[55]

But New York City was the great center to which immigrants came and a city very nearly inundated with foreign born in the late 19th and early 20th century. It had half as many Italians as Naples, as many Germans as Hamburg, and two and a half times as many Jews as Warsaw. Four-fifths of the population in 1890 was foreign born. Jacob Riis wrote of the city at that time: "A map of the city, colored to designate nationalities, would show more stripes than on the skin of a zebra, and more colors than any rainbow. The city on such a map would fall into two great halves, green for the Irish . . . , and blue for the Germans. . . . From down in the Sixth Ward . . . the red of the Italian would be seen forcing its way northward . . . to the quarter of the French purple . . . , to lose itself, after a lapse of miles, in the 'Little Italy' of Harlem. . . . Between the dull gray of the Jew, and the Italian red, would be seen squeezed in on the map a sharp streak of yellow marking the narrow boundaries of Chinatown."[56]

The new immigration raised questions about the assimilation to American culture and ways of those coming in. Indeed, since the population of immigrants was increasingly concentrated in cities and towns, particularly those of the northeast, and the foreign born were becoming majorities in some areas, the question might well have arisen as to who was going to be assimilated to what. Indeed, there was considerable support for some sort of immigration restriction. Even before the 1890s, Chinese immigration had been staunched by the Chinese Exclusion Act of 1882. Contract labor laws, too, were being prohibited. But by the mid-1890s, well before the tide of migration from southern and eastern Europe had reached its peak, Congress passed a bill requiring immigrants to pass a literacy test (1896). In support of this bill, Senator Henry Cabot Lodge of Massachusetts argued that it would

> bear most heavily upon the Italians, Russians, Poles, Hungarians, Greeks, and Asiatics, and very lightly, or not at all, upon English-speaking emigrants or Germans, Scandinavians, and French. In other words, the races most affected by the illiteracy test are those whose emigration to this country has begun within the last twenty years and swelled rapidly to enormous proportions, races with which the English-speaking people have never hitherto assimilated, and who are most alien to the great body of the people of the United States.[57]

President Cleveland vetoed the bill, and it did not become law. In the message which he sent to Congress, Cleveland indicated a concern with the coming of those who might promote turbulence and disorder, but he argued forcefully that the exclusion of such people would not be achieved by a literacy test. In his opinion, it would be "infinitely more safe to admit a hundred thousand immigrants who, though unable to read and write, seek among us only a home and opportunity to work, than to admit one of those unruly agitators and enemies of governmental control, who can not only read and write but delights in arousing by inflammatory speech the illiterate and peacefully inclined to discontent and tumult. Violence and disorder do not originate with illiterate laborers. They are rather the victims of an educated agitator."[58]

President Cleveland had put his finger on a problem that was indeed emerging. It was that the New Immigration brought with it an increasing number of radical agitators and revolutionaries. This is not to suggest that there were not native-born revolutionaries in America, but by all indications they were greatly outnumbered by the foreign born. This was abundantly obvious when the Communist Party was organized after World War I. Actually, two parties of that persuasion were organized during these years. According to some claims, there were about 27,000 members of the American Communist Party, "of whom only 1,900 were officially charac-terized as English-speaking. Over three-fourths of the membership was organized in Slavic, Baltic and Jewish language federations. The rival group, the Communist Labor Party, probably had about 10,000 members and was also overwhelmingly Slavic. . . . The alien nature of American Communism was revealed by the complaint of its leader, Charles Ruthen-berg, that in 1920 it didn't have five speakers able to present its case in the English language."[59] Jews have been especially prominent in the member-ship of the Communist Party, and one writer concludes tentatively that they may well have constituted a majority in the 1930s and 1940s.[60] They were more dominant in leadership positions than in membership.

The importance and impact of Communism, and more broadly socialism and collectivism, will be made clearer later on in this work. However, it should be pointed out here that their importance was much greater than the number who were members or the number who voted for Communist and avowed Socialist party candidates in elections would suggest. In view of the controversial character of the subject, it may be well, too, to emphasize what should be obvious. Most Slavs were not Communists. Most Jews were not Communists. Most of the New Immigrants were neither agitators, radicals, nor revolutionaries. However, they were probably more readily attracted to socialist or collectivist solutions to problems than were those of the older American stock. Certainly, city dwelling and working in factories tends to make collectivist solutions appear more plausible than does rural or small town life.

Moreover, the New Immigrants came into a country whose land was mostly claimed, whose cities were already large, and whose institutions were already fixtures. In contrast to earlier immigrants, they were under greater pressure to fit in rather than having the opportunity to shape the country to fit their desires. They were aliens in a strange land whose frame was already in place. The appeal of socialism is that it holds out the prospect of remaking society according to a different blueprint. This idea had especial appeal for what are sometimes referred to as "emancipated" Jews, i.e., Jews who have cast off all but the remnants of their religion and are more or less secular in outlook. These have shown a decided preference for a secular society, and were often drawn to socialism and Communism.

Be all that as it may, it is time now to examine the varieties of socialism that were beginning to have some impact in the latter part of the 19th century.

European Socialism

Socialism, as an idea, was formed by European thinkers, mainly in the 19th century. Although some of the ideas that went into it were stated in earlier times, it was definitely being advanced by the time of the French Revolution. The early socialists were mostly French: Morelly, Babeuf, Saint Simon, Comte, and Fourier. Robert Owen was an early 19th century British socialist. Then, near the middle of the 19th century came the Germans, Ferdinand Lassalle and Karl Marx. Thereafter, socialists were more common in other European countries.

In a very general sense, socialism is an ideology built around opposition to private property, in favor of public—"social" or, in practice, governmental—ownership of the means of production, the principle of equality in the distribution of goods, and an assortment of other programs which receive greater or lesser emphasis from time to time. Although Marx bitterly denounced utopians, all socialists are more or less utopians, and Marx in many ways the most utopian of all. But any attempt to define socialism must fall far short of the mark, for socialism is a vision of and a prescription for transforming man and the social world he inhabits. More-over, socialists differ with one another about the extent of the necessary change as well as how it shall be accomplished. That is a way of saying that there is more than one variety of socialism.

For practical purposes, however, there are two main varieties of socialism that survived the 19th century debates and have had a great impact on the 20th century. They are *revolutionary* socialism and *evolutionary* socialism. These two views differ both on the extent of the changes to be made and how they are to be accomplished. Thus each will be taken up separately.

1. Revolutionary Socialism

Although he was not alone in the field, Karl Marx originated and promoted the revolutionary socialism—usually called communism—which has had such an impact in the 20th century. Marx called his variety of socialism "scientific socialism." He believed that he could discern the direction that developments, or "forces" were moving in his day. Marx was a materialist, influenced by a German named Feuerbach in this persuasion. He was greatly influenced also by G.W.F. Hegel, and borrowed from him the idea of a dialectic at work in history. In contrast to Hegel's belief that ideas were the moving forces in history, however, Marx held that it was matter or materialistic forces that were at the root of the conflict.

Scientific socialism refers to the results Marx thought he obtained from his method; the method itself is called *dialectical materialism*. More precisely, Marx taught that the great moving force in history is the class struggle. The struggle is between those who own or control the means of production and the propertyless. In the Middle Ages, the two main classes

---

Karl Marx (1818–1883)

Marx was one of the most persistent socialist thinkers of his time, and was the main fount of 20th century Communism. He was born in a province of Prussia in what is now Germany and educated in German universities. Although his philosophical training might have prepared him for a teaching career, his radicalism, atheism, and materialism made the appointment to such a post unlikely. He married Jenny von Westphalen, of noble descent, and she stuck with him throughout the hard life he provided for her. So far as he ever earned his keep, it was in newspaper and book writing and revolutionary activity. He met Friedrich Engels in Paris in the 1840s, and they became fast friends and literary collaborators. Engels was the son of a wealthy cotton manufacturer and had the funds to help keep bread on Marx's table.

Marx's best known works are *The Communist Manifesto*, written in collaboration with Engels, *A Critique of Political Economy* (1859), and *Capital*, a three-volume work, the last two of which were completed and published by Engels after Marx's death. Most of the main ideas in socialism and communism can be traced from Marx, though he did not necessarily originate them.

had been the feudal nobility and the serfs. Out of that struggle had arisen the bourgeoisie, the townspeople and their culture. With the rise of industry, came the industrial workers (proletariats, in Marx's terms) and the capitalists. Marx predicted the coming demise of the middle class (the bourgeoisie), the concentration of industry in the hands of a few great capitalists, and a coming great struggle between capital and labor.

The result would be *the* revolution which would usher in socialism with the triumph of the proletariat. Although the revolution would occur at different times in different countries, it would eventually take place in all countries. This would be the last revolution for all time. A classless society would emerge, and government which, according to Marx, was simply a device by which the ruling class controlled the oppressed, would wither away.

The proletariat revolution would be a great transforming revolution. Everything in a society will have to be destroyed before the new society— socialism—will emerge. "The Communists disdain to conceal their views and aims," Marx declared. "They openly declare that their ends can be attained only by the forcible overthrow of all existing social conditions."[61] All existing conditions and relations must be abolished or destroyed so that social man may emerge:

> Religion, family, state, law, morality, science and art are only particular forms of production and fall under its general law. The positive abolition of private property and the appropriation of human life is therefore the positive abolition of all alienation, thus the return of man out of religion, family, state, etc., into his human, i.e., social being.[62]

The revolution was not only inevitable because of his predicted future course of history, as Marx saw it, but also because of what he claimed was an imbedded injustice in the economic system. The injustice he explained in terms of his labor theory of value. This is the theory that goods receive their value from the labor that goes into them. He described it this way: "The *relative values of commodities* are, therefore, determined by the *respective quantities or amounts of labour, worked up, realised, fixed in them.*"[63] In his view, then, the capitalists, who took a large portion of the prices of goods, were *exploiting*, i.e., taking advantage of, the workers. In the long run, the capitalists would accumulate more and more for themselves, and the workers would get less and less. This situation would set the stage for the communist revolution.

Of course, Marx's socialism was not scientific, nor was he much of an economist. Although he had the training of a scholar, he was a polemicist, a master of invective against those whom he hated (almost everyone), an agitator, given to poetic formulations of his ideas, a visionary, a founder of an atheistic faith or an anti-religion religion. This description of him was provided by Carl Schurz, a German immigrant who became a United States Senator: "The stocky, heavily built man with his broad forehead, with pitchblack hair and full beard, attracted general attention. . . . What Marx said was indeed substantial, logical and clear. But never did I meet a man of such offensive arrogance in his demeanor. No opinion deviating in principle from his own would he give the slightest consideration. Anybody who contradicted him was treated with hardly veiled contempt. Every argument which he happened to dislike was answered either with biting mockery about the pitiful display of ignorance or with defamatory suspicions as to the motives of the interpellant. I still well remember the sneering tone with which he spat out the word *bourgeois*. And, as bourgeois, that is to say, as an example of a profound intellectual and moral depravity he denounced anybody who dared to contradict his views."[64]

Any attempt to understand Marx and the destructive urge of Marxism must begin with the fact of Marx's profound alienation. He was for most of his life a man without a country, if country be taken to mean not only a nation but also religion, culture, and the sense of being a part of a received heritage. Marx's father and mother had been Jewish, but they became Lutherans in a predominantly Catholic community, converted, some said, so that the father could keep his government job. Karl Marx was baptized a Christian but in early manhood became a militant atheist, which he remained during the course of his life. He attended universities at Bonn and Berlin, but presented his doctoral thesis for his degree at the University of Jena, which he had never attended. He never had what could be called regular employment but earned such income as he did from writing and editorial work, and received aid from his one fast friend and frequent collaborator, Friedrich Engels. Though Marx married and fathered several children, the family lived from pillar to post so to speak, as he sought refuge first here, then there. He was frequently in trouble with the political authorities for his revolutionary activities, seeking refuge in Paris, in Brussels, and finally in London. His country, if he had one, was in his mind.

Even so, this alienated man, this man without a country, without traditional religious underpinnings, with few possessions, who could accept as friends only devout disciples, with only a boiling animosity toward his culture, who was usually aroused to write only out of opposition, set forth the doctrines which are today used to hold more than a billion people under control. Why? He set forth an earthly promise, a pseudo-religion, appealed to the destructive element in men, caught up some of the doctrines and notions about history gaining favor in his times, and bound it all together with a vision of a beatific future, when man should finally realize his potential on earth. His deepest appeal has always been to intellectuals, themselves all too often alienated from their culture.

Many have remarked the afterglow of religious images which lurk beneath the surface of Marx's vision. In a way, he had called forth an anti-Christian christianity. A lifelong student of Marxism describes it this way:

> In an age prepared for by nearly two thousand years of Christianity with its millennial expectations, when the faith of millions has grown dim, and the altar seems vacant of its image, Marxism has arisen to offer a fresh, anti-religious religion, a new faith, passionate and demanding, a new vision of the Last Things, a new Apocalypse, and a new Paradise.[65]

Undoubtedly, Marx stood Hegel on his head, as is commonly said, but he also stood Christianity on its head. For the love that impels Christianity, Marx substituted a virulent hate. Eternity is brought into time, spirit becomes matter, the Second Coming is transmuted into social revolution, the Incarnation is the socially aware proletariat, and communism is the hope of redemption. Marx did not say these things directly, but they underlie and give vigor to what he did say.

Karl Marx was the main fount of revolutionary socialism, which is embodied in the 20th century in world communism. However much it may have been distorted in the application, Marx provided the basic premise of Soviet Communism, Chinese Communism, Cuban Communism, and international communism in general. Modern revolutionary zeal and totalitarianism have sprung from the bitter denunciations, the destructive animus, and the messianic claims of Marx.

2. Evolutionary Socialism

Evolutionary socialism has had much greater direct impact on the United States than has revolutionary socialism. This variety of socialism is also known as democratic socialism, social democracy, and gradualism. Actually, evolutionary socialism takes on the coloration of each country in which it takes hold, and sometimes is not called socialism at all. In England, for example, the Labor Party became the vehicle of socialists; in the United States, socialism made the greatest strides in the 20th century, first under the wing who called themselves Progressives, and then later liberals. All this is a way of saying that the gradual approach to socialism has moved under a great many guises and names, and must often be identified by the character of programs being advanced rather than by the name of movements or parties.

Actually, Karl Marx contributed to evolutionary socialism, if he was not the only fount of it. In *The Communist Manifesto*, a pamphlet published in 1848, he and Engels set forth a program for a gradual movement toward the communist revolution. They said, "The proletariat will use its political supremacy to wrest, by degrees, all capital from the bourgeoisie'' and ''to centralize all instruments of production in the hands of the State. . . .'' To accomplish this, they said, it is necessary first ''to win the battle for democracy.'' Moreover, they set forth a ten-point program by which countries would move:

1. Abolition of property in land and application of all rents of land to public purposes.
2. A heavy progressive or graduated income tax.
3. Abolition of all right of inheritance.
4. Confiscation of the property of all emigrants and rebels.
5. Centralization of credit in the hands of the State, by means of a national bank with State capital and an exclusive monopoly.
6. Centralization of the means of communication and transport in the hands of the State.
7. Extension of the number of State factories and instruments of production: the bringing into cultivation of waste lands, and the improvement of the soil generally in accordance with a common plan.
8. Equal obligation of all to work. Establishment of industrial armies, especially for agriculture.
9. Combination of agriculture with manufacturing industries; gradual abolition of the distinction between town and country, by a more equable distribution of the population over the country.
10. Free education for all children in public schools. Abolition of children's factory labour in its present form. Combination of education with industrial production, etc.[66]

It might go without saying that most of these measures have been put into effect to a greater or lesser extent in most countries in the world, including the United States, in the 20th century.

The connection between evolutionary socialism and evolutionary theory in general was as close as the terms may suggest. Indeed, Marx saw the advantage to his theory of Darwin's ideas. He wrote Engels in 1860 that he had read ''Darwin's book on Natural Selection. Although it is developed in the crude English style, this is the book which contains the basis in natural history for our view.'' Or, as he wrote Lassalle in 1861, ''Darwin's book . . . serves me as a basis in natural science for the class struggle in history.''[67] Even so, there was a most important difference for Marx between his view of change and that described by Darwin. For Darwin, changes occurred gradually over long periods of time. By contrast, Marx believed in a dialectic of change, change that might come or culminate swiftly, ''a development in leaps and bounds,'' as V. I. Lenin described it, ''catastrophes, revolutions. . . .''[68] Thus, Marx was basically a revolutionist, not an evolutionist in the English sense.

Evolutionary socialism, or the gradual movement toward socialism, has taken root in many countries. But there is no political soil to which it is better suited than that of England. Since the mid-17th century, there has been little bent toward revolution in that country. The English have made many changes, but they have made them within the framework of their ancient institutions. They have kept monarchy, a House of Lords, and an established church through the centuries, though the monarch no longer rules, the Lords no longer have a significant legislative role, and religious toleration has long since become established policy. It was not surprising, then, that when they turned to socialism it was the gradualist variety. Moreover, the Darwinian conception of a slow and gradual change and improvement was most congenial to Englishmen. Substantially, the British developed the gradualist variety of socialism that had great impact on all the English-speaking peoples, and in much of the rest of the world.

Much of this was the work of the Fabian Society and the ideas spread by its members. The Fabian Society was organized in 1884. It was named for the Roman general Fabius, who was famed for his cautious military moves and delaying tactics. The Society took as its motto:

For the right moment you must wait, as Fabius did most patiently, when warring against Hannibal, though many censured his delays; but when the time comes you must strike hard, as Fabius did, or your waiting will be in vain and fruitless.

Whether the Fabian Society ever struck hard or not, it had considerable success in spreading its ideas of a gradual movement toward socialism between the mid-1880s and World War I. At the end of World War I, it began to play a leading role in the Labour Party, which was becoming a major party in England, thus had an increasing impact on the political course of England. Shortly after the founding of the Society, it drew into its ranks such accomplished publicists as the dramatist, George Bernard Shaw, Sidney Webb, Beatrice Potter (who married Webb), and Graham Wallas. Over the years, many other prominent English intellectuals and politicians were members or associated with the Society. In the 1920s, for example, the following people who were or became prominent were Fabians: Clement Atlee (Prime Minister of Britain after World War II), Stafford Cripps, R. H. Tawney, Michael Oakeshott, Rebecca West, C. E. M. Joad, Bertrand Russell, Malcolm Muggeridge, and Harold Laski. So prominent and dominant were these people that by the middle of the 20th century, almost everybody who was anybody in the intellectual world in Britain was a socialist, usually with a Fabian flavor.

The Fabians combined the ideas of socialism, democracy, and evolution, along with the belief in operating within the system, into an effective ideology. The Fabians were intentionally socialists, or, as they announced,

Sidney Webb
(1859–1947)

Webb was a longtime leader in the gradualist movement toward socialism in his native England as well as much of the rest of the English-speaking world. He was born in London and received his formal education there. Although he worked briefly in commerce, most of his career was spent in one or another kind of government service, first as a civil servant and then in elective and appointive offices. Webb joined the Fabian Society in 1885, wrote Fabian tracts, and eventually played a leading role in making the Labour Party the socialist party in England. Webb married Beatrice Potter, and the two of them joined their labors in trying to bring socialism to England. After the Labour Party became a major political party in the 1920s, Sidney Webb moved higher and higher in government circles, and eventually became a member of the House of Lords. The Webbs visited the Soviet Union in 1932 and published a laudatory book on *Soviet Communism* in 1935. They were no longer so attached to the gradualist approach to socialism.

"The Fabian Society consists of Socialists." Moreover, "It therefore aims at the reorganization of Society by the . . . extinction of private property in Land and . . . transfer to the community . . . of such industrial Capital as can conveniently be managed socially. . . ."[69] In short, they were in favor of confiscating private property in land and a large portion of the factories, and so forth.

Perhaps their most important idea, however, was the use of government to achieve socialism gradually. On the matter of the role of government, they said: "The Socialism advocated by the Fabian Society is State Socialism exclusively."[70] In short, government was their chosen instrument for the achievement of socialism. In this, the Fabians differed from most socialists of their day, and those who had preceded them. Most socialists had opposed government and political power in general. Government was the instrument of oppression. The Marxists quite often would not even participate in politics. When the time came, they expected to destroy the bourgeois state and that eventually the state would wither away when the class struggle was ended. However, the Fabians would have government actually administer socialism, and their view came generally to prevail eventually among socialists.

The tactics advanced by the Fabians were equally important, especially for Americans, who would eventually imitate them. Their favorite tactic was one they called "permeation." The word means to penetrate, to infiltrate, to pervade, and they had in mind political and social organizations. "In its most general sense, it meant that Fabians should join all organizations where useful Socialist work could be done, and influence them. . . ."[71] Once in an organization, whether a political party, a club, a member of a town council, or what not, they would use their influence to move them toward using government power over the economy.

The Fabians published a large number of tracts in which they described particular programs to be advanced, and how they should proceed gradually toward their goal. Fabian Tract #54, for example, came out for an old-age pension for the poor. Tract #127 pushed the idea of a minimum wage for workers. The first step toward that, it explained, would be to make studies to determine the minimum needs of basic goods for individuals and families. After that the government should be pressed to provide a minimum wage for its employees. That done, "A Minimum Wages Bill should follow, bringing all sweated trades within the scope of the law, and punishing all employers who, after a certain date, pay less than the legal minimum. . . ." Above all, however, they wanted to get government into the actual business of producing and distributing goods. This might be done first at the town and city level, moving on later to the national level. For example, Tract #90 argued for towns providing milk for their citizens:

> If we want good milk, let us establish our own dairy farms in the country and our milk stores in the city. Many of our large towns have spent enormous sums of money to provide their citizens with water; why should they not also provide them with milk? The arguments in favor of municipal water apply with greatest force to municipal milk. . . .

In tract after tract they argued for such things as municipal pawnshops, municipal slaughterhouses, municipal bakeries, and so on and on. Thus, the country would be moved gradually, step by step, toward socialism.

Collectivism in America

The above discussion is background here mainly for the spread of collectivist ideas in the United States, for the forming of organizations, and for the adoption of practices derived mainly from socialism. It should be noted at the beginning that socialism, when advanced under that name, was never popular in this country. There have been socialist political parties, and there have been Marxist, or Communist, parties, but none of these were very successful in electing candidates even at the local level. The nearest thing to being popular was the Socialist Party under the leadership of Eugene Debs in the early 20th century. But it was always a minor party, and it dwindled away into insignificance after World War I.

It might be supposed, then, that socialism, or, more broadly, collectivism, had little impact on the United States. Obviously, this is not the case in international relations, in view both of Communism in the 20th century and of socialist governments in many countries. They have provided much of the framework within which the United States has operated abroad. But neither has it been the case domestically. Note the following statement by Earl Browder, former head of the Communist Party of the United States, made in 1966:

> America is getting socialism on the installment plan through the programs of the welfare state. There is more real socialism in the United States today than there is in the Soviet Union.
>
> Americans may not be willing to vote for a program under the name of "socialism," but put it under another party label—whether liberal Republican or Democrat—and they're by and large in favor of the idea. . . .
>
> We have no real socialist party, no socialist ideology, but we have a large—and growing—degree of what 50 years ago would have been recognized as socialism.[72]

Some of his statements may be questionable—such as, the United States has more real socialism than the Soviet Union, or that this country has no socialist ideology—, but his main point about the prevalence of socialism is, if anything, an understatement.

The task here is not to describe the particular programs and policies by which America got this degree of socialism, that will be done later, but rather to explain how the groundwork was laid for this in the latter part of the 19th century. On the face of it, we are dealing with a contradiction. On the one hand, Americans rejected socialism when it was presented under that name. On the other hand, they have accepted and in some measure approved socialistic programs and policies, bit by bit and step by step, as they were presented under other names. What happened in large was this. Americans came to accept many of the premises and much of the outlook that informs socialism. That is, many Americans accepted the view that there are problems that can only be solved by collective action and that there is collective responsibility for dealing with social and economic problems. These ideas were advanced in a variety of ways in the latter part of the 19th century, by intellectuals, in an assortment of movements, by labor unions, for example, and by minor parties. Some particular examples may help to make clear how these changes were promoted.

One way that Americans were drawn into the socialist outlook was by being presented with large social problems, real or imagined, which were made to appear insoluble except by a collectivist approach. Karl Marx had one in his claim that workers were exploited by capitalists and by describing the solution as one in which the workers banded together to seize the instruments of production. An American, Henry George, presented a similar problem in a different light in his book, *Progress and Poverty*, first published in 1879. George claimed that great progress was being made in producing goods by the use of machinery. But this increasing progress was accompanied by spreading poverty, or so he claimed. In his own words,

> . . . The march of invention has clothed mankind with powers of which a century ago the boldest imagination could not have dreamed. But in factories where labor-saving machinery has reached its most wonderful development, little chldren are at work; wherever the new forces are anything like fully utilized, large classes are maintained by charity or live on the verge of recourse to; amid the greatest accumulations of wealth, men die of starvation, and puny infants suckle dry breasts; while everywhere the greed of gain, the worship of wealth, shows the force of the fear of want.[73]

George did not prove that his argument was valid; instead, he relied on the fact that there was poverty, though certainly no widespread starvation, and that at the same time many people were well off and some quite wealthy.

At any rate, George offered this explanation for the supposed paradox of increasing progress and spreading poverty. By individual land ownership arrangements, individuals were able to appropriate for their private use fruits of the land which neither their labor nor equipment had produced. They reaped the advantages of both the fertility of the soil and of superior location, advantages he believed rightly belonged to the community of men. He reasoned that in nature, the land belonged to all mankind, not to people individually. George proposed, therefore, that what he called the ''unearned increment on land'' be taxed and used for the benefit of all. This proposal was labeled a ''single tax.''

Progress and Poverty was a best-selling book and had sold 2 million copies by the early 20th century. George had a considerable influence on reformers generally, not so much for his particular program, however. It is true that he had and has disciples who have pushed various proposals for laws in accord with his ideas, but these have not generally had any substantial influence. Minus his collectivist bias, it is hardly more reason-

Henry George
(1839–1897)

George was born in Philadelphia, but lived much of his life in California and New York. He had but little formal schooling before going to sea as a youth. By turn, he was a sailor, a typesetter, and even a prospector for a time in the Pacific Northwest. Mostly, however, from 1858 to 1880 he made his living as a newspaperman and printer in San Francisco. He became very interested in land and government land policies in the 1870s, a subject which dominated much of his thinking for the rest of his life. A neo-physiocrat, George believed that the crucial economic question was who controlled and received the fruits of land. Thus, he developed his single tax idea, and it underlay the writing of his major work, *Progress and Poverty*. George convinced many people of the need for radical change and had a considerable influence both in the United States and England. In 1886, he ran for mayor of New York City, but was defeated. He is best known, however, for his single tax on land proposal.

able to conclude that the land belonged to everyone originally than that it belonged to no one, a much more common view. In any case, it would be highly disruptive and patently unjust to divest people of their property rights honestly acquired on such dubious grounds. Moreover, the scheme would be most difficult, if not impossible to carry out, nor is it at all clear it would achieve the ends claimed for it. The importance of his book was more despite his particular programs than because of them. It spread the idea that there was something drastically wrong with existing arrangements. It proposed a collective approach to the problem and the use of the power of government to make the necessary changes. And it subtly attacked the rights in private property. All this was grist for the mills of radicals and reformers; they could use the methods they extracted from it and slough off his particular programs.

Utopian literature played a much more direct role in preparing those who came under its influence for socialist programs. Although utopian fantasies have been written from time to time throughout the modern era, there was heavy concentration of them from 1885 to 1912, and the period of the 1890s was probably the most productive period in the history of utopian ideas. Some of the more important utopian productions, mainly by American writers, were: Ignatius Donnelly, *Caesar's Column* (1890), William Morris, *News from Nowhere* (1890), Thomas Chauncey, *The Crystal Button* (1891), Ignatius Donnelly, *The Golden Bottle* (1892), William Dean Howells, *A Traveler from Altruria* (1894), H. G. Wells, *The Time Machine* (1895), and Edward Bellamy, *Equality* (1897).

One book, however, may have been more important than all the others combined in planting the vision of utopia in America. It certainly gave great impetus to the production of utopias by its commercial success. The book was Edward Bellamy's *Looking Backward*, published in 1888. By 1890 the book had sold 200,000 copies, and it was in that year selling at the rate of 10,000 copies every week. Within two years after the publication of the

Edward Bellamy
(1850–1898)

Bellamy was a newspaperman, a novelist, and influential as the provider of a utopian blueprint for socialism in America. He was born in Massachusetts and studied both at Union College in New York state and in Germany. Although he denied any extensive study of socialist ideas, he must have been rather thoroughly acquainted with them, judging by his work. He was admitted to the practice of law, but he turned instead to newspaper and editorial work, first in Massachusetts and then in New York City. He began publishing light novels at the age of 30, and was only 38 when he published the utopian novel, *Looking Backward*, on which his claim to fame was to rest. Thereafter, he devoted himself to promoting reform, mainly through the Nationalist Clubs. *Looking Backward* was the most popular of the utopian fantasies published in his day. He wrote a much less well-known sequel, *Equality*, published shortly before his death.

book, 162 clubs located in 27 states were holding meetings. They were called Nationalist clubs, thus avoiding the stigma of socialism. A magazine, called *The Nationalist*, was founded by friends of Bellamy to spread his ideas. The Populist Party was much influenced by Bellamy, for an observer at the convention in 1892 declared that Bellamy's readers "were the brains of the convention. They were college professors, editors, artists, and authors. . . ."[74]

The book's considerable impact can be attributed in some part to the fact that there were a good many incipient socialists among intellectuals in America, and they got behind it and pushed its circulation. Bellamy did not mention socialism, and his clubs, too, avoided the term, as already noted. This irritated Henry Demarest Lloyd, an outspoken writer with a socialist bent, for he wrote Bellamy in 1896, "The movement we are in *is* International Socialism. . . . Why not recognize it and say so!"[75] But Bellamy was making socialism palatable to the American taste, not concerned with identifying the ideas with an unpopular term.

Looking Backward is a utopian fantasy or romance, set in the city of Boston in the year 2000. The main character of the story was mesmerized and put to sleep in 1887 and only awakened in 2000. His learning about all the changes that have occurred is the device used in the telling of the story. A great transformation has occurred, not only in Boston but also in the United States and the rest of the world. War has been banished from the face of the earth. There is no longer any crime to speak of, only occasional antisocial acts. There is no longer any corruption in politics, in fact, very little politics at all, no labor problems, and all destructive activities have disappeared. A vast surge of creativity and construction had emerged. These great changes were accomplished by a reorganization of the economy. All private production of goods and provisions of services were taken over by a kind of government. The economy was rationally organized—money abolished, income equalized, production scientifically planned, competition eliminated, and men bountifully supplied with goods and services. Labor was provided by an industrial army, in which every male between the ages of 21 and 45 was expected to serve.

How had all these things come about? Had there been a violent and prolonged revolution? Not at all. The change just occurred, as the result of an evolution. One of their learned men explained it this way:

> Early in the last [the 20th] century the evolution was completed by the final consolidation of the entire capital of the nation. The industry and commerce of the country, ceasing to be conducted by a set of irresponsible corporations and syndicates of private persons at their caprice and for their profit, were intrusted to a single syndicate

representing the people, to be conducted in the common interest for the common profit.[76]

And that, apparently, was that; everything just fell into place after that.

The transition from the old to the new society is vague in *Looking Backward*, but the description of what has emerged is quite detailed. Indeed, it is described in loving detail. The main character visits the department stores from which goods are obtained, and the distribution system from central warehouses is amply described. The system of state issued credit which replaces money is pictured minutely. There is no longer anything which could be called charity. Each person receives an income by virtue of his being a person, and this income is conceived as his by right. Any surplus is spent on public works, "pleasures in which all share, upon public halls and buildings, art galleries, bridges, statuary, means of transit, and the conveniences of our cities, great musical and theatrical exhibitions, and in providing on a vast scale for the recreations of the people."[77] Children are no longer dependent upon their parents, and the only family bonds are affectional. State governments have disappeared, and such power as remains has been centralized in Washington.

In the future, all things can be as seen through the eyes of a maker of fantasies, of course. People tend to dismiss utopias in just that way, and often deny either that they believe either in the possibility or even desirability of them. Even so, the vision of utopia in the future has played an important role in the thrust toward socialism in the United States. For one thing, it has provided an important vantage point from which to criticize the present situation. Things are bad, it may be alleged. In comparison to what, it is appropriate to ask? In terms of what they once were? No, in terms of what they could be. For another, programs advocated by reformers and politicians are advanced as bringing us into the better, if not perfect, society. But most important, where Bellamy's novel was concerned, all these marvelous things were achieved by collective efforts and largely according to socialist prescriptions.

Actually, collectivism was spread in America from several sources and in a variety of ways. Marxist and anarchist ideas were brought into the country most often by immigrants from Europe. A Marxian Socialist Labor Party was organized in 1877, but it did not become active until the 1890s, under the leadership of Daniel de Leon. In terms of minor parties, collectivist ideas were spread by the Greenback Labor Party, organized in 1878, and the Populist Party, organized in 1892. Labor unions and farmer organizations tended to embrace the class struggle idea, and so far as they attempted to act in concert as a group to obtain favorable political action, they were collectivist.

The Knights of Labor was the first clearly ideological national union. It was first organized in 1871, and grew to its peak following under the leadership of Terence Powderly. It was an industrial union, with a definite bias toward wage workers, though it welcomed into its ranks farmers as well. The only ones definitely excluded from its membership were liquor dealers, professional gamblers, lawyers, and bankers. Their announced object was "To secure to the toilers a proper share of the wealth they create. . . ." The most revolutionary of all the labor unions was the Industrial Workers of the World (I. W. W.), organized in 1905. It was a revolutionary union, with a heady tendency toward violence. The tendency toward revolution is clearly indicated in one of their songs:

> We hate their rotten system more than any mortals do.
> Our aim is not to patch it but to build it all anew.
> And what we'll have for government, when we're finally through
> Is One Big Industrial Union![78]

Several farmers organizations were formed which attempted to speak for farmers as a class in promoting government action. The Patrons of Husbandry, or National Grange, were first organized in 1867. Its greatest following was in the Midwest and Pacific states. Various Farmer's Alliances were formed in the 1880s. These organizations provided a part of the political base for the formation of minor parties, the thrust to railroad regulation, the pressure for government inflationary efforts. The great animating desire, at least of the leaders among farmer movements and their political offspring, was to use the government power to achieve their purposes. They were suffused with a naive faith in government power, as is indicated by this quotation from one of the leaders, Ignatius Donnelly: "We have but to expand the power of government to solve the enigma of the world . . . . There was a time when every man provided, at great cost, for the carriage of his own letters. Now the government . . . takes the business off his hands. There was a time when each house had to provide itself with water. Now the municipality furnishes water to all. . . . These hints must be followed out. The city of the future must furnish doctors for all; entertainment for all; business guidance for all. It will see to it that no man is plundered, and no man starved who is willing to work."[79] His was the voice of utopian socialism in its more alluring form.

Among the other men and movements which played a hand in spreading variants of socialism or collectivism were these. For a brief span of time in the 1890s, there was an American Fabian organization, which published a Fabian magazine. When Sidney and Beatrice Webb visited the United States, however, they concluded that there were constitutional difficulties in the way of following the British approach in America, and the organization eventually folded in America. The Social Gospel movement, spurred by such leaders as Washington Gladden and George D. Herron, made some impact in attempting to muster Christianity for reform and variants of socialism. The Progressive Education movement, although too complex for any brief characterization, began the task of mustering public education for social reform. In the 1890s, those who favored the collectivist approach were beginning to make some impact on the national political scene. That story will be told in greater detail in the next chapter.

Chapter 5
Political Climate
1877–1896

Our present tariff laws, the vicious, inequitable, and illogical source of unnecessary taxation, ought to be at once revised and amended. These laws . . . impose a burden upon those who consume domestic products as well as those who consume imported articles, and thus create a tax upon all our people.
—Grover Cleveland, 1887

Every contract, combination in the form of trust or otherwise, or conspiracy, in restraint of trade or commerce among the several States, or with foreign nations, is hereby declared to be illegal.
—Sherman Antitrust Act, 1890

Having behind us the producing masses of this nation . . . , we will answer their demand for a gold standard by saying to them: You shall not press down upon the brow of labor this crown of thorns, you shall not crucify mankind upon a cross of gold.
—William Jennings Bryan, 1896

Chronology

1877—Great Railway Strike.

1878—Bland-Allison Act.

1880—Election of Garfield.

1881—Assassination of Garfield.

1883—Pendleton Act.

1884—Election of Cleveland.

1886—Haymarket Riot.

1887—Interstate Commerce Act.

1888—Election of Harrison.

1890—July 2, Sherman Antitrust Act.

　　　July 14, Sherman Silver Purchase Act.

1892—Election of Cleveland.

1893—Panic of 1893.

1894—Pullman Strike.

1896—Election of McKinley.

Radical ideas and collectivism did not make any immediate impact on American government or politics in the last three decades of the 19th century. Indeed, the reformist thrust which had come to the fore during Reconstruction had largely played out by the early 1870s. Radicalism was mostly at the periphery during the next two decades, in unionism, in some farm organizations, among those pressing for free coinage of silver, and in relatively small third parties. Their beliefs made little imprint on the major political parties, though some measures were passed which signaled at least a bow or two in the direction of the thrust to control big business, which was a part of the political animus of radicalism and collectivism. The attempts to monetize silver, too, were in accord with the inflationary bent of some of the radicals.

In the main, though, during the years 1877 to 1896 neither of the major political parties favored major or drastic changes. The Democratic Party returned to a balance of power nationally after white rule was restored in the South. Indeed, with the South now solidly in the Democratic column, the Democrats could usually come close to a majority in national elections. Even so, the Republicans continued to dominate in the choosing of Presidents. In fact, only one man was elected to the presidency who was not a Republican. That was Grover Cleveland, who was also distinguished by being the only President who served two terms, separated by four years from one another. Neither party, however, usually controlled both houses of Congress at the same time. One house was usually Democratic and the other Republican. Thus, neither party exerted a predominant control over the government. The Republicans, however, were in the ascendance because of the presidency and a leading influence in the choice of members of the courts.

None of the Presidents who served during the years 1877–1897 was an especially strong executive, with the possible exception of Grover Cleveland. Certainly, none was a dominant and aggressive leader as Andrew Jackson had been or as Theodore and Franklin D. Roosevelt would be. They were all honorable men, and no scandal marked any of the administrations during these years. Rutherford B. Hayes, President 1877–1881, was a sturdy and independent man, but he had barely attained the office, and did not choose to run for re-election. James A. Garfield, a Republican, had served less than six months when he was assassinated by a disappointed office seeker. Chester A. Arthur, who succeeded him and served the remainder of the term (1881–1885), was suspect when he succeeded to the highest office. The Republican Party was divided into factions, and Arthur was associated with the patronage activities of the Republican "machine" in New York. Hayes had removed him from his post of collector of customs for the Port of New York because of his refusal to obey an executive order about appointments. Actually, Arthur acquitted himself well as President, both in the appointments that he made and in exercising the other powers of his office.

Grover Cleveland was elected President in 1884 in a spirited contest with the Republican nominee, James G. Blaine. Blaine was in many ways the outstanding Republican for nearly two decades and came close to the nomination on two other occasions. His failure to achieve the highest office was due more to political infighting than any lack of capacity for the office.

Grover Cleveland (1837–1908)

Cleveland was born in New Jersey, but his family moved to New York a few years later. He had to go to work as a youth rather than go to college, as he had planned, because of the death of his father. His political career began at Buffalo during the Civil War when he was appointed assistant district attorney. He had moved to the area a few years earlier, worked for several years, became a law clerk, and was admitted to the bar. Later, he served as district attorney and was elected sheriff of Erie county (in which Buffalo is located). Cleveland established a reputation for honesty, for being above petty partisan politics, and for acting consistently on high principles. He was elected mayor of Buffalo in 1881, governor of New York (by a landslide victory) in 1882, and President of the United States in 1884 on the Democratic ticket. He was renominated in 1888, but not elected, nominated again in 1892, and elected. Thus, Cleveland was three times nominated for and twice elected President. He used the veto on legislation generously, stood for sound money, was against the protective tariff, and acted to expand the civil service.

In any case, he was defeated by one of the most independent and principled men ever to be elected. Cleveland was of the Jefferson-Jackson school, and it was fitting that he should distinguish himself by his vetoes. He vetoed a large number of special pension bills passed by Congress to reward particular Union veterans of the Civil War. "Public business is a public trust," Cleveland insisted, and in contrast to his predecessors he attempted to determine the merits of each particular case. He also vetoed some rivers and harbors bills, a form of appropriation often tainted as "pork barrel" measures. Since he was the first Democrat elected to the presidency since the War, Cleveland took steps to bring Southerners back into the national counsels. He appointed L. Q. C. Lamar of Mississippi Secretary of the Interior and Augustus H. Garland of Arkansas Attorney General. His further efforts at conciliation were frustrated, however, when he issued the "Rebel Flag Order" to the War Department to return captured regimental colors to former Confederate units. Veterans of the Grand Army of the Republic created such a furor that he rescinded the order.

Cleveland's popularity waned during his first term, and a Republican, Benjamin Harrison, was elected in 1888. In addition, Republicans had majorities in both houses of Congress during the first two years of Harrison's term. He was the grandson of an earlier President, William Henry Harrison, a Union officer during the Civil War, and capable administrator. However, he gave Congress its head, and some measures were so unpopular that the Republicans lost control of the House of Representatives in the 1890 election. Harrison ran again in 1892, but was defeated handily in the electoral vote by Cleveland. Cleveland's second term was marred by the rising tide of Populism and other forms of radicalism.

Issues and Acts

Many 20th century historians, attuned to and in sympathy with the enlarged and much more assertive role of the federal government in American lives in this century, find fault with those who governed in the late 19th century for their restrained and less activist role. Above all, they tend to find the politicians more than a little dull and uninspiring. It is probably true that most of the politicians of this era would not have rated well as entertainers. It is not their basic task, however, to entertain us. Rather, they are chosen for the purpose of governing us, legislating, administering, and controlling the government, maintaining the peace, protecting the people from aggressors, and doing these things within the framework of the Constitution. There is much evidence that these things were done rather well during this period.

In the main, both parties had become somewhat conservative, and the leaders of neither were much inclined to push for drastic changes. To put it another way, issues dividing them were not sharply defined and contests did not often lead to dramatic confrontations. It was probably just as well, for there had been much more than enough drastic and dramatic change and confrontation during the Civil War and Reconstruction. It was a time for allowing the bonds of union to be formed again, for restoring some balance between the federal government and the states, allowing local government to reassert its role, and for allowing the branches of the federal government to resume their constitutionally prescribed roles. At least, that was going on in a generally peaceful setting during these years.

Even so, there were issues raised during the period, some reminiscent of earlier issues and others with greater portent for the future. Some of these issues, too, pointed toward an expansion of the role of the federal government that has come with a shift toward a collectivist attitude.

1. Civil Service Reform

Since the Age of Jackson, at least, there had been sporadic criticism of the appointment of government workers. The practice of allowing incoming Presidents to replace workers in office with those of their own choosing produced a "spoils system," according to those who championed the displaced workers. It may be that with the increasing number of government workers the appointment of workers had become burdensome for Presidents and their department heads, though few were ever heard to complain. New fears were raised with the emergence of what have been called "political machines" in big cities. A "political machine" is a party organization welded together and made effective by the handing out of political favors (contracts, appointments, aid of one kind or another) to the party faithful. "Boss" Tweed had been a notorious example of a leader of machine politics in New York City earlier. Senator Thomas Platt of New York was accused of being a Republican boss. At any rate, Platt and Senator Roscoe Conkling, along with Chester A. Arthur, were closely identified with a Republican faction known as the "Stalwarts," those who prided themselves òn being party men. They expected, too, that those of their persuasion would get the political plums when their party was in power.

James A. Garfield was of the faction known as "Half Breeds," not "Stalwarts." When he came to office he did not pass out the rewards solely to the party faithful. Platt and Conkling resigned their places in the Senate and applied to the legislature for re-election to them. This was a maneuver to gain a mandate from the New York legislature against Garfield's ignoring of Stalwarts in his appointments. The legislature refused to comply. It was in this general setting that a disappointed office seeker, Charles J. Guiteau, shot President Garfield in a railway station. As he stood over the wounded President, Guiteau declared: "I am a Stalwart and Arthur is President now."[80] His announcement was premature, for Garfield lived on for over two months, but he did die of the wounds. It was only the second time an

American President had been assassinated, which made it shocking, and it must have been especially unsettling to President Arthur who had been named by the killer as the beneficiary. In any case, he took great care to avoid favoring Stalwarts in the appointments that he made. Moreover, he became a champion of civil service reform, thus abandoning his former opposition to it. The assassination of Garfield gave impetus to the adoption of a reform measure, though the most effective preventive measures against assassinations had already been taken. Guiteau was tried, convicted, and executed, with all deliberate speed.

At any rate, the Pendleton Act, for the reform of civil service, was passed in 1883. The act authorized a Civil Service Commission to conduct competitive examinations of candidates for specified government posts. Actually, not more than one-tenth of appointive positions in the government were placed under civil service at that time. Presidents were authorized to extend the list from time to time, and outgoing Presidents have usually done so (to protect their appointees in their jobs). Once a civil service appointment had been made, an employee could not be dismissed for political reasons. It was illegal thereafter for them to be required to make contributions to political parties. Over the years, the percentage of government posts filled from civil service lists has been greatly increased.

No doubt, those government employees covered by civil service were benefited. Since they could not be dismissed for political reasons, their appointments became tenured for working life, in the absence of dismissal for incompetence, insubordination, or the like. And they did not have to pay tribute to get their appointments. Whether it benefited their employers—politicians and American taxpayers—is not so easily determined. Popular control over the government, so far as it is exercised, is by way of the political process. Thus, while it may sound attractive to keep politics out of appointment of many government employees, it should be kept in mind that this also reduces popular control over the government. Nor is it at all clear how or why tenured employees will be more likely to do their jobs more efficiently or be more responsive to the wishes of their employers. Most likely, much of the behavior which is denounced as "bureaucratic" could be traced to the insulation of workers from their employers under civil service. At best, civil service has been a mixed bag of benefits.

2. The Protective Tariff

Although the tariff came in for considerable debate and legislative activity during this period, it was not entirely a partisan issue. Republicans were generally protectionists, but Democrats were divided on the issue. Historically, they had tended to favor a tariff for revenue only and inclined toward free trade. By the 1880s, however, most of the Democrats in the Northeastern states favored protectionist measures, while those from the South and

West generally favored lower tariffs. Since the parties were generally fairly evenly divided in Congress, and since some of the Democrats voted with Republicans on this issue, high protective tariffs prevailed.

The basic tariff provisions were put into effect during the Civil War. Thereafter, over the next twenty years or so they were only slightly revised from time to time. Rates were high, and many goods were protected. Among the items covered by the Tariff Act of 1864 were: tea, sugar, molasses, syrup, snuff, tobacco, bar iron, wire, galvanized iron, tin plates, anvils, chains, trace chains, halter chains, fence chains, hammers and sledges, nuts and washers, axles, bed screws, hinges, nails, spikes, rivets, bolts, horseshoe nails, tacks, brads, pig iron, stoves, pipe, scrap iron, steel wire, skates, cross-cut saws, hand saws, knives, needles, coal, wool, woolens, belts, hats, blankets, dress goods, shirts, oil cloths, cotton and cotton cloth, spool thread, cotton bagging, china, glass, cloves, pepper, salt, gunpowder, and lemons.[81] During the 1870s and 1880s duties were slightly reduced several times, and more agricultural products were added to the list. So far as tariffs on agricultural products grown on large scale in the United States went, they were of little or no consequence. Americans produced these goods not only for the home market but for export as well. The caustic comment of a writer on the Tariff of 1883 is very much to the point: "As far as any significance of these duties on most of these agricultural products, either to the agricultural producer or the consumer, they were at that time of no economic importance whatever. They served only to throw dust in the farmer's eyes, and foster in him a sort of pacific feeling that he was sharing the benefits of the protective system."[82] Mostly, it was manufactured products that were protected from foreign competition by the tariff.

Although President Arthur made an effort to get the rates lowered, an attempt that was only partially successful, it was Grover Cleveland who made the most thorough attack on the protective system. He devoted a State of the Union Message to an argument for the reduction of the tariff. The occasion he used as justification was a treasury surplus. The government was taking in more in revenue than it was spending, and he thought the logical course was to reduce taxes, and about the only place to do that was with the tariff. Although what he said amounted to a spirited assault on the protective system, he denied that he was arguing for free trade. "The question of free trade is absolutely irrelevant," Cleveland said, "and the persistent claim . . . that all the efforts to relieve the people from unjust and unnecessary taxation are schemes of so-called free traders is mischievous. . . ."[83] Whatever his views on free trade, he undoubtedly thought it would be more effective to focus on the need to reduce taxes than upon the question of principle.

Cleveland's case against the tariff was thoughtfully made. He emphasized that the tariffs tended to raise the price to consumers, that in effect it was

Americans who were being taxed. If the goods were actually imported and sold in this country, the duties that were paid on them were added to the price which the consumer paid. If they did not buy foreign goods on which duties were levied but domestic manufactures instead, then if the tariffs worked as advertised Americans paid higher prices for the goods than they would have to do in the absence of the tariff. As for protecting the jobs of American workers, he noted that even those who might so benefit were "consumers with the rest"; and that a high tariff "results in a very large increase in the price of nearly all sorts of manufactures, which, in almost countless forms, he needs for the use of himself and his family. . . ."[84] He emphasized the desirability of American manufacturers and producers becoming competitive with foreign producers and exporting their goods. That way, there might be the same level of employment without penalizing American consumers to get it.

Chester A. Arthur (1830–1886)

Courtesy New York Historical Society

Arthur was the 21st President of the United States, succeeding to that office on the death by assassination of James A. Garfield. Born in Vermont, he was the son of a Baptist minister who had immigrated from Ireland. Arthur graduated from Union College, studied law, and began his practice in New York City. In the course of his practice before the Civil War, he handled some cases which brought him within the frame of the anti-slavery movement, and he had become identified with the Republican Party by the beginning of the Civil War. President Grant appointed him collector of customs in New York City in 1871, and he retained the post until 1879. Arthur's reputation suffered from the charges brought against him as collector of customs because of the association of the office with the New York Republican political "machine," but he received the vice-presidential nomination of the party in 1880 as a sop to the Stalwarts who were unable to nominate their candidate. Even so, he earned the respect of people generally by his open handling of the affairs of the presidency.

Cleveland's recommendations fell on a great many deaf ears, and no new tariff law was passed. However, with Republicans in control of both the House and Senate and Harrison, a Republican President, the protectionists were able to get a tariff bill to suit them. The McKinley Tariff of 1890 was probably the most thoroughgoing protective measure ever passed up to that time. The average duty rose to 49 per cent. On cotton manufactures, it was raised from 35 to 50 per cent, and on some linens it was even higher. In general, the duties on goods that were in competition with those produced in the United States were raised while those on goods little produced here were lowered. In consequence, the tariff brought in much less revenue than formerly, and did a much more precise job of protecting American industries from competition with foreign manufactures. The act also placed a number of goods from Latin American countries on the free list, but provided that the President could impose duties again if they discriminated against American goods in their duties.

Democrats ran against the McKinley Tariff in 1890, and won a majority of seats in the House. In 1892, they gained control of the Senate, and Grover Cleveland was returned to the White House. The Wilson-Gorman Tariff of 1894 did lower some of the duties and place wool on the free list. However, the protective system remained in effect.

3. Silver, Bimetallism, and Inflation

The United States government appeared to be on its way toward a full-fledged gold standard in 1875. The treasury had already ceased the coining of silver dollars in 1873. The outgoing Congress in late 1874 passed a bill authorizing the redemption of United States notes, i.e., the Civil War Greenbacks, in 1879, and thereafter began to reduce the number of them in circulation. The effect of these acts would be to place the United States on a gold standard, since all currency would be redeemable in gold, including the subsidiary silver coins. In taking these actions, the United States government was moving in the same direction as the major trading nations in Europe, which were abandoning silver for gold. Bimetallism had been a failure in general, for where there was a set ratio of exchange between the two metals—gold and silver—the least valuable one tended to circulate.

The well-laid plans of Congress did not quite work out, however. True enough, John Sherman, Secretary of the Treasury beginning in 1877, did successfully accumulate gold enough in the Treasury to redeem the Greenbacks. And, once it became clear that they would be redeemed, they traded at their full face value and people lost interest in redeeming them. But even before actual resumption of specie payments for Greenbacks had gone into operation, Congress had moved to reinstall bimetallism. Prices of agricultural produce and monetary wages declined in the mid-1870s. A Greenback-Labor Party was organized, which pushed for free coinage of silver, which they hoped would be inflationary. Also, large new quantities of silver were coming on the market from Western mines. Those with silver to sell hoped to get government to remonetize silver and thus raise the price.

The result of this agitation was the Bland-Allison Act of 1878. This act required that the Treasury purchase no less than $2 million worth of silver monthly and coin it as dollars. It was to purchase no more than $4 million in any given month. The coin could be deposited with the Treasury in return for certificates which would themselves be money for the purposes of the government. President Hayes vetoed the bill with some sturdy objections. He pointed out that silver dollars of the specified weight during the past year had been worth on the market only 90 to 92 cents. Silver dollars would, therefore, be overvalued. He argued that when people could pay their government obligations in silver or certificates, they would cease to pay in gold, and the government would be unable to meet obligations it had earlier contracted to pay in gold. That would be, he said, to act in bad faith. "National promises," Hayes argued, "should be kept with unflinching fidelity. . . . The nation owes what it has led or allowed its creditors to expect. I can not approve a bill which in my judgment authorizes the violation of sacred obligations."[85] Congress was not greatly impressed with the position of Hayes and overrode his veto to make the bill a law.

Actually, the Bland-Allison Act never succeeded fully in its object or in fulfilling Hayes' fears of replacing silver with gold in government coffers. Gresham's law holds that bad money will drive good money out of circulation when both are legal tender. In this case, silver should have driven gold out of circulation. The process was delayed, however, by some unusual circumstances. First, the government had a large quantity of gold reserves on hand in anticipation of the resumption of specie payments. Since the Greenbacks were now "as good as gold" they continued to circulate, and thus the gold could be used to stave off the change to silver. Second, the Treasury only bought the minimum amount of silver each month. In consequence, most of the silver minted did not go into circulation. Grover Cleveland pointed out in 1885 that somewhat over 215 million silver dollars had been coined to that date. Of that amount, approximately 50 million had gone into circulation and 165 million were in storage by the government. In effect, the United States was still on the gold standard.

Even so, President Cleveland called for the repeal of the Bland-Allison Act in 1885 and warned that trouble lay ahead if this were not done. His analysis was much more thorough than Hayes' had been. He pointed out that if the Treasury continued to buy $2 million in silver per month, paying for it with gold, government would end up with only silver in its reserves. Then, Gresham's law would come into effect, and the cheaper (or overvalued) silver would drive gold out of circulation. He noted that all who had savings would be hurt by having to take the depreciated silver currency, and that when gold had gone out of general circulation the result would be a practical contraction of the money supply, not an increase of it, as many supposed.

John Sherman
(1823–1900)

A younger brother of the famous General Sherman, Sherman was an organizer of the Republican Party, was elected to the House of Representatives in 1855, moved up to the Senate in 1861, and served in that body until 1897, with only four years away (1877–1881) as Secretary of Treasury under President Hayes. He was involved with the formulation of most of the monetary laws of the government from the Civil War to the time of his retirement from the Senate: the National Banking Act, the resumption of specie payment, the administration of the Bland-Allison Act during the early years, and the Sherman Silver Purchase Act. He was the sponsor as well of the Sherman Antitrust Act. Sherman was born in Ohio, and studied and practiced law there before going into politics. His long service in Congress made him the thread of continuity in the Republican Party from the Civil War to the end of the century.

Congress did not act, however, on his reasoned appeal. Instead, in 1890 Congress passed a much more drastic silver measure. It passed the Sherman Silver Purchase Act. The Treasury was required to purchase 4½ million ounces of silver per month, if that much was offered for sale. The Treasury was to pay for the silver with bonds which were to be redeemable in gold or silver, at the discretion of the Secretary of the Treasury. At least a part of the silver purchased was to be coined in dollars. Congress further declared it to be government policy to have a currency of both gold and silver (bimetallism).

Congress had succeeded in placing the Treasury in a squeeze from which it was not fully relieved until 1900. It was committed to redeeming Greenbacks in gold, and to their reissue once they were received. Moreover, Treasury officials believed that they needed a reserve in gold of at least $100 million to take care of this situation. After the passage of the Silver Purchase Act, it had a much larger quantity of Treasury notes outstanding. By Congressional proclamation, the Treasury could redeem these in gold or silver, but it could only exercise this discretion by refusing to pay in gold, thus threatening gold as a circulating medium. That would have been to fail to comply with the command of Congress that both metals should circulate. Silver was now even more overvalued in relation to gold than formerly. The situation was impossible to deal with effectively, and could only worsen as more silver had to be bought.

There was an almost immediate, fairly severe drain on the Treasury's gold reserve. It had been about $200 million at the beginning of 1890, but had sunk to $117 million in November of that year. The Treasury was able to weather this particular siege, but in 1892 there began a severe drain of gold to foreign countries. This was further aggravated by the continued exchange of silver for gold, by way of the Treasury notes, so that by April, 1893 the gold reserve had sunk below $100 million. A panic ensued, the Panic of 1893, and the demand for liquidity increased. President Cleveland asked Congress to repeal the Sherman Act, and it did repeal that portion of the act which required the purchase of 4½ million ounces of silver per month. But it left in effect the law requiring keeping the Treasury notes in circulation, and the siege upon gold continued. The Treasury was able to maintain a gold supply in reserve only by selling government securities for gold, with successive bond issues. The crunch was eventually ended by the increase in the supply of gold from mining in the late 1890s.

4. The Regulation of Business

The federal government made its first tentative thrust toward the regulation of privately owned domestic businesses in the latter part of the 19th century. There was an element of such regulation in the national banking system and involvement with the money supply, stemming from the time of the Civil War and Reconstruction. Otherwise, the United States government had not been much involved with domestic regulation of business before the late 1880s, at the earliest. The two acts which signalled this major shift were the Interstate Commerce Act of 1887 and the Sherman Antitrust Act of 1890. Regulation means the laying down of rules for the conduct or operation of some undertaking. In practice when government regulates it tends to establish control over what it regulates. The businesses involved here were privately owned. Ordinarily and in general, the owners of private property lay down the rules for undertakings to be carried on with their property and exercise control over them. (That does not mean, of course, that owners may commit crimes with impunity on their property or that they may use their property in such ways as to do damage to the persons or property of others without being subject to legal action by those whom they damage. Rather, it means that with exceptions for general laws which apply to everyone, and in pursuit of peaceful ends, they regulate and control their property.) Government regulation, then, came into conflict with the regulation which owners ordinarily exercise over their property—or the "rights of property," as that is sometimes called. Government regulation did entail, at least potentially, taking some of the rights over property which owners have and vesting it in the public. In short, it would be (or could be) socialistic in tendency. Thus, the thrust toward regulation owed some of its impetus to radical and revolutionary ideas.

Actually, the thrust toward regulation had a variety of sources and motivations behind it. State and local governments never entirely abandoned some forms of commercial regulation, and the United States government did exercise some control over foreign commerce. Moreover, the federal government was constitutionally empowered to regulate commerce among the states and with the Indians. The United States often did regulate commerce with the Indians, but had not usually concerned itself much with commerce among the states. With the coming of interstate railroading and the development of nationwide businesses, those who were pushing for regulation turned to the United States government. It became clear by the mid-1880s that if those engaging in interstate business were to be subject to regulation the federal government would have to do it. And there were groups pushing for regulation.

Some of these wanted to control the railroads for their own ends. People in small towns wanted the same rate and service advantages as cities sometimes obtained. Small shippers wanted the same rates as large shippers. Farmers were often told that they were being taken advantage of by railroads in the high rates that were charged. Big businesses were described in such a way by agitators that people were induced to fear them. Some of the demagogic tactics of agitators come out in the following quotations. On the rapacious character of the railroads, a speaker for the National Farmer's Alliance declared that "the railroads are now menacing the peace and prosperity of the country in a far more grave and dangerous manner than was thought of by the people a half-century ago. Their power to centralize population, to control the commerce of the country, to build up a city or tear it down, to prosper one businessman and ruin another, to control legislatures and Congress, to pack courts, is what the people have come to fear."[86] Sockless Jerry Simpson proclaimed that "It is a struggle between the robbers and the robbed." And, a Populist manifesto described the situation this way: "On the one side are the allied hosts of monopolies, the money power, great trusts and railroad corporations, who seek the enactment of laws to benefit them and impoverish the people. On the other are the farmers, laborers, merchants, and all other people who produce wealth. . . ."[87]

What of these charges against the railroads, to take them first? Were they public enemy number one, arrayed against the American people? On the face of it, that does not appear to have been the case. Railroad equipment was improved as new technology became available, and service was usually bettered by these improvements. As far as rail rates were concerned, they usually declined from the 1870s to the early 20th century. In 1868, the average railway revenue per ton mile was about 1.9 cents; by 1900, this had been reduced to only a little more than .7 cents. The greatest benefits from rail service went to consumers. Americans quickly became accustomed to having on the shelves of their stores products from all over America and from much of the rest of the world. They not only could have them with great predictability, but they could also have them much cheaper than ever before in the latter part of the 19th century.

None of this is meant to suggest that there was not some truth to some of the charges leveled against the railroads. They did engage in some of the practices decried by their critics. They did sometimes charge more for a short haul than for a long haul, give rebates, give preferential rates to large shippers, favor some cities, or especially cities, over small towns, form pools for dividing up revenue between points, give out free passes to assorted people, and the like. But prior to 1887 none of these were illegal actions, and it is not at all clear on what grounds they were matters of public concern. It is true that some railroads had received various sorts of aid from states as well as the federal government to induce private entrepreneurs to build, but it is by no means clear that this compromised their status as private property.

At any rate, some states undertook to regulate railroads by what were sometimes called Granger laws, since they had been sponsored by the Grange in the Midwest. After the courts ruled that states could not regulate beyond their borders, the effort to get regulation shifted to the national government. Congress obliged in 1887 by passing the Interstate Commerce Act. The act applied to all rail lines operating in more than one state by crossing their boundaries. It provided that all charges made by the railroads must be just and reasonable. It established an Interstate Commerce Commission, composed of five members appointed by the President, who were empowered to determine when rates were unjust and unreasonable, but the Commission was not empowered at that time to fix rates. The act prohibited pooling operations, discriminatory rates, drawbacks, and rebates, and made it illegal to charge more for a short haul than a long haul of goods of the same character over the same line. The Commission was also empowered to conduct investigations of the railroads, to summon witnesses, and compel (by way of Federal courts, if necessary) the production of contracts. rate structures, and other materials. It was also given authority to require railroads to make annual reports and adopt a uniform system of accounting.

The Interstate Commerce Commission was the first (in a long line) of the regulatory commissions. The powers granted to it embraced what have usually been described as quasi-legislative, quasi-executive, and quasi-judicial functions. In short, what the Constitution had put asunder by the separation of powers the Congress united in a single body in regulatory commissions. By denominating the railroads "common carriers," a phrase derived from Medieval common law, Congress vested the Commission with powers which doubtfully descended from the power to regulate commerce and prohibited acts which were not generally illegal in the use of private property or in private business undertakings. The main thing the act did in this last regard was to interfere with the railroads' right to set prices and enter into contracts on mutually agreeable terms with customers.

In the market, prices are arrived at by the consent of willing buyers and sellers. Buyer and seller may or may not haggle over prices; a formal contract may or may not be drawn; and services and prices may or may not be tailored to meet the needs of particular buyers. It is not uncommon, for example, for sellers to sell larger quantities at a lower unit price than where only a single or a few units are bought. The ability of the railroads to do any of these things was now circumscribed. They could not strike individual bargains with groups of passengers or large shippers. In short, the power of the railroads to dispose of their services on terms agreeable to them was circumscribed. Congress did not deign, of course, to make clear what would constitute "just and reasonable" rates. Indeed, Congress indicated very little awareness of the thicket into which it was entering by prescribing such things. It was sufficiently leery of its rule about short and long hauls (with good reason) that it authorized the Commission to make modifications within the rule. But about "just and reasonable" rates it expressed no qualms. A "just price" is a metaphysical concept involving such abstract and practical complexities that if one could be worked out for any one good of a certain quality it would be obsolete before it could be charged. At any rate, Congress dumped the burden of determining such mundane things on the Commission and went on to more exalted general tasks.

Congress proved its innocence even more decisively in 1890 when it passed the Sherman Antitrust Act. This act was prompted by fears that had been aroused by the growth of large businesses and combines, that they would come to monopolize the provision of particular goods by buying out or driving out all competitors. The Standard Oil Trust had been the first and most dramatic of these. It was feared, or alleged, that such organizations would use their dominant positions to charge extortionate prices and otherwise take advantage of consumers. The Marxist vision of a time when businesses would grow larger and larger until only a few giants remained probably provided added dimensions to these fears. The proclaimed purpose of this legislation was to maintain or restore competition among providers of goods and services.

The first section of the Sherman Act prohibits any contract, combination, or conspiracy in restraint of trade among the states or with foreign nations. The second section prohibits any "person" to "monopolize, or attempt to monopolize, or combine or conspire with any other person or persons, to monopolize any part of the trade or commerce among the several States, or with foreign nations. . . .'' The third section elaborates somewhat on the provisions in the first section, and the rest of the act deals mainly with empowering Federal courts to enforce it.

The key word in the first and third sections is "restraint." If the word means what it is taken to mean in common usage, it would involve the use of intimidation, threats, force, or violence. Since the prevention or punishment of such acts are the main business of government, laws to that end are unexceptionable, as a rule. The second section, however, is peculiar, to say the least. The key word in it is "monopolize," and it makes it illegal for any person or combination or conspiracy to *attempt* or monopolize any portion of trade or commerce among the states, and so forth.

The first peculiarity is that "monopoly" is an ambiguous word, yet Congress did not define it or specify what constitutes a monopoly. Historically, a monopoly had been an exclusive privilege granted to some person or company to produce a good, provide a service, or carry on trade with some region. Such monopolies had been granted by monarchs or whoever exercised the power of government. Sixteenth-century English monarchs granted such monopolies in great number, so that by the beginning of the 17th century they had acquired a bad reputation. Even so, the English government continued off and on to grant exclusive privileges, also known as patents and franchises, in the 17th century, and American colonies often did the same. By the early 19th century the very word monopoly had become odious, though some exclusive franchises were still granted in the United States for the building of bridges, and the like. In the latter part of the 19th century, there was apparently a concerted effort to shift the odium that had attached to monopolies granted by government to large private companies and corporations. Thus the word came to mean something like this, as defined in a dictionary: "exclusive control of a commodity or service in a particular market, or a control that makes possible the manipulation of prices." The major thing to note here is that while the government grant of a monopoly was a definite thing, the newer definition of the word points to nothing definite that may have happened and is, therefore, vague and imprecise. In short, monopoly had become a highly ambiguous term.

Granted that this newer meaning was the one Congress had in mind in the Sherman Act, there is a second and even greater peculiarity. Congress ostensibly intended by this act to encourage competition, yet if the wording of the act is taken literally it makes effective competition illegal. It prohibits attempts to monopolize trade. Yet every competitive effort to increase business by any tradesman, every providing of better service or higher quality goods at a lower price, could be reasonably interpreted as an *attempt* to monopolize trade. If there were two grocery stores in a remote village, and one of them went out of the business, the remaining store, by this definition, would be a monopoly. The storekeeper, in the words of the law, "shall be deemed guilty of a misdemeanor, and, on conviction thereof, shall be punished by fine not exceeding five thousand dollars, or by imprisonment not exceeding one year, or by both. . . .'' Or, if the two storekeepers were to combine their businesses, they might be equally guilty. (Technically, the law might not apply if the village did not draw customers from two or more states.) In any case, any competitive act involving trade or agreement between two or more competitors might conceivably be deemed a violation of this strange provision.

In section 2 of the Sherman Antitrust Act, Congress had called into being a species of crime that did not theretofore exist, one which entailed no necessary injury to anyone, one which was ill defined, vague, and imprecise. It is still on the books, and has apparently served two functions over the years. It gives aid and comfort to those who wish to believe that somehow giant combinations are prohibited. Its other function has been to provide an arbitrary weapon with which to intimidate businesses and exercise government power over selected companies. The Sherman Act did not so much regulate business as attempt to intimidate it. Attorneys general, Presidents, and lawyers have sometimes brought suit, and some large businesses have been dismantled. Even larger and more dominant ones often escape, however, and great holding companies have been formed many times since. The only definite result of the measure is that aside from banks which perform trustee functions no business has since 1890 called itself a trust.

Regulation and the Courts

Neither the Interstate Commerce nor Sherman Antitrust acts had any immediate great impact either on railroads or large businesses. Not only were the powers either vague or so indefinite as to limits as to invite some caution in their assertion but also the courts, and especially the Supreme Court, were inclined to restrain regulatory power. The degree to which the federal government may regulate private property under the Constitution was very much in doubt as well as the extent of any regulatory authority. But now there was also a question of the degree to which private property could be regulated by the states under the Constitution. The 14th Amendment prohibits any state to "deprive any person of life, liberty, or property, without due process of law. . . .'' There is no reason to doubt that government could so regulate the use of property as to deprive their owners of some portion or all of it. For example, the setting of rail rates could deprive a railroad of its property. The rates could be set so low that it would bankrupt a railroad, or so high that shippers could not afford to pay them. These would be rather clear cases of depriving the railroads of the effective uses of their property. Less drastic rates would produce less obvious results, of course.

There was still the question, however, of the authority of governments to set the rates at all, for that would be interfering with a right ordinarily reserved to ownership. Then, there was the difficult and much debated question of what constituted "due process of law." If a legislature prescribed rates, for example, would that be in accord with or in violation of due process of law? Ordinarily, a legislature acts by prohibiting some action. (It may also act positively, as in levying taxes, for example.) Those who are accused of violating the act may then be accused and taken through all those procedures by which the person may be found guilty or not, and, if guilty, have his life, liberty, or property taken from him. Did the setting of rates by the legislatures, or by commissions, go around these procedures?

The Federal courts avoided absolute positions on these matters in the latter part of the 19th century, but their general tendency was to restrain and limit such exercise of legislative power. One of the first major decisions of the Supreme Court regarding state powers and the 14th Amendment, that of *Munn vs. Illinois*, maintained that state powers of regulation over certain kinds of property could be exercised. Speaking for a majority of the Court, Chief Justice Waite held: "Property does become clothed with a public interest when used in a manner to make it of public consequence, and affect the community at large. When . . . one devotes his property to a use in which the public has an interest, he . . . grants to the public an interest in that use in which the public has an interest, and must submit to be controlled for the common good." The suit involved the setting of maximum rates for the storage of grain by the legislature in Illinois. The Court held that as a matter of public interest and states could exercise such power of regulation. As to whether or not "statutes regulating the use, or even the price of the use, of private property necessarily deprived an owner of his property without due process of law. Under some circumstances they may, but not under all."[88] In the case before them, the Court ruled that the state regulations did not violate the 14th Amendment.

By the mid-1880s, however, the Supreme Court had begun to limit and restrain such exercises of state power. For one thing the composition of the Court was changing, and several of the new appointees to the Court were conservative property-minded men. Stephen J. Field, already on the Court, was of that persuasion, and others much nearer to his persuasion came on the Court: Horace Gray, 1882, Chief Justice Melville Fuller, 1888, L. Q. C. Lamar, 1888, and Edward D. White, 1894. In 1890, the Supreme Court negated a Minnesota rate law. It did so on the grounds that there was no provision for trying the matter in the courts. Justice Samuel Blatchford, speaking for the majority, said: "If the company is deprived of the power of charging reasonable rates for use of its property, and such deprivation takes place in the absence of an investigation by judicial machinery, it is deprived of the lawful use of its property, and thus, in substance and effect, of the property itself, without due process of law and in violation of the Constitution of the United States."[89] In the following years, the high court also negated such state laws as those prescribing hours of labor. In 1905, a majority of the Court (*Lochner vs. New York*) nullified a law fixing the maximum hours of bakers on the grounds that it took away their liberty of contract. Justice Peckham gave the opinion that "There is no reasonable ground for interfering with the liberty of a person or the right of free contract, by determining the hours of labor, in the occupation of a baker. . . . They are in no sense wards of the state. . . ." If the state could extend its powers in this way, he went on, "Not only the hours of employees, but the hours of employers, could be regulated, and doctors, lawyers, scientists, all professional men, as well as athletes and artisans, could be forbidden to fatigue their brains and bodies. . . ."[90]

It should have come as no surprise, then, that the Supreme Court would confine and limit the application of the Interstate Commerce and Sherman Antitrust acts. In 1896 and 1897, the high court denied that the Interstate Commerce Commission had been invested with what amounted to quasi-legislative and quasi-judicial powers. The fixing of rates, it said, was a legislative power, and had not been conferred on the Commission. Nor could it take the place of courts in determining the facts of cases that came before it. In short, the Commission could do very little about rail rates. In the Supreme Court decision, *United States vs. E. C. Knight Co.*, the majority held that manufacturing was not commerce, and that combinations engaged in manufacturing (or, for that matter, any other sort of production of goods), were not subject to the Sherman Act.

Even so, there were developments in the law in the late 19th century which indicated a shift away from the reliance upon the law and the Constitution as something of great fixity. For one thing, when the majority acted to delimit the power of governments to regulate by particular devices it still affirmed the power to regulate private property in the public interest. And it did so quite often on the basis of common law rulings stretching back into the distant past or upon such vague sources as powers inherent in sovereignty. (For example, in *Julliard vs. Greenan*, the Supreme Court held in 1884 that the federal government had the power to issue paper money and make it legal tender on the basis of its sovereignty, though there was no constitutional warrant for the decision.) In short, judges were going beyond the Constitution increasingly for support for their rulings.

For another thing, a different view of the law known as legal realism was beginning to make an impact. The crucial aspect of this view was that rulings should take into account conditions that prevailed. That may have provoked Justice Oliver Wendell Holmes, Jr.'s vigorous dissent in the case of *Lochner vs. New York*. He admonished his fellow justices that "The 14th Amendment does not enact Mr. Herbert Spencer's Social Statics. . . ." Moreover, "a Constitution is not intended to embody a particular economic theory, whether of paternalism and the organic relation of the citizen to state or of *laissez faire*."[91] Despite the fact that this was a *non sequitur*—no one

Oliver Wendell Holmes, Jr. (1841–1935)

Courtesy Library of Congress

Holmes was born in Boston, educated at Harvard, fought in the Civil War, studied law at Harvard afterward, and went into private practice for a few years. He was the son and namesake of a prominent Massachusetts physician, poet, essayist, and novelist, inherited some of his father's wit, but was bent more toward scholarship than imaginative literature. Holmes edited *The American Law Review* for several years and contributed articles to it over the years. He taught constitutional law and studied broadly in the common law. In 1881, he published an important treatise, entitled *The Common Law*. In 1882, he accepted an appointment to the Massachusetts supreme court, and became chief justice of that tribunal in 1899. However, he was appointed associate justice of the United States Supreme Court in 1902, and served with that body until he retired at the age of 90 in 1932. Holmes was best known for his dissenting opinions over the years. He tended to make a broad interpretation of the Constitution, dissented frequently from the majority opinion of the Court, and was the forerunner of the judicial use of the Constitution for expanding the powers of government.

had cited Spencer in support of the position, and there were much older arguments for the right to dispose of one's services on one's own terms—it has been a favorite quotation of historians over the years. But legal realism had a much more clear-cut impact a few years later. Louis D. Brandeis, a Boston attorney, presented what came to be known as a "Brandeis Brief" to the Supreme Court in 1903 in defense of an Oregon law regulating the hours of labor of women in employments using machines. His brief consisted of two pages of constitutional argument and over a hundred pages of factual and statistical material in support of his contention. The Court was apparently so overwhelmed by this flood of evidence that it allowed the statute to stand, thus reversing its position in *Lochner vs. New York*. Women had become, in the words of the Court in the earlier decision, "wards of the state," and in a few years men would be accorded the same status. The important point here, however, is the Brandeis Brief, and what its use and admission has done to the consideration of questions of law. In the 20th century, it has become commonplace for courts to listen to or read vast quantities of evidence, much of it irrelevant by almost any standard, before making rulings. Judges are invited to make their decisions on the basis of tendentious materials rather than attending to law and precedent. Virtually overwhelmed by factual details, they are invited to rule on the basis of their sympathies.

In any case, only the first major thrust of regulation has been dealt with here. It would become a tidal wave in the 20th century.

The Rise of Labor Unions

Perhaps the greatest disturbance of the relative political tranquility of this period was the rise of labor unions. There had been a few labor unions, generally local trade or craft associations, from the early years of the Republic. There had even been some sporadic growth of union activity, as in the 1830s. But it was only after the Civil War that large unions were formed, and after the growth of nationwide businesses, particularly railroads, that violent activities claimed national attention. Although the following figures probably exaggerate the actual impact, the Industrial Commission of 1900 reported that between 1881 and 1900 there had been a total of 22,793 strikes involving 117,000 businesses. Undoubtedly, most of these were local and brief, but there were a few of much more extensive character and impact.

The Civil War was hardly over when the first major effort to form an inclusive national union took place. Under the leadership of William H. Sylvis, a National Labor Union was set up in 1866. It claimed several hundred thousand members, but the membership was quite diverse, and it soon resembled more of a political party with the single purpose of advancing the interests of workers than a labor union. It broke up in the early 1870s. The Knights of Labor began to take shape in the early 1870s under the leadership of Uriah Stephens. It was only after 1879, when Terence V. Powderly became its president, that it grew large. At the height of its following it had as many as 700,000 members in the mid-1880s. The Knights was composed of individual members, not groups or unions, was radical in tendency, but the leadership opposed the strike as a weapon. At one time or another, the Knights favored an eight-hour work day, the abolition of child labor, government ownership of railroads and telegraph, paper money, an income tax, and the organization of cooperatives. Despite the opposition of the leadership to strikes, the Knights were prominent in a successful strike against the Missouri Pacific railroad in 1885, but failed the next year against the Texas and Pacific. In the late 1880s, the membership declined, and the organization soon disappeared.

Even before its decline had set in, however, a much more firmly based national union organization was being formed. In 1886, the American Federation of Labor was organized by Samuel Gompers. The AF of L, as it became known, was an association of trades unions mainly, organized on the basis of the federal system, and composed of local unions, sometimes organized nationally as trades. Gompers tried to keep the unions out of direct involvement in partisan politics and focused on union efforts to get higher pay, shorter hours, and the like. He succeeded well enough that the federation which he forged has continued down to the present time.

Generally speaking, though, it was the local union, or the organization according to craft or skill, such as the railroad brotherhoods, not national organizations and their leadership, that was at the heart of most union activity during these years. Labor unions posed a considerable problem for governments, both local and eventually national. They differed essentially from most other groups or organizations in that they tended to use force, intimidation, and violence, especially during organization campaigns and strikes. Moreover, their most potent weapon generally was the threat of striking and about the only good they offered was to refrain from striking. These tactics brought unions into conflict with government, because government is given a monopoly within its jurisdiction of the use of organized force and is charged by the citizenry with protecting them from the use of force upon them. Union activities, then, tend to turn into contests with government, as unions challenged the government's monopoly of the use of force.

That is not the way unions have described their undertaking, of course. They have tried to justify their use of force on the grounds that workers were being taken advantage of by employers. To counter the wealth and dominant position of employers, they claim that it is necessary for workers to band together and use their numerical advantage. Socialism, especially Marxism, provided them with the ideological ammunition to support these claims. Workers constitute a class, in this view, a class that is exploited by employers. Marx's labor theory of value provided the bluntest argument for this case. He held that workers contribute the whole of the value to goods, but that the capitalists who add nothing to the value of the goods keep a large portion of what is paid for the goods for themselves. Workers must become class conscious, according to this formulation, and engage in a class struggle with employers (or capitalists) for what is theirs. Unionism was one approach to doing this.

American unions have not usually been avowedly Marxist though some of their leaders and rank and file members, have been that, or some other variety of socialists. But they have usually claimed that workers were being taken advantage of by employers and that the contest was with them. Thus, when they strike or organize or engage in boycotts it is the workers against management (or the capitalists). Here is how one friend of the union movement described the justification of action:

> It is hardly disputed that capital, under our modern industrial system, is receiving more than a just share of the fruits of labor, and the laborer is receiving relatively less and less of the profits of his toil. . . . The distribution of wealth is not according to one's worth to society, but according, in large measure to the skill of some in appropriating to themselves the fruits of the labor of others. . . .[92]

What follows is a statement of the justification and purpose of unionism made by a group of labor leaders, including Samuel Gompers of the AF of L, in 1894:

> The trade union movement has its origin in economic and social injustice. . . . It stands as the protector of those who see the wrongs and injustice resultant of our present industrial system, and who by organization manifest their purpose of becoming larger sharers in the product of their labor, and who by their efforts contribute toward securing the unity and solidarity of labor's forces; so that in the ever-present contest of the wealth producers to conquer their rights from the wealth absorbers, we may . . . work out . . . the final emancipation of labor.[93]

In short, unionists claim that workers are being done out of a portion of what is theirs and that employers (managers, capitalists) are the villains of the piece. The solution, they say, is to organize and contest with them.

As a general charge against all employers, the union claim is ridiculous, on its face. Far from enriching themselves at the expense of their employees, in any given period of time, some businesses fail, go broke, declare bankruptcy, or simply go out of business. It does not follow, however, that those employers who usually make a profit do so at the expense of their employees. A business may be well managed, produce some good for which there is a ready market, serve its customers effectively, purchase materials more wisely, and so on. Once it is admitted that capital plays an important role in production, that enterprisers deserve some reward, that management is essential to organized production, no general charge of "exploitation" of workers is sustainable. This is not to suggest that either particular workers or even all those in a plant or who work for a particular company may not have some grievance. That is true, however, in all relationships involving two or more people and cannot be fruitfully charged to employee relationships.

In any case, it is largely an illusion that unions are organized primarily against employers. The conflict ordinarily is not directly between management (or capital) and labor. It is basically between unionists and other workers or would-be workers. This is not to deny that employers may be injured by strikes, boycotts, and other coercive or violent union activities. Nor is it to deny what has already been confirmed, that unions may pose a challenge and contest with governments, or that consumers and other businesses may be inconvenienced by union activities. Rather, it is to say that the intimidations, threats, and such violence as may be used by unionists is usually aimed directly at other workers.

This is seen most clearly when there are strikes and unions maintain picket lines. Those who try to enter struck plants to go to work are subject to abusive language, threats, and often violence. Generally, management personnel can go and come at will at struck plants, with no harm threatened or done to them. It is quite otherwise in regard to workers—those who stay on the job when the union calls a strike (called "scabs" by unionists), union members who return to work during the strike (called "rats"), or replacement workers (called "strikebreakers"). These are subject to the full wrath of those on the picket line and other strikers. This has been so from the early 19th century onward. When shoemakers went on strike in Philadelphia in the early 19th century, six journeymen stayed on the job. "The strikers kept up a sharp eye for them and when they briefly emerged one Sunday night to visit a nearby tavern, beat them up severely."[94] A more striking example occurred in 1880 in Leadville, Colorado when the Miner's Union struck, and some of the owners tried to operate their mines:

> The managers employed every available man who could handle pick or shovel, hold a drill or swing a sledge. The strikers used every means at their command to keep men from going to work and to pull out those who were at work. . . . Every day, and sometimes twice each day a "Committee," composed of several hundred strikers, made the round of the mines that were working. . . . Fists, clubs, and sometimes pistols were used, but without fatal results.[95]

Thousands of examples of union violence against other workers could be found in American history, some much more violent, and including such things as attacks upon workers' homes, property, and killings. There have been isolated instances, of course, of unionists attacking management. One violent organization, composed of the Molly Maguires, did assault managers and foremen connected with the coal mines in Pennsylvania in the late 19th century, but this movement was exceptional and short-lived. Generally, union intimidation, threats, and violence have been aimed at other workers.

In no sense is this contest of unions with other workers incidental. It is at the heart of what unions have to do to accomplish their goals. Economically, workers in similar undertakings are in competition with one another, in competition for the best jobs which they can perform. Thus, workers in a factory doing similar work, or those who may wish to work there, are in competition with one another. To overcome this, unions attempt to promote class solidarity, and those who do not bow to that view are the enemy, hence, "scabs," "rats," and the like. Even more important economically, unions attempt to raise the wages and reduce the hours of work and the work load of their members. They attempt to do this most directly by reducing the supply of labor, artificially, to given employers or industries. That is the purpose of the picket line ordinarily, to keep out all those who would work for the pay being offered. In general terms, they attempt to monopolize employment so as to restrict it to their members and those who will work under their terms.

What unions attempt, or aim at, is to form an alliance with employers to exclude nonmembers from employment. That is the fundamental purpose of the labor contract between unions and employers, though unions often take less than that. The idea of such an alliance between employers and unions was stated rather candidly by John L. Lewis, a union leader, in 1901. He explained why miners' unions were conferring with the coal operators:

> As I understand it, it is for the purpose of wiping out competition between us miners first, viewing it from our side of the question; next for the purpose of wiping out competition as between the operators in these four states. When we have succeeded in that . . . , then as I understand the real purpose of this movement, it is that we will jointly declare war upon every man outside of this competitive field. . . .[96]

In short, unions and employers in particular undertakings should form an alliance to keep out competition.

It was hardly surprising that employers did not rush to enter into such alliances with labor unions. It was hardly in their interest to do so ordinarily, since they would be denying themselves access to willing workers on the market who might do better work for lower wages. Moreover, labor contracts only ran for some period of time, and employers might have their operations disrupted by strikes at some future time. Nor was the legality of such agreements by any means clear. For employers to join with unions in excluding some workers (and their products sometimes) from the market would make them subject to prosecution for conspiracy or combination in restraint of trade. Indeed, unions were often charged with such offenses in the 19th century without the connivance of employers. And courts often ruled against such union activity. For example, in *The People vs. Fisher*, a New York court had this to say in 1835 about such combinations:

> . . . The man who owns an article of trade or commerce is not obliged to sell it for any particular price, nor is the mechanic [worker

with machines] obliged to labor for any particular price. He may say that he will not make coarse boots for less than one dollar per pair, but *he has no right to say that no other mechanic shall make them for less.* . . . If one individual does not possess such a right over the conduct of another, no number of individuals can possess such a right. All combinations therefore to effect such an object are injurious, not only to the individual particularly oppressed, but to the public at large. . . .[97]

In general, it can be said that labor unions had no standing at law throughout the 19th century, but that action was only taken against their members when they disturbed the peace or suit was brought against them by someone.

It was into this somewhat confused situation that large labor unions appeared after the Civil War and some large and disruptive strikes occurred. Until 1890, there was no Federal law which applied to them, and Federal forces only went into action upon requests from governors of states to put down resistance to their authority or quell rebellions. After the passage of the Sherman Antitrust Act in 1890, the federal government was authorized to take action on its own initiative in matters affecting interstate commerce. The major disruptions illustrate more clearly the contest between unions and government than between unions and other workers or employers, but these latter were always in the wings if not at the forefront of events.

The first disturbance which had national dimensions was the one known as the Great Railway Strike of 1877. It began in Baltimore, when some of the crewmen on the B & O refused to remove trains after they received pay cuts. The railroad hired replacements, but when the strikers refused to leave the rail yards they were arrested. But there was trouble ahead in Martinsburg, West Virginia, when the crew refused to take the train through. The railroad asked for aid from state troops, but they met resistance as well, and a striker was killed. The governor requested Federal troops, and when several hundred arrived the trains began rolling again. Open warfare broke out in Pittsburgh after crewmen on the Pennsylvania Railroad refused to move a train pulled by two connected engines. The sheriff was unable to quell the ensuing uprising, even with the aid of state troops; strikers attacked the troops, surrounded them, and finally drove them off with gunfire. The strike spread across Pennsylvania; the governor assembled a large force to march against them; and Federal troops armed with artillery joined in the fray. Disturbances spread to several states in the Midwest, and Chicago became the scene of extended disorder. The United States Army was eventually able to restore peace there as elsewhere.

An even more spectacular series of events occurred in 1886 in Chicago in what has gone down in history as the Haymarket Riot or Massacre. This riot was preceded by strikes, but it also was fomented by radicals, mostly of foreign extractions (usually called anarchists, for their opposition both to capitalists and to government). Cyrus McCormick, owner of a harvester works in Chicago, had refused to accept a union to represent his employees. When pressed, he closed his factory and opened it later with nonunion workers. Conflict between the union workers on strike and the workers who replaced them was frequent and bitter. Meanwhile, organized labor generally launched a campaign for the 8-hour day with a general strike. McCormick granted this boon to his workers and gave them a half-day off to celebrate. Striking workers greeted them with abusive language when they left the factory. These were joined by other unionists who were on strike nearby, and the situation became dangerous. The police were called; the strikers challenged them, and several of the strikers were killed.

Radicals promoted a protest meeting to be held the next night at Haymarket Square with provocative circulars printed in both German and English. The heading read: "Revenge! Revenge! Workmen to Arms!" The body of the circular was a verbal assault on the police:

> Men of labor, this afternoon the bloodhounds of your oppressors murdered six of your brothers at McCormick! Why did they murder them? Because they dared to be dissatisfied with the lot which your oppressors assigned to them. They demanded bread, and they gave them lead for an answer.[98]

In the course of the meeting which ensued at Haymarket Square, a squad of police arrived and asked the crowd to disperse. Instead, the crowd was belligerent, and someone threw a bomb into the midst of the police, killing one and wounding others. A battle ensued: seven policemen were killed and over sixty others were wounded. Four people in the crowd were killed. Subsequently, several of the radicals were arrested, tried and convicted for incitement to murder, and four of them were eventually executed.

The Homestead Strike of 1892 brought on not only a contest between government and the unions but also between unions and a private force of Pinkerton detectives. The strike occurred at the Homestead (Pennsylvania) plant of Carnegie Steel, which was headed by Henry C. Frick. When a steelworkers' union struck Homestead in 1891, Frick tried to operate the plant without them. The plant was surrounded by strikers, and the sheriff came to the site with 100 deputies, but this force refused to cross the picket lines. Instead, the sheriff urged negotiations, and the strike was settled. However, when the plant was struck the following year, Frick determined not to rely very heavily on the sheriff for protection. Instead, he placed an order for guards with the Pinkerton Detective Agency because, as he said, "it would be necessary to protect our own property and secure new workmen."[99] Three hundred of the Pinkerton men tried to reach the struck plant by boats on the river, but they were repulsed by strikers, and several detectives were killed. They tried twice more but finally surrendered to the strikers, who then took over the plant and held the guards captive. The sheriff asked the governor for troops, and 7,000 troops were sent. They removed the strikers, and Frick regained control of the plant. In the midst of these developments an anarchist shot and stabbed Frick but failed in the effort to kill him.

The Pullman Strike of 1894, centered around Chicago but extending outward in its impact, brought new factors into play in a labor uprising. In this one, the United States government became directly involved, rather than as a backup force. The Sherman Antitrust Act was invoked, and a court injunction was used. The injunction (both from state and Federal courts) was now on its way to becoming a major device in dealing with union disturbances. Only 28 injunctions were issued dealing with these in the 1880s; 122 were issued in the 1890s, 328 from 1900 to 1909, and 446 from 1910 through 1919.

Eugene V. Debs
(1855–1926)

Courtesy Tamiment Institute Library

Debs was the leading socialist in the United States during the first two decades of the 20th century. He was the Socialist Party candidate for President five times from 1900–1920. Born in Indiana, he was schooled in his native state and started out his working life as a locomotive fireman. He had a brief career in local politics in the 1870s before returning to the railroads and becoming a unionist. Debs organized the American Railway Union, led the Pullman Strike of 1894, and was sentenced to prison for violating a court order during the strike. While in prison, he studied socialist literature and thereafter became a writer and publicist for socialism and industrial unionism. Among socialists, Debs was an oddity—a native born American—and that plus his writing and speaking ability made him the choice of the less violent socialists as their leader. He was sent to prison once again during World War I for espionage and was even a candidate for President while there. He did much to familiarize Americans with socialist ideas.

Actually, Pullman Strike is a misnomer for the events that brought action by the federal government. There *was* a Pullman strike, but it was not the direct cause of the Federal intervention. It could more aptly be called the American Railway Union Boycott. When the workers in the Pullman plant near Chicago went out on strike, the American Railway Union, under the leadership of Eugene V. Debs, who later ran for President several times on the Socialist ticket, proclaimed a boycott of Pullman cars on the trains that they worked. The Associated Railroads of Chicago determined that they would continue to pull Pullman cars. The rail workers refused to pull the cars, and the railroads replaced them with workers who would. The strikers attempted to prevent the movement of trains, and the mails could not go through on a regular basis. The United States government got an injunction against the American Railway Union. The strikers ignored the injunction, and Federal troops were sent to Chicago to maintain order. Debs and other leaders were arrested, tried, and sentenced for violation of a court order. The strike was now broken.

Union conflicts with governments did not end in 1894, but they were generally less violent over the next several decades. As already noted, the injunction was increasingly used by governments to restrain unions. Violence and intimidation by unions were much more apt to be aimed at nonunion and replacement workers than against armed force. President Cleveland appointed a United States Strike Commission, which had some trenchant comments about labor union disturbances. "They are war," it said. "These barbarisms waste the products of both capital and labor, defy law and order, disturb society, intimidate capital, convert industrial paths where there ought to be plenty into highways of poverty and crime, bear as their fruit the arrogant flush of victory and the humiliating sting of defeat, and lead to preparations for greater and more destructive conflicts. . . ."[100] The Commission recommended that the government encourage labor combinations, as it had capital formation, in the interest of industrial peace. The Commission showed little awareness, however, of the nature of unionism, who it was organized against, or how it acts to achieve its purposes.

Populism

The Populist movement of the 1890s was the first political movement animated by collectivist and radical ideas to make much of a national impact. It had only meager successes, so far as elections went, but it championed programs which, in altered form, were eventually enacted, and it made a considerable impact on the future direction of the Democratic Party. Actually, the political party which has often been called Populist was formally named the People's Party. Several state conventions took steps toward its organization in 1890, and a national organization was set up in

1891. In 1892, the People's Party nominated James B. Weaver of Iowa as its presidential candidate. He carried several Western states, but won less than 10 per cent of the popular vote in an election in which Cleveland was elected President and the Democrats took control of both houses of Congress. A number of Populists, however, won election at the local and state level as well as seats in Congress. The Populists nominated William Jennings Bryan, the Democratic candidate for President, as their candidate as well in 1896. He lost to the Republican candidate, William McKinley, and thereafter the following of the Populists dwindled away. Thus, the Populists were only important nationally for five or six years, but during that period they altered the political climate considerably.

The Populist movement was built mainly on the Farmers' Alliances which had been organized in the 1880s as a focus of discontent among farmers, especially in the West (including Midwest) and the South. Although farm prices fluctuated from time to time, they had generally declined over the years from the Civil War through the mid-1890s. Several things contributed to this price decline. One was the great increase in agricultural production, as much more land was opened up for cultivation with the building of the railroads. This increase in production was also greatly aided by cheap land made available by governments and the railroads themselves, who had received large land grants. Another contributing factor was that much of American farm produce was now sold on the world market, and prices there tended to set an upper limit for prices in America. Prices, in general, tended to decline, for manufactured products and transportation as well as farm products. There were some declines in the money supply as well, particularly as the notes of national banks were retired. And, of course, particular farmers were impoverished by droughts, heavy rains, mismanagement, and all the reasons that may lead to failure in farming.

Of course, farmers, like most of the rest of us, are subject to assorted discontent with their lot. Their undertaking is unusually exposed to the elements, and they cannot determine in advance how much they will produce. Aside from all these things, however, a large portion of farmers were coming to produce primarily for the market, and even the world market. From time immemorial, most farmers have produced primarily for their own needs (plus those of the landlord, if any). To the extent that they now produced for the market, they were engaged in business. Yet they often had neither the talent nor understanding for business, nor have they accustomed themselves easily to the vagaries of the market. It was easy for them to believe that they were being victimized by the railroads, by merchants, by warehouses and owners of grain elevators, by the middlemen, that they were the true producers of wealth, yet others were enriching themselves at their expense. In short, many farmers were ready prey for demagogues and politicians touting political solutions for their problems.

Populist ranks were filled not only by farmers but also by unionists, particularly the Knights of Labor, and assorted radicals of one stripe or another. At a convention in Topeka in 1890, at which a call was made for a People's Party, the delegates consisted of "forty-one Alliancemen, twenty-eight Knights of Labor, seven Patrons of Husbandry [Grangers], ten members of the Farmers' Mutual Benefit Association, and four single-taxers."[101] The leadership contained utopians, hard-bitten farm leaders, rabble-rousing politicians, silverites, and assorted collectivists promoting panaceas for the farm problem. Utopians, particularly followers of Edward Bellamy, were very much in evidence in the Populist movement.

The Populist leaders were under the sway of an idea. In the broadest terms, that idea was socialism—the belief that it is the business of society to look after and provide for the needs of every one of its members. A contemporary historian pointed out that "Populists may claim, as many of them do, that they are not socialists, and that they are opposed to socialism; the fact remains that their attitude is socialistic. Their demands for government correction of evils are socialistic. They believe that government can do better for individuals, in many cases, than the individuals can do for themselves. Furthermore, their proposals are the very ones advocated by socialists."[102] After the Democrats had adopted a Populist-leaning platform in 1896, Archbishop John Ireland of Minnesota deplored the "spirit of socialism that permeates the whole movement which has issued from the convention at Chicago."[103]

Populists described the struggle and its protagonists in various ways. It was "the people" against Wall Street, labor against capital, farmers and workers against men of great wealth. Mary E. Lease, the fiery woman leader among the Populists, declared that "Wall Street owns the country," that the United States has "a government of Wall Street, by Wall Street, and for Wall Street. . . . The West and South are bound prostrate before the manufacturing East. . . . Kansas suffers from two great robbers, the Santa Fe Railroad and the loan companies. The common people are robbed to enrich their masters. . . ."[104] The Populists wanted to use government as the means to set all this right, in their view. Jacob S. Coxey, who led a motley throng of people in a march on Washington in 1894, said: "We are here to petition for legislation which will furnish employment for every man able and willing to work; for legislation which will bring universal prosperity. . . ."[105] Lorenzo Dow Lewelling declared, "I claim it is the business of Government to make it possible for me to live and sustain the life of my family."[106]

As for their particular programs, Populists were most concerned to break the money power, the bankers especially, over them. They claimed that the money power over them was exercised by way of the gold standard. Populists wanted plentiful money; they wanted silver to trade on a par with gold, but they wanted more than that. They wanted paper money, issued and backed by government. To Ignatius Donnelly the gold standard was "the silly superstition of some prehistoric nation." It was like an iron band crushing the poor to death. If there were only an international paper money, "The world, released from its iron band, would leap forward to marvelous prosperity. . . ."[107]

The Populist platform of 1892 called for "a national currency, safe, sound, and flexible, issued by the general government," with no involvement by the banks, free and unlimited coinage of silver, a graduated income tax, a postal savings bank (a bank for the people provided by the government), government ownership of railroads, telephone, and telegraph, and that all land held by corporations beyond their actual needs be returned to the government for distribution to real settlers. The Party also expressed "sentiments" in favor of measures to make the government more responsive to the will of "the people": the secret ballot, the direct election of Senators, restriction of Presidents to a single term, and the use of the initiative and referendum to obtain legislation. For organized labor, they favored shorter hours, immigration restriction, more stringent restrictions on contract labor brought in from abroad, and abolition of the Pinkerton detective system.

The Populists did not originate these ideas for the most part—most of them had been bandied about by radicals for a number of years—but they did give them much greater currency. Moreover, though Populists were never in position to pass any of them, in one way or another most of them became a part of programs that did become law in the 20th century. Most important, perhaps, they exerted a major influence on the Democratic Party from 1896 onward, contributing to a radicalization of the leadership which has not yet been abandoned in the 20th century.

The Democratic Convention which met in Chicago in 1896 turned its back on Grover Cleveland and came out for free and unlimited coinage of silver. It nominated as its standard bearer William Jennings Bryan, who had, in a speech before the Convention, signified his sympathy with the Populist direction. "Upon which side will the Democratic party fight," Bryan asked rhetorically, "upon the side of 'the idle holders of idle capital' or upon the side of 'the struggling masses'? . . . The sympathies of the Democratic party . . . are on the side of the struggling masses. . . .There are two ideas of government. There are those who believe that if you will only legislate to make the well-to-do prosperous, their prosperity will lead through on those below. The Democratic idea, has been that if you make the masses prosperous, their prosperity will find its way up through every class which rests upon them."

> You come to us and tell us that the great cities are in favor of the gold standard; we reply that the great cities rest upon our broad and fertile prairies. Burn down your cities and leave our farms, and your

cities will spring up again as if by magic; but destroy our farms and the grass will grow in the streets of every city in this country.[108]

Bryan was defeated in the ensuing election, and he was defeated the other times he would run for President, but he had drawn the Populist spirit into the Democratic Party, and the party of Jefferson and Jackson made a fateful turn, however hesitant, in the direction of socialism.

William Jennings Bryan (1860–1925)

Bryan was the foremost leader of the Democratic Party from 1896 to 1912, though he was never elected to national office. He was three times a candidate for President, but achieved national office only by serving as Secretary of State for several years under Woodrow Wilson. He was born in Illinois, studied law in Chicago, and was admitted to the bar. After practicing law for several years in Illinois, he moved to Nebraska and was soon deeply involved in politics. As a Senator from Nebraska, Bryan came to national attention for his advocacy of unlimited coinage of silver. With his stirring oratory, he captured the hearts of many of the delegates to the Democratic Convention in 1896 and the nomination for President. He traveled more miles and made more speeches than any candidate ever had before, but he lost the election. Bryan ran again in 1900 and 1908, but lost both elections. Even so, he championed many reforms——popular election of Senators, the creation of a department of labor, national prohibition, and women's suffrage—which were eventually adopted.

Chapter 6
Progressivism

> *We are Anglo-Saxons, and must obey our blood and occupy new markets, and, if necessary, new lands. . . . Like England, we will establish trading posts throughout the world, we will cover the oceans with our merchant marine . . . ; great colonies will grow about our posts of trade, and American law, American order, American civilization, and the American flag will plant themselves on shores hitherto bloody and benighted.*
>
> **—Albert J. Beveridge, 1898**

> *Church and State are alike but partial organizations of humanity for special ends. Together they serve what is greater than either: humanity. Their common aim is to transform humanity into the kingdom of God.*
>
> **—Walter Rauschenbusch, 1907**

> *Legislation is powerless to eradicate racial instincts or to abolish distinctions based upon physical differences, and the attempt to do so can only result in accentuating the difficulties of the present situation. . . . If one race be inferior to the other socially, the Constitution of the United States cannot put them on the same plane.*
>
> **—Plessy vs. Ferguson, 1896**

Chronology

1898—

February—Sinking of the *Maine*.

April—Resolution for War against Spain.

July 3—Destruction of Spanish Fleet at Santiago.

July 7—Annexation of Hawaii.

December—Treaty of Paris ending Spanish-American War.

1899—North Carolina imposes racial segregation on trains.

1900—Open Door Policy in China.

1901—Enactment of the Platt Amendment.

1902—Publication of *The Pit* by Frank Norris.

1904—Publication of Ida Tarbell's *The History of the Standard Oil Company*.

1906—Publication of Upton Sinclair's *The Jungle*.

1907—William James publishes *Pragmatism*.

1909—Publication of Croly's *The Promise of American Life*.

Populism had hardly been turned back and its following begun to dwindle away when a new surge of reform swept over America in the early 20th century. It is generally called Progressivism, and it had a much broader following and greater impact than did all the third party, reformist, and collectivist movements of the latter part of the 19th century. Indeed, Populism, with its predominantly rural following, never had much chance of electoral success, even when it was allied with the silverite Democrats. It depended too much on the conflict between rural and urban America at a time when America was becoming much more urban, and when wealth was being concentrated in the cities. At any rate, the Progressive appeal was much broader and comprehended farmers, industrial workers, and Americans generally. That part of Populism which was absorbed by the Democrats served well as a basis of reformism, which was the hallmark of Progressivism. Indeed, several of the Populist reform proposals were adopted and actually enacted by the Progressives. Moreover, in contrast to Populism, Progressivism made a considerable impact upon the Republican Party in the early 20th century, particularly by way of Theodore Roosevelt.

The Progressive Ethos

Progressivism—a name bestowed on it mainly by historians—did not come to the fore as a third party as Populism had. It was much broader and less precise than that. It emerged as a movement or ethos in the early 20th century and embraced much of the reform impetus which arose or came into focus. A third party was organized in 1912, the Bull Moose Party, which was an instrument largely for pushing the election of Theodore Roosevelt to the presidency. There was a Progressive Party afterward, mainly in the mid-1920s, but it was made up mostly of the more radical Republicans. The progressive ethos went mainly into the New Deal in the 1930s, and so much of it as remained came to be called Liberalism, a considerable distortion of an older set of ideas once known by that name.

Progressivism did not come to the forefront during hard times, though it is a part of the reform lore that reform surges occur at such times. On the contrary, the period from the late 1890s until World War I was unusually prosperous. The United States had the most extensive rail transport system of any large country in the world. American manufactures, which had been growing greatly in recent decades, grew and expanded even more vigorously. New inventions and devices were being rapidly developed: the telephone, electric lighting, the automobile, the streetcar, and even the airplane. Motion pictures were being made, though the industry was still very much in its infancy. The marketing of goods was developing apace, and Henry Ford was showing the way with the automobile how to produce and sell even the more expensive of them to more and more customers. Farmers enjoyed unprecedented prosperity during most of these years. Gold had been discovered in Alaska in 1896 and was mined in large quantities in the ensuing years. The surge of prosperity was only briefly interrupted by a banking panic in 1907. Thus, while the reformers did advance economic reforms, they did so in a framework of general prosperity.

But the impulse behind progressivism was not some temporary emergency. Progressivism was an ideology which had hold in the minds of a goodly number of American intellectuals by the early years of the 20th century and which joined together ideas which had broad appeal to many Americans. It was the result, in the first place, of the joining of the idea of progress to reform, of the dawning belief that progress could be achieved by the aggressive use of government power. The linking of government instituted reforms to the idea of progress was a masterstroke. Americans generally believed to a greater or lesser extent that progress was taking place. The signs of ongoing progress were all around, or so people generally believed, progress in transportation, rapidity of communication, and in devices of one kind or another. By linking this idea to reform, reformers made it appear that those who opposed their efforts were opposed to progress.

Darwinism gave great new impetus to the idea of progress, as explained earlier. It made progress a kind of universal phenomenon, driven, so some held, by natural forces. An American sociologist, Lester Frank Ward, had advanced the notion which has been called reform Darwinism. His basic idea was that man had moved into a new stage of evolution by the development of mind so that he could control the course of development by reforms so as to insure improvement and progress. His chosen instrument, along with that of an increasing number of reformers, was government.

Progressivism also embraced two other powerful ideas. They were democracy and nationalism. By the late 19th century, the idea was gaining ground that the United States was a democracy, or that it ought to be anyway. Reformers began to latch on to democracy in the latter part of the 19th century, pushed for popular control over government to be expanded, and linked this to progress and progressivism. They linked it to broader and deeper reform, too, by identifying democracy with equality, and proposing to use the power of government to make men more nearly equal. The expansion of the power of the central government and the use of that power to transform not only America but the world setting as well was a part of the progressive ethos. The result was what Theodore Roosevelt called the New Nationalism.

1. Pragmatism

Several intellectual developments undergirded and gave particular thrusts to the reform effort we are calling progressivism in general. One of these was in philosophy itself, and it was done by Americans. A philosophy, or pseudo-philosophy, known generally as pragmatism, was advanced in the late years of the 19th and early years of the 20th century. The term was coined by Charles Sanders Peirce, a rather obscure thinker who received his undergraduate degree at Harvard and later advanced his ideas in lectures at Johns Hopkins, Harvard, and Lowell Institute. William James, a Harvard professor, publicized pragmatism, and John Dewey, a professor at Columbia, gave even greater currency to the idea.

Pragmatism is not so much a philosophy as a way of doing without philosophy. So far as it is a philosophy, it is a philosophy of process, of change, in a word, of flux. The pragmatists held that everything in the world is continually changing, growing, altering, and becoming. Theirs is a philosophy built on evolution, ongoing and never-ending evolution which never reaches the point of fixity. Theirs was a root and branch assault on the inherited philosophy, in the belief in an enduring order, an underlying reality, or in any such thing as human nature or the nature of anything. There are no absolutes, fixities, natures, or properties. Peirce held that pragmatism will "serve to show that almost every proposition of ontological metaphysics is either meaningless gibberish . . . or else is downright absurd."[109] James declared that the notion that there are absolutes "clashes with other truths of mine. . . ." Therefore, "I personally just gave up the Absolute."[110] Dewey pointed out that in the older philosophy truth and falsity "are thought of as fixed, ready-made properties of things themselves. . . . This view is radically challenged by the pragmatic conception of truth. . . ."[111]

The central concept of pragmatism, according to those who advanced the idea, is that the truth of any thought, so far as it contains any, consists in the effects or results of believing and acting on it. As James said, "we need only consider what conceivable effects of a practical kind the object may involve. . . . Our conception of these effects, whether immediate or remote, is then for us the whole conception of the object. . . ."[112] In practice, Dewey said of "ideas, meanings, conceptions, theories, systems . . . ," that if they are "instrumental to an active reorganization of the given environment . . . , then the test of their validity and value lies in accomplishing this work. If they succeed in their office, they are reliable, sound, valid, good, true."[113] Undoubtedly, it is important to discover whether a thing performs its function well or not. This is especially true for gadgets, devices, machines, plans, programs, and the like. It is easy enough to see, for example, that the questions John Dewey poses might be just the ones we would want answered about a washing machine. That they comprise all that it is important to know is not equally clear, however. Surely, it is important to know about human nature, the laws of nature, principles, morality, and anything that can be discovered about an order in the universe.

John Dewey
(1859–1952)

Courtesy Columbiana Collection, Columbia University

Dewey was a philosopher, an educational innovator, and a reformer. He was the founder of the progressive education movement, and he strove to alter radically both the content and purpose of schooling so that it could be used to reconstruct society. Dewey was a pragmatist, greatly influenced in his views by William James, but he eventually called his variety of pragmatism "instrumentalism." He was born in Vermont, graduated from the state university, and did his postgraduate study at Johns Hopkins. Subsequently, he taught at several midwestern universities before being called to teach in the philosophy department at Columbia University in 1904.

Dewey was a prolific writer, exercised great influence from his post at Columbia, and lectured extensively in foreign lands. His great emphasis was upon democracy (by which he most often meant equality), the individual child, and society. He worked to substitute the authority of the class and peer group for that of the teacher and the learning to be mastered. In that way, he emphasized, the child would be socialized and schooling made relevant to him. He was much involved with social reform over many years, showed sympathy for the Communist "experiment" in Russia in the 1920s and 1930s, and pressed American schooling in the direction of socialism.

The pragmatists cast all these latter matters aside, relegating them to the junkheap of history, so to speak. They wanted nothing to do with any enduring order or fixities; they wanted to believe or did believe, as Peirce put it, that "The universe as a whole is open-ended. . . ."[114] These ideas set the stage for continuous and ongoing reform. If there is no fixed nature of anything or any enduring order, then it must be possible to reshape man and the world about us according to our wills. All things become possible; and reform and remaking things becomes man's purpose. William James said, *"Theories thus become instruments. . . .*We don't lie back on them, we move forward, and, on occasion, make nature over again by their aid."[115] Dewey more pointedly held that with the traditional philosophical concerns out of the way, it would "encourage philosophy to face the great social and moral defects and troubles from which humanity suffers . . . ; in short upon projecting an idea or ideal which . . . would be used as a method of understanding and rectifying social ills."[116] Pragmatism, then, cleared the ground and prepared the way for ongoing social reform.

2. Progressive Education

Another intellectual development which arose with progressivism and was of a piece both with pragmatism and reform was the Progressive Education movement. It was largely the brainchild of John Dewey, who was associated with the spread of pragmatism as well, but many other reformers were interested also in changing the character of schooling and using the schools as a major instrument for transforming society. To Lester Frank Ward, according to one historian, "education was the 'great panacea'—for political as for all other evils."[117] Albion Small, a disciple of Ward, declared in the 1890s, "Sociology knows no means for the . . . reform of society more radical than those of which the teachers hold the leverage. . . ."[118] In 1911, Charles A. Ellwood wrote that the schools should be used as "the conscious instrument of social reconstruction."[119] During the same period, David Snedden noted that the schools were the "only educational institutions which society, in its collective and conscious capacity, is able to control." Thus, it should be possible through them to introduce an education which proceeded "from the broadest possible conception of society reconstructing itself."[120]

It was John Dewey and his disciples, however, who conceived of an educational program suited to this purpose. Dewey went to Columbia University in 1904, and Teachers College there became the center for the diffusion of the ideas of progressive education over the country. William H. Kilpatrick, a student and disciple of Dewey, "taught some 35,000 students from every state in the Union at a time when Teachers College was training a substantial percentage of the . . . leaders of American education. . . . In the hands of the dedicated, compelling Kilpatrick, the chair became an extraordinary strategic rostrum for the dissemination of a particular version of progressive education. . . ."[121]

Progressive education advanced under the banner of progress, implying that it was the latest and the best. No doubt about it, in the early twentieth century progressive education was the latest, but whether it was the best was another matter. Indeed, whether it would be education at all would be a good question. Progressives carried on a continual assault on traditional education, charging it with being taken up with rote learning, education for the upper classes rather than children generally, with being authoritarian, and unsuited to children. Dewey said that the "traditional scheme . . . imposes adult standards, subject matter, and methods upon those who are only growing slowly toward maturity."[122] He called for "modification of traditional ideals of culture, traditional subjects of study and traditional methods of teaching and discipline. . . ."[123] As usual, however, he probably understated his case, for Dewey appeared to be more concerned with the abandonment of traditional education than its modification.

Dewey's pragmatism left little room for education as it has been conceived over the centuries. Aside from the most basic of the fundamentals—reading, writing, and arithmetic, say—education, or at least formal education, has been concerned with the learning and literature of the past. It has been premised on the belief that philosophers, historians, essayists, scientists, and theologians have discovered and learned much. But pragmatists would have none of that. They wanted to cast aside the religious and humane learning, experience, and revelations and to launch out into the uncharted sea of the future, armed only with the determination to experiment and find out what would work in transforming man and his world.

Why bother with schools at all, it might be asked? Whether the progressives in education had a good answer or not, they did see a purpose in formal education. The child did need to be trained to adjust to changing conditions, of course. And, he needed help in developing a favorable attitude toward social reconstruction. In their own language, they wanted to "socialize" the young. To foster this, they emphasized the importance of what they called "child-centered" education, that is, focusing on the values and desires of children rather than using the schools to inculcate what adults wanted. Thus, they would be able to change schooling, change the child, and send him forth to change the world. Spontaneous participation by the children in the classes was one of the progressive ideals. By participation the children would learn to adjust to one another, would be socialized, and be fitted to conformity to the wishes of the group.

The term which tied all this together for John Dewey, and for his followers generally, was "democracy." Dewey took this term, which Americans were coming to accept as describing their political system, and used it as a word to conjure with. Democracy, for him, was the ultimate good, the *summum bonum*, the thing to be striven for above all else, and that which his educational system was bent on achieving. What did it mean? It meant whatever Dewey would have it mean, at least for him; it meant equality, freedom, concern for others, participation in the "formation of the values that regulate the living of men together . . . ,"[124] "primarily a mode of associated living, of conjoint communicated experience,"[125] and so on and on. Above all, though, "democracy" was a word to be used to change schooling in the direction that he wanted. What he wanted to do was build a new social order along what is generally known as socialistic lines. As he wrote, on one occasion: "the schools will surely . . . share in the building of the social order of the future. . . .They will of necessity . . . take an active part in determining the social order."[126]

Over the years, the progressives had a great impact on schooling in the United States. They contributed much to the development of schools of education, whose graduates eventually took over much of the direction of schooling from their key position in teacher's colleges, in state education departments, and as teachers. The progressive impetus underlay such things as consolidation of schools, centralizing control over the schools in state departments of education and eventually in the United States Department of Education, undermining the authority of teachers, changing the content of textbooks, making learning humanistic, and encouraging children to participate in classroom discussions. These changes did not all come about in the early years of the 20th century, of course, but the direction was conceived and the ideas spread during these years. Progressive education not only applied progressive ideas to the schools but also contributed to the mood of progressivism generally.

3. The Social Gospel

Progressivism received crucial aid in its push to reform and make over society from the social gospel movement. The social gospel movement within Christianity did not spring full blown upon America in the early 20th century, nor was it simply the work of a few prominent preachers. It had been building momentum for several decades before that. A scholar of the movement says that "Study of an extensive and varied literature indicates . . . not only that the social gospel originated in the early years of the gilded age [1880s, say] but also that its prophets were legion [numerous] and their message an integral part of the broad sweep of social and humanitarian efforts."[127] Even so, there were leaders in the movement, among them, Washington Gladden, Richard T. Ely, W.D.P. Bliss, George D. Herron, and Walter Rauschenbusch, and the movement was making a considerable impact on the older established Protestant churches by the early 20th century.

The social gospel movement was an effort to utilize Christianity as support for transforming the social order. Social gospellers had generally imbibed considerable doses of socialism, Marxism (usually second hand), utopianism, and were often influenced in their thinking by such Americans as Henry George and Edward Bellamy. Such influences are fairly clear in Washington Gladden's description of the tendencies of the times:

> The tendency of wages to sink to starvation point, the tendency of the workmen's share of the national wealth to grow constantly smaller, the tendency of commercial crises and depressions to become more frequent and disastrous . . .—all these are, as I believe, the natural issues of an industrial system whose sole motive power is self-interest, and whose sole regulative principle is competition.[128]

Social gospellers were often most vociferous in their condemnation of the American economic system: private property, the profit motive, corporations, and competition. Walter Rauschenbusch, whose condemnation of the economic system showed the clearest signs of Marxist influence, said that "Competitive commerce exalts selfishness to the dignity of a moral principle. It pits men against one another in a gladiatorial game in which there is no mercy and in which ninety per cent of the combatants finally strew the arena."[129] George D. Herron, described best, perhaps, as a Christian socialist, proclaimed that "The economic system denies the right of the sincerest and most sympathetic to keep their hands out of the blood of their brothers."[130]

The notion that a social and economic system can itself be sinful was largely an invention of the social gospellers. Christianity is profoundly individualistic, and sin is something that individuals commit. The social gospellers also departed from the basic Christian sources in proposing to use the power of government to transform society and usher in the Kingdom of God, though they were not quite so original in this. At any rate, they pushed for government intervention in the economy and much more vigorous government activity. Gladden, who was one of the earliest of the social gospellers, said:

> The limits of governmental interference are likely to be greatly enlarged in the immediate future. . . . It may become the duty of the state to reform its taxation, so that its burdens shall rest less heavily upon the lower classes; to repress monopolies of all sorts . . . ; to regulate or control the railroads and telegraphs; to limit the ownership of land; to modify the laws of inheritance; and possibly to levy a progressive income tax. . . .[131]

Richard T. Ely declared that it is "as truly a religious work to pass good laws, as it is to preach sermons, as holy a work to lead a crusade against filth, vice, and disease in slums of cities, and to seek the abolition of the

disgraceful tenement-houses of American cities, as it is to send missionaries
to the heathen."[132] George D. Herron maintained that "It is the vocation of
the states . . . to so control property, so administer the production and
distribution of economic goods, as to give to every man the fruit of his
labor, and protect the laborer from the irresponsible tyranny of the passion
of wealth."[133]

By 1912, Walter Rauschenbusch could rejoice in print that the social
gospel was catching on, and indeed it was. Old line churches were pushing
for reform, particularly in the matter of working conditions and labor
unions. As early as 1887 the Episcopalians set up a Church Association for
the Advancement of the Interests of Labor. In 1901, the Congregationalists
provided for a labor committee. The largest of the Presbyterian denominations established a department of church and labor in 1903. In 1908,
a general conference of Methodists announced that it stood

> For equal rights and complete justice for all men in all stations of
> life. . . .
> For a living wage in every industry.
> For the highest wage that each industry can afford, and for the most
> equitable division of the products in industry that can ultimately be
> devised.
> For the recognition of the Golden Rule, and the mind of Christ as the
> supreme law of society and the sure remedy for all social ills.[134]

Though churches often worded their statements in language that evoked
ancient Christian doctrine, they were in fact embarking on the support of the
use of government power to achieve their announced ends.

4. The Muckrakers

Reform got its most dramatic push in the early 20th century from those
whom Theodore Roosevelt described as "muckrakers," those who exposed
the underside of human undertakings to public view. Muckraking was a
journalistic undertaking that flourished especially from 1902 to 1912. It was
carried on mainly in magazines, although a number of the series of articles
first published in that medium were also published as books. *McClure's*
magazine took the lead by the publication of Ida Tarbell's *History of the
Standard Oil Company* serially, beginning in 1902. Lincoln Steffens, also
of *McClure's*, did a series of articles on the interrelationship between
politicians and businessmen in such big cities as St. Louis, Minneapolis,
and Philadelphia. These were published in book form in 1904 as *The Shame
of the Cities*. He followed this with revelations about goings on in a variety
of state governments. These exposés proved highly popular and other
magazines began following suit: *Everybody's*, *Munsey's*, *Cosmopolitan*,
Colliers, and *American Magazine*. First and last, all sorts of businesses and

political organization were subjected to muckraking: the Senate got a going over in David Graham Phillips' *Treason of the Senate*, meatpackers in Charles Edward Russell's *The Greatest Trust in the World*, the railroads in Ray Stannard Baker's *The Railroads on Trial*, the stock market in Thomas W. Lawson's *Frenzied Finance*, life insurance in Burton J. Hendrick's *The Story of Life Insurance*, and labor relations in Baker's *The Right to Work*.

The muckrakers who relied more or less on facts and interpretation were joined in the fray by novelists, who could allow their imaginations free play in depicting conditions. Frank Norris made a scathing attack on the Southern Pacific Railroad in his novel, *The Octopus*, and painted a fictional picture of the control of the wheat market by speculators in *The Pit*. David Graham Phillips gave an account of how the quest for money corrupts in *The Great God Success* and told of a country girl drawn into prostitution in *Susan Lennox, Her Fall and Rise*. Robert Hunter's *Poverty* indicted capitalism for the fate of the hungry, and John Spargo's *The Bitter Cry of the Children* condemned child labor and the system which was supposed to make life so

Upton Sinclair
(1878–1968)

Sinclair was a novelist who gained a popular following by his lurid fictional exposés of conditions in a system dominated by wealth. He was born in Maryland and graduated from City College of New York. He gained wide recognition for his novel, *The Jungle*, published in 1906. It was a fictional depiction of conditions in the Chicago stockyards and meatpacking plants. Its publication gave impetus to the passage of the Pure Food and Drug Act, though Sinclair had in mind arousing sympathy for the workers. Much of his book production could be accurately classified as socialist propaganda. Among the exposé novels were: *King Coal* (1917), *The Profits of Religion* (1918), *The Brass Check* (1919), and *Money Writes!* (1927). He received a Pulitzer prize for *Dragon's Teeth* (1942). Sinclair was defeated in his campaign for governor of California in 1934 on the Democratic ticket.

hard for them. In the *Iron Heel*, Jack London described the American economic system as brutal and oppressive.

The composite picture that emerged from the muckraking, both factual and fictional, was of an America that was corrupt and corrupting, of state and local governments dominated by bossism and rapacious men of wealth, of an economic system that drove the poor to the wall and took advantage of large portions of the population, of grasping businessmen, and of government gone awry. That it was a distorted and overdrawn picture there should be no doubt. Even those who researched and wrote with considerable care, such as Ida Tarbell, were often factually accurate, but nonetheless myopic.

Two things especially tended to place views of the muckrakers out of kilter. One was utopian idealism, which often underlay what was written, in which they subtly compared the reality they saw, or thought they saw, with the perfect world that ought to be. The world about us and actual people's behavior always comes off rather badly from that perspective. The other is what Ludwig von Mises, the Austrian economist who migrated to America during World War II, called the "Anti-Capitalistic Mentality." That is, they had a highly developed sense of superiority and contempt for those who built businesses, operated large enterprises, and gained wealth in the process. Thus, muckrakers were often blind to the accomplishments and the benefits conferred by these men on people generally. They saw the profits but not the goods made available, the sometimes unsavory practices but not the morality which generally pervades productivity, the labor of children in factories but not the labor that has been the lot of children in most times and places.

5. Domestication of Socialism

Some of the muckrakers were active socialists, including Upton Sinclair, for example, who gained early fame with his fictional exposé of the meatpacking industry in *The Jungle*. John Spargo, mentioned above, and Jack London were also socialists. But whether they were avowed socialists or not, muckrakers generally provided grist for the mills of socialists in particular and the more ardent advocates of reformism in general. At any rate, there were Americans who were conceiving and presenting plans for drawing the country into socialism gradually by way of reform in the years before World War I. Three who eventually made some impact with their ideas along these lines were Herbert Croly, Walter Weyl, and Walter Lippmann. Croly published a book entitled *The Promise of American Life* in 1909. This book is reckoned to be especially important because it influenced Theodore Roosevelt in formulating his New Nationalism in 1912.

A considerable portion of Croly's work was to fit the need for reform and the way to go about it into the American framework. He was, in effect, domesticating socialism. Both Jefferson and Hamilton had championed ideas which contained hints of the course to be pursued, according to Croly. Alexander Hamilton had a vision of using the government to advance national well-being. But Hamilton had been antidemocratic, as Croly saw it, and had set forth too narrow a program, at least for twentieth-century conditions. Thomas Jefferson, on the other hand, had contributed to the development of democratic sentiment, but he was individualistic, not nationalistic. The Whigs, too, had a national vision, but their development of it was quite incomplete. Croly drew his conclusion: "The best that can be said on behalf of this traditional American system is that it contained the germ of better things. The combination of Federalism and Republicanism . . . pointed in the direction of a constructive formula."[135] What Croly was getting at was that Americans ought to take the seeds of nationalism and democracy from their past and join it to a program of social reconstruction.

Fundamentally, though, neither Croly nor Weyl or Lippmann, who helped him to establish *The New Republic* magazine, were concerned with preserving the American past and traditions. Croly said that his program for Americans would "in certain essential respects emancipate them from their past. . . ."[136] Weyl made clear his attitude toward the centerpiece of the American political tradition, the Constitution, when he said: "The Constitution of the United States is the political wisdom of a dead America."[137] Walter Lippmann put his view of the American past equally bluntly. We have "to substitute purpose for tradition," he said. "We can no longer treat life as something that has trickled down to us. We have to deal with it deliberately, devise its social organization, alter its tools, formulate its method, educate and control it."[138]

All three men were gradualists, setting forth a gradual path toward socialism within the American context. They did not avow their socialism; so far as they gave a name to it, they used such terms as nationalism, social democracy, and democracy. Lippmann had been a member of the Intercollegiate Society of Socialists when he was a student at Harvard, but by the time he began writing he had apparently decided it was wiser to drop that appellation. But there can be no doubt that they believed that government should take over the control of the economy in the name of society, whether by outright ownership or through regulation. Lippmann proposed to do this in the name of the nation: "It means that you have to do a great variety of things to industry, invent new ones to do, and keep on doing them. You have to make a survey of the natural resources of the country. On the basis of that survey you must draw up a national plan for their development."[139]

Croly suggested the gradual approach this way: "the man who believes in the ultimate necessity of government ownership of railroad road-beds and terminals must be content to wait and to watch. The most that he can do for the present is to use any opening which the course of railroad development affords . . . ; and if he is right, he will gradually be able to work out . . . some practical method of realizing the ultimate purpose."[140]

Weyl left no doubt of his devotion to the gradualist approach. He declared "that the surest method of progress is to take one step after another. The first step, often uncontested (*because* it is only one step), leads inevitably to others."[141] He suggested, by way of example, if government wanted to get possession of rich mineral lands, the thing to do would be to go after it with the "sword of a gentle tax in the one hand and the olive branch of a fair purchase price in the other. . . ."[142] Lippmann envisioned a gradual transformation in America, when "Private property will melt away; its functions will be taken over by the salaried men who direct them, by government commissions, by developing labor unions. The stockholders deprived of their property rights are being transformed into money-lenders."[143]

Progressivism, then, was infused with the spirit of social transformation. That spirit was derived largely from socialism. But pragmatism provided a philosophical way to avoid the onus of socialism. Each move could be considered separately, treated as a social problem to be solved, and tested by how it worked. The spirit of transformation began to gain a hold on Americans from a variety of directions: by way of unionism, by the fears raised about big business, by the social gospel, by progressive education, and so on. In the early 20th century, most Americans believed more or less strongly in private property, freedom of enterprise, that people should manage their own affairs, and usually rejected socialism when it was offered to them by that name. Even so, the piecemeal approach was beginning to have its impact, as many people who would not have socialism whole were nonetheless attracted to its premises when considering them bit by bit.

The Imperial Surge

There were two sides to the progressive coin. One was the bent to domestic reform, which has been largely emphasized thus far. The other was the penchant for foreign intervention. Although not all those who were domestic reformers favored policies of foreign intervention, the two things did share common bonds. For one thing, they were both forms of intervention. Domestic reform usually involved some sort of government intervention in the economy or lives of Americans (particularly if it had as its object the transformation of society) as foreign intervention involved intervening in the affairs of foreigners. For another thing, foreign intervention was often impelled by a similar spirit to that of domestic reform. It was a spirit which evinced itself in the use of government power to set things right, to reform and reshape them, whether domestic or foreign. It should be noted, too, that the thrust to domestic reform occurred more or less simultaneously with the acquisition of empire and increasing foreign intervention by the United States. Often the same people were more or less deeply involved in both.

Actually, there was more than the above might suggest behind the American acquisition of empire and becoming more aggressive in intervening in Latin America during the progressive period. American commerce and foreign trade had grown with the economic growth of America in the latter part of the 19th century. Major European nations went on a surge of acquiring colonies and establishing favorable trade positions, particularly in Africa, Asia, and the islands of the Pacific. A united Germany was pushing outward in the world to compete with Britain and France. Imperial Russia was expanding southward and eastward and definitely seeking to expand in the Far East around the turn of the century (fighting a war with China 1894–95 and with Japan 1904–1905). The Spanish Empire was on its last legs so to speak, and the colonies under Spanish rule were ineffectively governed. All this provided a setting in which it was easy to believe that the United States must become actively involved or left out.

A strong navy was the key to such involvement at the time. In the last decade or so before the turn of the century, the older ships of the United States Navy were being replaced with steel ships powered by steam. Thus, the country had a trim and modern navy, though hardly of the size of the British. The United States had a man with a vision and the ability to express it, Admiral A. T. Mahan. He published a book on *The Influence of Sea Power upon History* in 1890. It pointed up the decisive role of naval power in world affairs, particularly following the discovery of America and had great influence not only in America but in Europe as well. Mahan drove the point home in an article published in the same year:

> Whether they will or no, Americans must now look outward, [he wrote]. The growing production of the country demands it. An increasing volume of public sentiment demands it. The position of the United States between the two Old Worlds [Europe and Asia], and the two great oceans, makes the same claim. . . . The tendency will be maintained and increased by the growth of the European colonies in the Pacific, by the advancing civilization of Japan, and by the rapid peopling of our Pacific States. . . .[144]

Darwinian ideas may have had a decisive impact at the intellectual level for this new American expansion, and they certainly linked it to progressivism. As already pointed out, these ideas gave new support to the belief in progress, and one aspect of progress was the expansion of civilization to the far corners of the earth. There were men ready with justifications for the more civilized nations to use force to extend civilization. Among Americans, there were thinkers who believed that not only was Anglo-Saxon culture superior to that of others in crucial respects, particularly the American variety, but also that it was their duty, nay, even burden, to extend its blessings to other peoples. In the struggle for survival, the Reverend Josiah Strong maintained, the time was coming (he wrote in 1885) when America must join in the struggle and assert itself to the fullest. When that happens

> . . . this race of unequaled energy . . .—the representative, let us hope, of the largest liberty, the purest Christianity, the highest civilization—having developed peculiarly aggressive traits calculated to impress its institutions upon mankind, will spread itself over the earth. If I read not amiss, this powerful race will move down upon Mexico, down upon Central and South America, out upon the islands of the sea, over upon Africa and beyond. And can any one doubt that the result of this competition of races will be the "survival of the fittest"?[145]

Several politicians had begun to take an expansionist line similar to this by the late 1890s. Senator Henry Cabot Lodge would defend the acquiring of an empire on grounds similar to these. But Senator Albert J. Beveridge of Indiana, both a Progressive in seeking domestic reform and an eager proponent of expansion, best exemplifies the various connections. "We are Anglo-Saxons," he said in 1898, "and must obey our blood and occupy new markets, and, if necessary, new lands. . . .We go forth to fight for humanity. . . . In the name of the mighty minds of every party and of every English-speaking land . . . , we welcome the golden dawn of the republic's full-grown manhood. . . ."[146] That there were elements of condescension toward less civilized or uncivilized peoples should be clear. Indeed, the whole business of domestic reform as well as foreign intervention entailed elitism—the belief that an elite using the power of government would do what was "best" for people rather than allowing them to manage their own affairs. That was an important connecting link between the two kinds of intervention.

The United States acquired an overseas empire in the years 1898–1901. There was a sense, of course, in which the United States was an empire from the outset. The United States was composed of states which differed significantly from one another and of peoples who had migrated here from various lands, in addition to the native Indians. Also, from the beginning the United States claimed territory not yet organized into states. But there were important differences between this older empire and the new one. Except for the region around New Orleans, territory had generally been sparsely settled. The Spanish colonies acquired were different, too, in that they had no significant population of older American stock. All the territory acquired before 1898 (excepting a naval base or so) was in North America, and, except for Alaska, had been contiguous with older states or territory. The Northwest Ordinances and the Constitution had provided the means for the dissolution of the older territory by division into territories and eventual admission to statehood. It was not generally believed that the territory acquired off the shores of America would ever become an integral part of the United States (although Hawaii has), and thus it had the makings of an empire, by the usual understanding of the term.

1. Annexation of Hawaii

The Hawaiian Islands were officially annexed to the United States in July, 1898. Although this was in the midst of the Spanish-American War, it had only an incidental connection with it. The treaty of annexation had been signed the year before. Hawaii was at the time an independent republic, but it had been a kingdom until the early 1890s. The islands had become known to the rest of the world as a result of Captain James Cook's voyage there in 1778. Pearl Harbor on the main island became a port of call for many ships in the course of the 19th century. American missionaries went there and converted the natives to Christianity. The United States acted as a kind of protector of the independence of Hawaii from any attempts of other nations in the latter half of the 19th century. Descendants of American missionaries became involved with sugar production and other commercial activities, and, though they were very much a minority, began to look toward annexation to the United States. In 1893, they engineered the overthrow of the ruler, Queen Liliuokalani, and asked for annexation by the United States. President Cleveland, however, doubted that the government truly represented the people of the islands, and he thwarted the efforts at annexation.

President McKinley, who succeeded him, was much more favorably disposed toward the move. Thus, a treaty was worked out in 1897 and presented to the Senate for approval. That body was not so enthusiastic, however. But when the Spanish-American War broke out, and the United States became involved in the Philippines, the desirability of a mid-Pacific naval base became more pressing. Even then, there was doubt that the necessary two-thirds could be mustered in the Senate for ratification of the treaty. The result was achieved in another way; it was done by joint resolution of Congress, which required only simple majorities in each of the houses.

2. Spanish-American War

The Spanish-American War was a brief conflict. Congress adopted a war resolution on April 20, 1898, and a peace treaty was signed at Paris on December 10 of the same year. Most of the fighting occurred from May into August, and the Spanish asked for terms of peace in July. It was mainly a naval war, since neither side had time to muster extensive land forces. Despite its brevity, it was a far-flung war, since it involved naval action in the Philippines as well as naval and land action in the Caribbean.

The United States entered the war because of developments associated with Cuba. Not to acquire Cuba, for the war resolution specifically committed the United States not to take Cuba but to support Cuban independence (the Teller Amendment). The reasons for the United States going to war were both more complicated and less direct than that. A revolt broke out in Cuba in 1895. The rebels were not well organized nor able to maintain any continued government over the island. They engaged in

William Randolph Hearst (1863–1951)

Hearst was a newspaper and magazine publisher who increased the public impact of these by giving them greater popular appeal. He was born in San Francisco, the son of a politician and newspaper publisher, and he studied for two years at Harvard. He left college to pursue his interest in newspaper publishing, acquired control of the San Francisco *Examiner*, and then moved into the New York City market by purchasing the *Morning Journal*. The *Journal* soon had the largest circulation in the country as a result of Hearst's aggressive use of illustrations, colored magazine sections, glaring headlines, sensational articles, and political activism, especially in foreign affairs. His papers backed William Jennings Bryan in 1896 and helped to stir up the war fervor which erupted in the Spanish-American War.

Courtesy William Randolph Hearst, Jr.

The dramatic accounts of Spanish atrocities earned Hearst's papers the dubious distinction of practicing "yellow journalism." Before World War I, Hearst had bought papers in other large cities, notably Chicago and Boston, and by 1925 he had forged a newspaper empire consisting of papers in major cities in every section of the country. He was also deeply involved in politics as a Democrat over the years, served two terms in Congress, ran unsuccessfully for mayor of New York and for governor of the state. He contributed most notably, however, to sensational journalism.

guerrilla warfare, making sporadic raids in which they destroyed sugar mills and devastated plantations. The insurrection was sparked by the depression in the sugar market which followed the American adoption of the Wilson-Gorman Tariff in 1894 and by Spanish government policies which allegedly favored the white inhabitants. The Spanish government used harsh methods to quell the rebellion. General Valeriano (''Butcher'') Weyler was assigned to the task, and he went about it by rounding up rebels and sympathizers and confining them in concentration camps.

American sympathy for the rebels was aroused by the ''yellow journalism'' of William Randolph Hearst's New York *Journal* and Joseph Pulitzer's New York *World*. They gave lurid accounts of brutal treatment of rebels by ''Butcher'' Weyler and conveyed the impression that the Cuban insurrection was an event of the character of the American War for Independence. The United States government protested the mistreatment of the rebels, and in 1897 the Spanish government yielded by agreeing to recall General Weyler and reform its confinement policies. The rebels were not satisfied with this, however, and the ''yellow'' American press continued to fan the fires of popular resentment. Some of the younger Republicans, notably Theodore Roosevelt and Henry Cabot Lodge, were urging greater American involvement in the Cuban crisis.

The Spanish government had shown considerable willingness to correct abuses to conciliate opinion in the United States, but in February 1898 two events occurred which led to war. One is known as the de Lôme Letter, and the other the sinking of the battleship *Maine*. The letter was written by the Spanish minister to the United States Dupuy de Lôme; it was private correspondence but was taken from the mails in Havana and turned over to Hearst's paper, which published it. De Lôme described President McKinley as ''weak and a bidder for the admiration of the crowd, besides being a would-be politican who tries to leave a door open behind him while keeping on good terms with the jingoes of his party.''[147] The publication of this letter inflamed American opinion, and a few days later an even more dramatic event took place. The *Maine* had been sent to Havana in January. On February 15, it was blown up in the harbor by an explosion which killed 260 officers and sailors. A naval inquiry found that the *Maine* had been destroyed by a submarine mine, but who planted the explosive has never been determined. Many Americans assumed that the Spanish government had been behind it, and ''Remember the *Maine*'' became the battle cry of the war. Actually, it is more likely that it was done by someone in the rebel camp, since the insurgents had been trying to draw the United States more directly into the conflict for several years.

If that was the intent of those who did it, it succeeded. Even so, the United States did not go to war immediately. Instead the government put pressure on Spain for an armistice to end the fighting and to close the concentration camps. By the time Spain was ready to make these concessions, however, McKinley had decided for war, and Congress supported the war resolution.

The Navy was prepared to engage the Spanish fleet once war had been declared. The Pacific fleet, under the command of Commodore George Dewey, was at Hong Kong in the late winter of 1898. Theodore Roosevelt,

William McKinley (1843–1901)

McKinley was the 25th President of the United States, serving for a few months more than one term (1897–1901). He was born in Ohio, attended Allegheny College in Pennsylvania for a while, left to teach school, served in the Union Army during the Civil War, studied law afterward, and was admitted to the bar. He was a lifelong Republican and was elected to Congress for that party in 1876. Except for one term, he served in the House of Representatives until 1891. In that year, he was elected governor of Ohio, and in the ensuing election he was chosen once again for that position. In 1896, he was elected President. In Congress, McKinley had distinguished himself by his interest in government finance, especially the tariff, and he authored the McKinley Tariff of 1890. He ran for President on a gold standard platform and as a known advocate of the protective tariff.

McKinley's presidency was a time both of economic prosperity at home and expansion abroad. His standing with the electorate was such that he was handily re-elected in 1900. McKinley had the satisfaction, too, as he began his second term, of seeing Cuban independence begun and effective governments set up in Puerto Rico and the Philippines. In the summer of 1901, he embarked on a tour of the United States, which ended for him on the return leg at Buffalo in September. There he was shot down by an anarchist, Leon Czolgosz, and he died of the wounds a few days later.

Assistant Secretary of the Navy at the time, notified him to attack the Spanish in the Philippines if war should come. A few days after the war began, Dewey sailed from the coast of China and was ready for battle at Manila Bay on May 1. Although the Spanish had a larger fleet, Dewey had superior armament and seamen, and they made quick work of them, sinking or capturing everything in sight between breakfast and lunch of May 1. Dewey became an almost instant hero, and as soon as Congress could authorize the rank, he was made an admiral. He did not have the soldiers, however, to take Manila, much less the Philippines, so he waited several months until a force could arrive to launch the assault. Meanwhile, a German and British fleet arrived and he had to take a strong stand to maintain his position. When American troops arrived, they were reinforced by rebel forces under the command of rebel General Emilio Aguinaldo (a rebellion having been going on in the Philippines for some time). Manila fell on August 10.

The fighting proceeded much more slowly in Cuba. The Spanish fleet in the Atlantic did not arrive at Santiago de Cuba until May 19, and the American fleet under the command of Commodore Winfield S. Schley did not get there until May 29. He was joined a few days later by another fleet, but the Spanish fleet already occupied Santiago harbor and had the protection of land batteries as well as its own guns. An assault upon the Spanish fleet was too risky under these circumstances, so none was made until land forces could arrive to improve the situation.

The Army was skeletal in size (only about 30,000 men) and ill equipped when war broke out. Congress acted quickly both to authorize increases in the regular army and a volunteer force. But accomplishing this, along with providing the necessary equipment, proceeded much more slowly. An expeditionary force under General William Shafter sailed from Tampa June 14. Theodore Roosevelt managed to be in this force as a lieutenant colonel in the "Rough Riders," a voluntary regiment of cavalry which he had helped to organize after leaving the Navy Department. The army landed on Cuban soil in late June. This force moved to gain command of the heights overlooking Santiago Harbor. This they achieved by winning the Battle of San Juan Hill on July 1. Roosevelt and his "Rough Riders" were involved in this charge, and he achieved fame as a gritty soldier for his part in it. The army was now in position to launch artillery fire upon the Spanish fleet in the harbor. The fleet tried to run the American blockade on July 3, and in a naval battle lasting four hours it was destroyed. The Spanish navy hardly existed any longer, and the Spanish were in no position to continue the war. On July 17, the Spanish garrison in Santiago surrendered.

On July 4, American forces took possession of Wake Island in the Pacific. July 25, United States troops occupied Puerto Rico after encountering little opposition. The next day the Spanish government used the offices of the French ambassador at Washington to request peace terms. By the terms of a preliminary agreement signed on August 12, hostilities were to cease and a treaty was to be worked out at Paris. Work on the peace treaty was concluded on December 10.

3. United States Acquires Colonies

Although the Spanish-American War had not been fought for the announced purpose of acquiring the Spanish colonies, that was the outcome of the treaty bringing it to a close. By the terms of the Treaty of Paris, the United States acquired the Philippines, Puerto Rico, and Guam. In return for the cession of the Philippines, the United States paid $20 million to Spain. As already pointed out, the United States annexed Hawaii during the course of the war. This country also laid claim to Wake Island in 1899, and formally occupied it in 1900. A far-flung empire had been acquired.

In addition, the status of Cuba had not been settled. By the terms of the Treaty of Paris, Spain surrendered all claim to Cuba. However, Cuba had no established government of its own, nor had the steps been taken to establish one. Although American commitment to the independence of Cuba was not altered, a military government was set up to govern the country during the transition. General Leonard Wood headed the military administration, and he instructed the Cubans to call a constitutional convention in 1900. The convention was held; a government was provided for; and the Cubans prepared to hold elections and govern themselves. The Cubans had, however, envisioned more independence for themselves than Congress had in mind. A Platt Amendment to the army appropriation bill in 1901 defined a special relationship between Cuba and the United States. It prohibited Cuba to make any treaty with a foreign power impairing its independence. Cuba was not to contract any debt in excess of its ability to retire with ordinary revenues. If necessary, the United States was authorized to intervene in Cuba to maintain Cuban independence or to preserve order. And, Cuba was to agree to sell or lease to the United States lands for naval stations. Under pressure, the Cubans made the provisions of the Platt Amendment a part of their constitution. Cuba had, in effect, become a protectorate of the United States.

The Philippines posed the largest problem and the most difficulties of the new possessions. In the first place, Spain had only been persuaded to cede them to the United States most reluctantly. Indeed, by his own account President McKinley had great difficulty in deciding to obtain them. He said that he ''walked the floor of the White House night after night until midnight'' struggling with this matter before reaching a decision on the Philippines. Finally, he reasoned in this way to a conclusion:

> (1) That we could not give them back to Spain—that would be cowardly and dishonorable;

(2) That we could not turn them over to France or Germany—our commercial rivals in the Orient—that would be bad business and discreditable.

(3) That we could not leave them to themselves—they were unfit for self-government . . . ;

(4) That there was nothing left for us to do but to take them all, and to educate the Filipinos, and uplift and civilize and Christianize them. . . .[148]

In the second place, the whole business of acquiring possessions, especially the Philippines, provoked a full-scale debate in the Senate when the Treaty of Paris came before that body for ratification in early 1899. The Democrats and Populists were generally opposed to the acquiring of possessions, and they were joined in this sentiment by several Republicans. The main argument was that it ran contrary to the American tradition, that United States policy since the founding had been for independence of peoples and not imperialism, and that such populated countries as the Philippines and Puerto Rico were of a different culture and hardly likely to be integrated into the United States. However, William Jennings Bryan, the Democratic leader, favored ratification to end the war; he thought the status of the Spanish colonies could be determined later. His view prevailed sufficiently to obtain a two-thirds majority for ratification.

In the third place, the United States had only militarily occupied Manila on the large island of Luzon. The Philippine Islands form an archipelago of more than 7,000 islands. Only about a third of them even have names, and there are about a dozen large ones. The total land area is only a little less than that of Great Britain, and the Philippines extend over a much broader area. The Spaniards had never succeeded in subduing all the tribes, but once they had withdrawn there was no effective government in control. The Americans had hardly laid claim to the islands before a major rebellion began. The irony of it was that Americans had encouraged the return of Emilio Aguinaldo and helped him and his rebel force obtain arms. They had used them against the Spanish. But once it became apparent that the Philippines were not to have their independence under the Americans, Aguinaldo led a revolt against them. At one point there were 70,000 American troops ranged against an almost equal number of Filipinos. The organized resistance had just about broken down by the end of 1899, but guerrilla warfare continued until 1902.

America's imperial surge was short, if not sweet. Except for the Panama Canal Zone and Virgin Islands acquired over the next several years, it had all taken place over a six-month period. The United States had acted in haste, and so far as it did, it could repent at leisure. That is not to say that the electorate did not generally approve what had taken place. Judging by the next election, the one in 1900, it did. McKinley's electoral vote was 292 to

155 for William Jennings Bryan, his Democratic opponent once again. For Bryan, imperialism had been the paramount issue of the campaign. The Democratic platform had roundly condemned the action in the Philippines, saying:

> We condemn and denounce the Philippine policy of the present Administration. It has embroiled the Republic in an unnecessary war, sacrificed the lives of many of its noblest sons, and placed the United States, previously known and applauded throughout the world as the champion of freedom, in the false and un-American position of crushing with military force the efforts of our former allies to achieve liberty and self-government.[149]

Such rhetoric was to no avail.

Even so, it is at least plausible to suppose that if America had not been caught up in circumstances calling for action, and swept onward by a temporary fervor for expansion, the deliberate decision would have been to avoid getting an overseas empire. The Philippines and Puerto Rico posed problems difficult to deal with either in the traditional framework or any other. Moreover, the United States was drawn into intricate involvement in world affairs, both with European and Asian countries, such as had usually been avoided in the past. The acquiring of colonies may have set the stage for other foreign interventions, because such intervention was to mount in the years before and through World War I and its immediate aftermath.

The Open Door in China

Indeed, the United States had not even consolidated its hold upon the Philippines before the government had become involved with the situation in China. The Chinese Empire had been tottering on the brink of dissolution for more than half a century. European countries had been picking at the edges of China during this period, gaining a port here, a trade concession there, and lopping off a bit of territory when they could. The process was accelerated by the Sino-Japanese War (1894–95). This brief conflict revealed both the weakness of China and the growing strength of Japan. China's days as an independent empire appeared to be numbered. Russia began to take charge in Manchuria; France was expanding its influence from the south; and Germany was eager to carve out its own sphere of influence. The United States government was very much interested in expanding trade with China and fearful of being squeezed out.

Thus, Secretary of State John Hay took steps in 1899 to keep China open to American trade. He proposed that all interested nations join him in subscribing to an Open Door policy for China. The British had proposed a similar idea to the United States the year before, but Hay decided to act on

John Hay
(1838–1905)

Hay was a diplomat, lawyer, poet, biographer, essayist, and public speaker of note. He was born in Indiana, graduated from Brown University, studied law in the office of Abraham Lincoln, and was admitted to the bar. His most prominent political position was as Secretary of State (1897–1905) under Presidents McKinley and Roosevelt. He was in a crucial position during the years when the United States became much more actively involved in world affairs: directing the peace negotiations concluding the Spanish-American War, taking the initiative in setting up the Open Door policy in China, in persuading Russia to withdraw forces from Manchuria, making the treaty with Great Britain which opened the way for a United States controlled canal through Panama, and negotiating treaties with Panama and Colombia. Hay had a long preparation for the position as Secretary of State, for he had served with United States legations in Paris, Vienna, and Madrid, and as ambassador to Britain. Also, he was an editorial writer for five years for the New York *Tribune*, and devoted much time to writing over the years.

Courtesy Brown University Library, John Hay Collection

his own to get agreements from all interested nations. Hay sent Open Door notes to Britain, Germany, Russia, France, Italy, and Japan suggesting that these countries join with the United States in pledging to keep China open to trade with all nations. Although the answers that he received were far from conclusive, he announced in early 1900 that the Open Door was in effect.

Meanwhile, trouble was brewing in China which came to a head in the Boxer Rebellion in 1900. The Boxers were an anti-foreign group of Chinese who wanted to throw the "foreign devils" out of their country. They launched an attack on foreign traders, missionaries, representatives of foreign governments, and anyone other than native Chinese, harassing and subjecting them to indignities, as well as bodily harm. Foreigners took refuge, when they could, in the embassies in the capital city of Peking. However, they were far from safe there, for the Chinese government was in sympathy with the Boxers. This became clear when the German minister ventured out into the streets of Peking on his way to lodge a protest with the Chinese government. He was killed by a Chinese soldier in uniform. Several governments, including the United States, agreed to send troops to relieve the situation. A total of about 20,000 troops of these various nations were dispatched to Peking. They managed to fight their way to the city and to occupy it.

The situation was ripe for the partition of China among the occupying powers. However, Secretary Hay took the initiative in sending notes to the other powers that stated the American position that the territorial integrity of China should be maintained, that all rights of friendly powers should be observed, and that equal and impartial trade should be open to all within the Chinese Empire. This was a restatement and elaboration of the Open Door policy. All troops, except those of Russia in Manchuria, were withdrawn in late 1901. It remained the policy of the United States in the following years to maintain the Open Door in China.

Racial Segregation in the South

It is not customary to discuss racial segregation in connection with Progressivism and the acquisition of an overseas empire. That is, however, the appropriate context for dealing with it. Not only was segregation imposed, in the main, during the last years of the 19th century and the early years of the 20th, but also it was a reflex of Populism-Progressivism, with their bent to reform, government intervention, popular government, and the imperial attitude. The same men who made demagogic attacks upon business in the South also made demagogic attacks upon the Blacks, for example. To see what happened more clearly, it helps to distinguish between racial *segregation* and racial *separation*. Racial separation may be defined as people of the two races being separated from one another by choice and custom, not by legal prescription. Racial segregation could then be distinctively used to refer to legally prescribed and required separation of the races.

Racial separation began to take place as soon as slavery was abolished. Under slavery, there were no segregation laws, nor, strictly speaking, were whites and Blacks separated. The ordinary relationship between white and Black was that of master and slave. The distinction between them was more functional than racial. Blacks often attended church with whites, though in a separate section, and slaves would be likely to ride side by side with their masters in public conveyances. But with the abolition of slavery the old ties were broken, and such new ones as developed were generally individually chosen or contracted over the succeeding two and a half decades or so. It is safe to say that Blacks and whites worshiped separately in their own churches and that social functions generally were separate.

The public school movement had hardly got underway in the South, and to the extent that Blacks attended school they were separate from those of the whites. As public funds were provided, that continued to be the rule. As for what took place in private establishments providing public services—stores, hotels, eating places, saloons, transportation, and the like—it was ordinarily left to the owners or managers to determine whom they would serve and under what conditions. There is some evidence that separation was by no means the universal rule in privately owned businesses. An Englishman traveling through the South in 1879 reported that in the use of

Booker T. Washington (1856–1915)

Washington was the founding head of Tuskegee Institute in Alabama and led it as it grew from a church and a shack to a college with more than 40 buildings. He was born a slave on a plantation in Virginia. After the Civil War, he worked in a coal mine. He got an elementary education by attending a night school, and worked as a house servant for a family which encouraged his efforts at learning. Washington worked his way through Hampton Institute as a janitor, attended a seminary, and returned to Hampton as an instructor. His appointment to a fledgling teacher training school at Tuskegee set the stage for him to emerge as a Black leader.

Washington's especial concern was that the students there should prepare themselves for work in the South as it then was. He advised them to live peacefully within the system, to learn skills, trades, and work habits that would enable them to improve their position. By recommending this course, Washington endeared himself to many whites both in the North and the South. With this philosophy, he was able to build a respected college for Blacks at a time when the badge of inferiority was being firmly fastened upon them.

transportation facilities "the humblest black rides with the proudest white on terms of perfect equality. . . ." A Southerner reported from South Carolina that "The negroes are freely admitted to the theatre in Columbia and to other exhibitions, lectures, etc. . . .In Columbia they are also served at the bars, soda water fountains, and ice cream saloons, but not generally elsewhere." A black man from the North who traveled through the states of the Confederacy in the 1880s observed that without regard to race on the railroads "a first class ticket is good in a first class coach," that "Negroes dine with whites in a railroad saloon," and that he could "go into saloons and get refreshments even as in New York."[150] In government buildings and political activities Blacks were generally accorded equal treatment in the 1870s and 1880s.

The situation began to change rapidly in the 1890s, and the move was on to establish separation by legal segregation. Some important changes preceded and accompanied this move toward segregation. The development of manufacturing on a considerable scale and the growth of cities increased the frictional possibilities of contacts between the races. This was especially so with the coming of streetcars and much more widespread rail transportation. The attitude toward the role of government was changing nationally as well. The move to regulate privately owned business opened the way for imposing segregation as regulations. While slavery had a racial base, it had earlier been widely supposed, at least by the more thoughtful, that important differences between the races were cultural rather than racial in origin. That is not to say that cultural differences were not reckoned to be important, but they were not necessarily fixed. Darwinism emphasized heredity and focused attention on the much greater fixity of traits that could be thought of as racial. The Federal courts were making it clear that they would not apply the Fourteenth Amendment so as to restrain states in segregation efforts, *per se*. In *Plessy vs. Ferguson*, the Supreme Court ruled segregated cars on the railroads were not unconstitutional so long as the facilities were equal (hence, the doctrine, "separate but equal"). It was of much importance, too, that a goodly number of Southern states adopted new state constitutions which contained provisions aimed at making it more difficult for Blacks (as well as whites, in some instances) to vote.

Among these devices were literacy tests, the poll tax, and so-called grandfather clauses. The last was of little significance for very long, since it had to do with enfranchising those whose ancestors could vote before the abolition of slavery. The poll tax and literacy test did not necessarily discriminate on the basis of race. A literacy test could (and sometimes did) eliminate whites as well as Blacks from the voting rolls. The poll tax was entirely color blind. It was cumulative (had to be paid annually from the time one was eligible to vote or in a lump sum if registration occurred at some later point in life), and poll tax receipts had to be presented upon demand at the polls. It was the White Democratic Primary, however, by which Blacks were most effectively disfranchised. The Southern states maintained that their Democratic parties were private associations, and they proceeded generally to exclude Blacks from voting in them. Thus, those Blacks who could qualify to vote could only vote in the general elections. This was quite often pointless, because the white South had become solidly Democratic, and nomination by the Democrats was, as it was often said, "tantamount" to election. So it was that a device promoted to make elections more democratic—the primary—was used to exclude blacks.

As they were excluded from effective voting and politicians no longer needed to appeal to them to get elected, Blacks lost the political means for opposing segregation, if that was their desire. The acquiring of overseas possessions in which the people were to be treated differently, to be governed by appointed officials, and to have self-government delayed was used to justify different treatment and segregation of the Blacks. The editor of the *Atlantic Monthly* noted that "If the stronger and cleverer race is free to impose its will upon 'new-caught sullen peoples' on the other side of the globe, why not in South Carolina and Mississippi?"[151]

Above all, though, it was the Populist and Progressive bent to reform and regulation that set the stage for segregation. Both pressed, too, for making government more responsive to the popular will. In the South, politicians were not long in learning that the way to stir up popular fervor among many white voters was to turn on Blacks. Senators Benjamin R. Tillman of South Carolina and James K. Vardaman of Mississippi were examples of men who were demagogues of that flavor as well as vigorously opposed to big business. Tom Watson of Georgia was slow to take up the racial gauntlet, but he too turned to it as a means of gaining support eventually.

In any case, legal segregation laws came forth in great variety and number in the years before World War I. The first segregation law generally adopted separated white and Black passengers on trains. Most Southern states had such laws by 1900. Following that came separation on street cars: North Carolina and Virginia in 1901, Louisiana in 1902, Arkansas, South Carolina, and Tennessee in 1903, Mississippi and Maryland in 1904, Florida in 1905, and Oklahoma in 1907. Steamboats were segregated in states where this was an important mode of transportation. Some states provided strict segregation rules for factories. For example, South Carolina "prohibited textile factories from permitting laborers of different races from working together in the same room. . . ."[152] Segregation was also applied in various ways in some states to mental institutions, hospitals, jails and prisons, public parks, athletic events and contests, housing, public telephone booths, and elevators. By World War I, widespread legal segregation had been established in the states of the old Confederacy and neighboring states. That did not end the thrust toward legal segregation, and it was extended to other areas in ensuing years. For example, in 1930 a Birmingham ordinance prohibited Negroes and whites to play dominoes or checkers together.

Since segregation has since fallen under general condemnation, some further observations about it may be made. Segregation laws applied to and restricted whites as well as Blacks. Two things modified this formal equality, however: the laws were imposed by whites generally, and it was done in a context in which white supremacy was proclaimed and Black inferiority was assumed, when it was not stated. Most likely, segregation and separation reduced racial tension and conflict in the South. After all, reducing opportunities for collisions might be expected to have that impact. Lynchings, which had been on the rise before the establishment of segregation, tended to decline afterward. Moreover, the worst race riots in the first half of the 20th century occurred in the North. The under side of this was that Blacks had been set aside in the law as constituting a separate class or caste, and that they have often acted as if they were.

But in the late 19th and early 20th centuries there was no major movement among Blacks to counter political disfranchisement and segregation. On the contrary, Booker T. Washington, the most prominent Black leader of the period, advised members of his race to meet indignities and injustices with "few words and conservative action," "to suffer in silence," and exercise "patience, forebearance, and self-control in the midst of trying conditions."[153] Instead of becoming embroiled in politics and confrontations, Washington advised Blacks to study, improve themselves, learn mechanical and industrial skills, become disciplined workers, and prepare themselves to compete successfully in the market place. He held that this approach offered the best opportunity for progress.

Chapter 7
Progressives in Power

I stand for the square deal. But when I say that I am for the square deal, I mean not merely that I stand for fair play under the present rules of the game, but that I stand for having those rules changed so as to work for a more substantial equality. . . .
—Theodore Roosevelt, 1910

And the day is at hand when it shall be realized on this consecrated soil,—a New Freedom,—a Liberty widened and deepened to match the broadened life of man in modern America. . . .
—Woodrow Wilson, 1912

In this widespread political agitation . . . , there may be distinguished . . . three tendencies. The first of these tendencies is found in the insistence. . . that . . . corrupt influence in government—national, state and city—be removed; the second tendency is found in the demand that the structure . . . of government . . . be so changed and modified that it will be more difficult for the few, and easier for the many, to control; and, finally, the third tendency is found in the rapidly growing conviction that the functions of government at present are too restricted and that they must be increased and extended to relieve social and economic distress.
—Benjamin Parke De Witt, 1915

Chronology

1901—Assasination of McKinley, Roosevelt becomes President.

1902—Roosevelt directs suit to dissolve Northern Securities Company.

1903—Establishment of Department of Commerce and Labor.

1904—Roosevelt Corollary to Monroe Doctrine.

1906—

June 29—Hepburn Act.
June 30—Pure Food and Drug Act.
June 30—Meat Inspection Act.

1907—Roosevelt appoints Inland Waterways Commission.

1908—

May—Aldrich-Vreeland Act.
November—Election of Taft.

1909—Mann-Elkins Act.

1911—United States intervenes in Nicaragua

1912—Election of Wilson.

1913—

February—Adoption of 16th Amendment.
May—Adoption of 17th Amendment.
December—Federal Reserve Act.

1914—Clayton Antitrust Act.

1916—Federal Farm Loan Act.

Progressives were in power nationally from 1901 to 1921, that is, from the time of the assassination of President McKinley to the end of Wilson's second term. That is not to say that they always dominated the national government during this period, but they played a dominant role throughout. Both major political parties were very much under the influence of progressivism. The three Presidents who served—Theodore Roosevelt, William Howard Taft, and Woodrow Wilson—professed to be progressives, though Taft's progressivism was questionable, and Wilson tried to distinguish his brand from that of Roosevelt in the election of 1912. As Progressives, they tended to identify progress with an expanded role of government, favored greater popular participation in government, government intervention in the economy, especially to control big business, were bent toward efforts to transform society in a variety of ways, and were more than a little inclined to become involved in foreign affairs. World War I was, of course, more than an interlude in this period, but the character of American participation in it was more than a little influenced by progressive ideas.

Progressivism was not exclusively a national phenomenon, however; Progressives were also highly influential in state, municipal, and other local governments. There, the thrust was to restructure governments so as to make them more professional, to increase the role and power of voters, regulate business, and reform or transform communities. So far as restructuring governments was concerned, the notable changes pushed for by Progressives were: primaries for nominating party candidates, adoption of initiative, referendum and recall to give voters direct access to government, and reorganizing city governments by having the government run by a hired city manager rather than an elected mayor, or having a commission system rather than a council. Actually, neither the commission nor city manager system made city government either more popular or democratic. Instead, they were moves toward having experts run the cities. Indeed, there was much of such elitism in the progressive movement.

Progressives at the local and state level moved in a number of directions to reform or transform society. Building codes, which began to be adopted in cities during this period were an attempt to alter the quality and character of dwellings. City zoning ordinances, while they did not become widespread until the 1920s, were nonetheless an extension of the progressive impetus to direct and control the development of cities. While building codes especially were often adopted on the claim that they would improve housing conditions for the poor, their impact was usually to make housing more expensive and thus more difficult to acquire for the poor. Progressives pressed at the local and state levels also to get increased government financing for schools. If a state did not already have compulsory attendance laws, they pushed to have that done, or to extend the number of days a year of schooling and the number of years a child was required to attend.

Marcus A. Hanna (1837–1904)

Courtesy Library of Congress, Brady-Handy Collection

Mark Hanna was a coal magnate, developer of street railways, involved in banking and finance, a political leader, and United States Senator. He was born in Ohio, grew up in Cleveland, and attended Western Reserve University. Afterward, he went into his father's wholesale grocery business, and went on from there to become one of the leading businessmen in Ohio. His interest in the fortunes of the Republican Party led him to become involved in state and national party activities. He played a prominent role in the nomination and election of McKinley to the presidency in 1896. As a result of his demonstrated political tact and astuteness, he was elected chairman of the Republican National Committee. In 1897, Hanna was appointed to the Senate, and served in that body until his death. He was often thought of as the "power behind the throne" of McKinley, but after Roosevelt became President, his influence in the executive branch declined.

Nowhere was the desire to use government to transform society more transparent, however, than in the prohibition movement, which achieved its ultimate goal just after World War I. The Women's Christian Temperance Union and the Anti-Saloon League had been pushing for prohibition of alcoholic beverages before the progressive movement. A Prohibition Party had even been formed to support its own slate of national candidates, though they gained little support. Progressives, however, gave a shove to reform in all sorts of directions, and by 1917 nineteen states had prohibition laws on the books. States were also very active in regulating business, as indicated.

It was at the national level, however, that progressives in power established progressivism as a direction. While the history of what happened in the states is important, the states differed too much from one another for ready generalization. Progressivism in the South was often different from that in the East, and a governor like Braxton B. Comer in Alabama hardly resembled Hiram Johnson in California, though Johnson was almost ready at one point to segregate the Japanese as Comer accepted the segregation of Blacks. Moreover, this is primarily a national history, and the focus is properly there.

Two men, more than any others, made collectivist reform respectable in America. They were Theodore Roosevelt and Woodrow Wilson. Before them, reformism had been a minority movement, and it was tinctured with the radicalism from which it had sprung. Roosevelt and Wilson were nothing if not respectable. They were of older American stock, untouched except most indirectly by foreign radicalism. Their political careers were mainly in the older established political parties, Roosevelt in the Republican, until his temporary break with it in 1912, and Wilson in the Democratic. They were both college men, trained at old prestigious universities, Roosevelt at Harvard and Wilson at Princeton. Both, too, went to law school, Roosevelt at Columbia and Wilson at Virginia, though neither was attracted to the practice of the law. They were men of ideas, Roosevelt probably out of his almost universal interest in everything, but Wilson had a Ph.D. from Johns Hopkins, wrote extensively on history and government, and was called to the presidency of Princeton. Above all, they were eminently qualified for the task of making reformism respectable, for they had been nurtured in the most prominent of American institutions and were successful members of the prevailing society.

Both Roosevelt and Wilson, too, showed the way to thrust the whole government toward collectivist reforms. They asserted presidential leadership in the government. Presidents had always taken the lead in foreign relations, of course, because they have the constitutional responsibility for doing so. But in domestic legislation, the prescribed constitutional role of the President is negative—the veto. They cut a path around this difficulty. The initiative for legislation is vested in the Congress. Roosevelt took the lead in setting forth programs which shifted the initiative to him.

Roosevelt referred to his program in 1904 as a Square Deal, by which he meant to indicate that he would be working for a square deal for all elements in the population. "Over half" of his message to Congress in 1904 "was given over to proposals for new economic and social legislation."[154] He called for the federal government to pass an employer's liability act for its employees and those of contractors employed by the government. There were requests for such things as requiring the use of safety devices on railroads, regulation of hours of labor of railroad workers, giving the Interstate Commerce Commission power to establish rail rates, establishing a Bureau of Corporations to license interstate businesses, the instituting of a variety of reforms in the District of Columbia, and so forth.

Most likely, Roosevelt did not foresee that when he used the phrase Square Deal to stand for his program that the notion would catch on with other candidates. In any case, it did. Roosevelt called his program in 1912 the New Nationalism, and Wilson called his the New Freedom. Although the practice was begun by a Republican, thereafter only Democrats have used it. Thus, we have had Franklin D. Roosevelt's New Deal, Harry S. Truman's Fair Deal, John F. Kennedy's New Frontier, and Lyndon B. Johnson's Great Society. Since the 1960s no Democrat (or Republican) has come forth with a name for a program of change. Two things at least may have drawn the candidate's minds away from this approach. One is the conservative resurgence which has dimmed the glitter of major social and economic changes. The other is that while pressures for change have still been made, presidential candidates have not seen fit to fly the banner of social transformation. But even if this practice has now been abandoned, it had a large impact on America while it was being used.

Strangely, historians have never agreed upon a generic term for these named programs for asserting presidential leadership to make major changes. Indeed, few appear to have given thought to the phenomenon or to the dimensions of its significance. It would be appropriate, as the present writer suggested some years ago, to call them Four-Year Plans (or, if they occur before the beginning of a President's first term, perhaps Eight-Year Plans).[155] After all, they are plans, and the presidential term is four years. The phrase is borrowed from the Stalinist plans of the late 1920s and 1930s for reconstruction of the Soviet Union. These were usually called Five-Year Plans. Here is Joseph Stalin's description of the first five-year plan, begun in 1928:

> The fundamental task of the Five-Year Plan was, in converting the U.S.S.R. into an industrial country, fully to eliminate the capitalist elements, to widen the front of Socialist forms of economy, and to create the economic base for the abolition of classes in the U.S.S.R., for the construction of Socialist society. . . .
> The fundamental task of the Five-Year Plan was to transfer small

and scattered agriculture to the lines of large-scale collective farming, so as to ensure the economic base for Socialism in the rural districts and thus to eliminate the possibility of the restoration of capitalism in the U.S.S.R.[156]

Granted that the presidential Four-Year Plans were different in very important ways from the five-year ones in the Soviet Union, there were nonetheless enough essential likenesses to make the analogy interesting. The Soviet plans were not election devices, whereas those in the United States tended to be in some measure. The American plans were introduced earlier than the Russian, though that does not much matter. There should be no doubt, however, that the Soviet plans were much more thoroughgoing, plus being brutally imposed, such as forced collectivization of agriculture in which millions died, than anything that was ever done in the United States. In a word, the Soviet plans were revolutionary. Those in the United States were not, certainly not those of Roosevelt and Wilson. Even so, there were essential similarities which make the use of analogous generic terms appropriate.

Both the Soviet and American plans were for using the power of government to control the economy. The Russian plan was revolutionary; the American one was evolutionary, if it be accepted that the basic direction was toward greater control and direction of the economy—to take the management of economic affairs away from individuals and voluntary groups and vest them increasingly in the collective or government—i.e., socialism. Neither Roosevelt nor Wilson professed to be socialists, and they probably did not think of themselves in that way. Yet they set forth visions that would tilt the country in that direction. This may be clearer from their descriptions of the New Nationalism and New Freedom. What Roosevelt sought, according to historian Richard Hofstadter, was "A strong centralized State, extended government interference in economic life. . . ."[157] Roosevelt himself said, "The New Nationalism puts the national need before sectional or personal advantage. . . . This New Nationalism regards the executive power as the steward of the public welfare. It demands of the judiciary that it shall be interested primarily in human welfare rather than property. . . ."[158] Wilson said of his New Freedom, "I believe that the time has come when the government of this country, both state and national, have to set the stage . . . for the doing of justice to men in every relationship of life. . . .Without the watchful interference, the resolute interference, of the government, there can be no fair play between individuals and such powerful institutions as the trusts. Freedom today is something more than being let alone. The program of a government of freedom must in these days be positive, not negative merely."[159]

In sum, both the New Nationalism and the New Freedom were programs to use government to rearrange and control matters in America. The New

Deal, in the 1930s, was a much more thoroughgoing Four-Year Plan, but the programs of Roosevelt and Wilson pointed the way to that.

Roosevelt in Power

Thomas C. Platt, Republican "boss" of New York, had pressed the nomination of Roosevelt for Vice-President in 1900. The Vice-President during McKinley's first term, Garret Hobart, had died in 1899, and Platt saw the vice-presidency as the place to hold in check Roosevelt's restless energy, or at least to get him out of New York state where he had been a thorn in his flesh. Neither McKinley nor Senator Mark Hanna, his close political adviser, were enthusiastic about the prospect. Hanna is alleged to have remarked, when the nomination was being discussed, "Don't any of you realize that there's only one life between this madman and the White House!"[160] Roosevelt had support in the party, however, both because he was the hero of San Juan Hill and his other political activities, including his stint as governor of New York. Thus, he was nominated for Vice-President.

But Platt was foiled by events in his effort to relegate Roosevelt to vice presidential obscurity. On September 6, 1901, McKinley was shot by Leon Czolgosz, an anarchist. The wound was fatal, and McKinley died on September 14. Thus, Roosevelt became President less than a half-year into McKinley's second term. There was a weird logic to the assassination of political figures by anarchists. Since they were opposed to all government, some of them tried to attain their goal by the direct route, namely, by killing government leaders. Anarchists were associated in the public mind and often in reality with revolutionary socialists and what would become communists.

Roosevelt was hardly the sort of man to accept any strict constructionist view of the powers of the President, once he had risen to the office. He took a much more generous view of his powers than that, inclining toward the position that the President might do whatever was not prohibited by the Constitution. "I believe in a strong executive," he admitted in 1908. "I believe in power; but I believe that responsibility should go with power, and that it is not well that the strong executive should be a perpetual executive . . . , that one man can hold it for no more than a limited time."[161] By 1912, his idea of what those limits should be, if any, must have changed, for he offered himself for office once again in the latter year. In any case, Roosevelt believed not only in a strong executive but also a vigorous one. Roosevelt was a man of many interests, threw himself into involvement in these interests, was a live wire, to say the least, favored action to contemplation, wanted to be where the action was going on, and tended to make things happen.

Roosevelt had exhibited most of these traits before the presidency could have been anything more than a gleam in his eye, if that. He had hardly been elected to the New York state legislature, his first political undertaking, before he was pressing for the impeachment of a prominent judge. When he left the legislature, he moved to the Dakotas and was soon embroiled in bringing law and order to the west, organizing vigilante groups, serving as deputy sheriff, and making life difficult for cattle thieves. He returned to New York City in 1886 to save that metropolis from Henry George by running for mayor. Neither he nor George won the election, but he was soon in the thick of things once again by serving on the Civil Service Commission, where he fought to expand the civil service. Following that, he was appointed president of the police board of New York City, making himself

Theodore Roosevelt (1858–1919)

Roosevelt was the 26th President of the United States and was the youngest, at 43, to take on the duties of that high office up to that time. Only Jefferson, among those who had served as president, had such a variety of interests and accomplishments. Roosevelt was, at different times, a state legislator, rancher, biographer, historian, naturalist, bureaucrat, police commissioner, Assistant Secretary of the Navy, regimental commander in the army, governor, Vice-President, President for nearly two terms, and world traveler. The chances are good that he was the most prolific writer ever to hold high office in the United States. Roosevelt was a frail and sickly boy, but by dint of exercise and determination he developed into a healthy and strong man, capable of enduring the strenuous life of a cowboy, soldier, and an explorer in the far reaches of a tributary of the Amazon. He was a reformer throughout his political career, gravitated toward the limelight, and made reform respectable through his efforts. When the United States entered World War I, he offered his services to raise a division of outdoorsmen. Some 250,000 men indicated their willingness to follow, but President Wilson declined the offer.

heard by fighting corruption and working to install a merit system. After McKinley's election, for the first time, Roosevelt was made assistant secretary of the Navy, and on his own initiative he ordered Admiral Dewey to prepare for action in the Philippines. When war broke out, he resigned his position, helped organize a cavalry unit, the Rough Riders, and helped to lead them in taking San Juan Hill. He was hardly back from the war before the Republicans nominated him to be governor of New York. After his election, his reformist urges so aggravated some of the New York politicians that they could hardly wait to make him Vice President.

Roosevelt was, then, what is sometimes called a mover and a shaker, and he was not long in demonstrating this attribute as President. By the Knight decision in 1895, the Supreme Court had cast doubt upon the constitutionality of any attempt by the government to break up large business combinations by applying the Sherman Antitrust Act. In the year that Roosevelt became President two large mergers had been made: one establishing United States Steel and the other forming a rail combine in the Northwest by Northern Securities Company. In early 1902, Roosevelt ordered the attorney general, Philander C. Knox, to file an antitrust suit against Northern Securities, which was a holding company. Despite the efforts of business leaders to get Roosevelt to call off the suit, he persisted with it. In 1903, a Federal court ordered the dissolution of the company, and the next year the Supreme Court affirmed the decision. Much of Roosevelt's reputation as a "trust-buster" arose from this case.

Roosevelt also became involved in the coal strike in 1902. The anthracite miners' union struck in the fall, raising the specter of a coal shortage during the winter. Roosevelt called upon the union and the operators to arbitrate the dispute. The union agreed, but the operators led by J.P. Morgan and George F. Baer refused at first, maintaining that this was their decision as to how it should be handled. Roosevelt persisted, and eventually the strike was ended by an arbitrated settlement. This was the first time that the President had intervened in labor relations of employers, but it was not to be the last.

1. The Panama Canal

Roosevelt added further luster to his macho image in the way he acquired rights to territory for building a canal, but he hardly improved feelings toward the United States in Latin America. Interest in a canal through Central America somewhere had mounted following the Spanish-American War. The time involved in getting ships from the Pacific to the Atlantic had been dramatized by the long voyage of the battleship *Oregon* around the Cape during the war. With possessions in the Pacific to be guarded, the urgency of a short cut between the oceans was further increased.

There were difficulties in the way of digging such a canal however. One was that the United States had an agreement with Britain—the Clayton-

Bulwer Treaty—made in 1850 requiring that if either country sought to build a canal it would have to be undertaken as a joint venture by both. This difficulty was finally removed by the Hay-Pauncefote Treaty in 1901. The treaty permitted the United States to build a canal, control and fortify it, but provided that the canal was to be open to the ships of all nations on equal terms. The other main difficulty was deciding upon a route and acquiring the rights to the territory. A French company had attempted to dig a canal through the Isthmus of Panama, the shortest distance between the oceans, in the nineteenth century, but the project had failed. The successor French company offered to sell its rights to the United States for $109 million. At that price, a presidential commission concluded that it would be less expensive to dig a canal along a longer route through Nicaragua. Both Congress and the President agreed on the Nicaraguan route. However, an agent of the company, Philippe Bunau-Varilla, and William N. Cromwell, an adventurer involved in the undertaking, got the price of the rights reduced to $40,000,000. That, plus the fear of volcanoes in Nicaragua and the timely eruption of one, induced Congress to authorize the purchase of the French rights and proceed with the Panama route.

Panama belonged to Colombia, however, and the Congressional act stipulated that before proceeding with this route, the United States must acquire a zone across Panama from Colombia. Secretary of State Hay managed to negotiate a treaty with Tomás Herran, Colombian minister to the United States, which granted a canal zone 6 miles wide across Panama on quite favorable terms. The Senate ratified, but after lengthy considera-tion, the Colombian Senate rejected it. They were motivated in part, at least, by the belief that when the French company's charter expired in 1904 the United States would offer better terms. Roosevelt was furious with the Colombians, denounced them as "inefficient bandits," and gave serious consideration to seizing Panama. Indeed in 1911 he declared, "I took the Canal Zone and let Congress debate. . . ."[162]

That is not exactly how it occurred, however. Bunau-Varilla and Crom-well helped to organize a revolt against Colombia in Panama. The revolu-tion was proclaimed on November 3, 1903. The day before, Roosevelt dispatched warships to Panama, invoking an old treaty which authorized the United States to keep order in the Isthmus, and thus preventing Colombia from sending troops. On November 6, the United States recognized the independence of Panama as a republic. A few days later, as soon as Bunau-Varilla could get to Washington, the Hay-Bunau-Varilla Treaty was negotiated. The treaty provided that the United States would guarantee the independence of Panama, granted a Canal Zone 10 miles wide across Panama forever, in return for which the United States paid $10 million upon ratification and $250,000 per year beginning 9 years after ratification.

Work on the Panama Canal began in 1904, and the canal was opened to traffic in 1914. Congressional Democrats mainly remained dissatisfied with the way the route had been acquired, but they were powerless to do anything about it.

2. Roosevelt's Foreign Policy

Roosevelt's posture toward foreign nations might be summed up by his saying, "Speak softly and carry a big stick." He may not have always spoken softly, but he did have a large club to back him up before his terms in the White House were completed. Under his prodding, Congress authorized and a large and powerful navy was built. Ten battleships and four cruisers were voted between 1902 and 1905, and between 1906 and 1913 either one or two dreadnoughts were authorized each year. In 1906, the United States Navy was rated second only to that of Great Britain.

Roosevelt was as available and inclined to become involved in foreign disputes as domestic ones. His first occasion to become involved was in a dispute between Venezuela and several European powers. Venezuela's dictator, Cipriano Castro, went deeply into debt to European investors. When he failed to pay the debts or submit the question to the Hague Tribunal, Germany and Great Britain imposed a blockade, and, when they were joined by Italian vessels, bombarded Venezuelan ports. When the Germans had a year earlier notified the United States that any intervention would not result in permanent occupation, Roosevelt had observed that the United States did "not guarantee any State against punishment if it misconducts itself, provided that punishment does not take the form of acquisition of territory by any non-American power."[163] Following the bombardment of Venezuelan ports in 1902, Castro asked Roosevelt to propose arbitration. He did so to the European powers; they agreed, and the issue was eventually resolved by the Hague Tribunal.

However, Roosevelt took a different stance when the Dominican Republic was in danger of foreign intervention. This time, the United States was invited to supervise the customs houses to see that the receipts were used to pay foreign debts. However, a dispute arose over the apportioning of receipts, and it looked as if one or more European powers might intervene. Roosevelt thus issued what has since been called the Roosevelt Corollary to the Monroe Doctrine in 1904. In his annual message to Congress in that year, Roosevelt assured the rest of the world that this country had no territorial ambitions in the Western Hemisphere. But, and this was his statement of the Corollary, in cases of "Chronic wrongdoing, or an impotence which results in a general loosening of the ties of civilized society," the situation may "ultimately require intervention by some civilized nation, and in the Western Hemisphere, the adherence of the United States to the Monroe Doctrine may force the United States, however reluctantly . . . , to the exercise of an international police power."[164] Roosevelt's words could be construed to mean that if it becomes necessary for any power to intervene in any nation in the Western Hemisphere that nation will be the United States. Indeed, that is the construction that has been placed upon it.

But suppose some European nation should intervene to collect debts, say. What would the United States do? Would the country go to war against that nation? Roosevelt attempted to clarify his position in his message to Congress in 1905. He indicated that if some Latin American nation should do damage to some other nation, the United States would only interfere to prevent some foreign nation from taking possession of it. On the matter of debt, he said that the United States would not go to war to prevent the collection of a just debt. On the other hand, the United States would not permit some foreign power to take over the customs houses of any Latin American country. In short, the United States would protect the territorial integrity and nationhood of Latin American countries from outside interference, and intervene in their affairs when it judged that to be necessary.

In the Orient, Roosevelt's main concern was the continued promotion of Hay's Open Door Policy in China and keeping a balance of naval power in the Pacific. Russia continued to be troublesome in Manchuria, leading the President to consider more vigorous action against Russia. As it turned out, however, the Japanese were ahead of him on that. They launched a naval attack against the Russian fleet in 1904, precipitating the Russo-Japanese War. Indeed, the Japanese were so successful in their prosecution of the war that the balance of power in Asia and the Pacific might be threatened. However, the Japanese government was in such financial difficulties that despite their victories they asked Roosevelt to mediate the dispute. This he agreed to do, and a settlement was reached in the Portsmouth Conference in the United States in 1905.

Japan's swift victory over Russia surprised, if it did not shock, the other powers in the world. Russia had been reckoned to be one of the great powers of the world, whereas Japan had only recently opened its land to the rest of the world and had hardly become a factor on the world stage. Following the war, Japan continued to build its naval power and was becoming a potential threat to the Philippines as well as the stability of the Orient generally. At just this juncture, trouble arose between the Japanese and the United States. The Hearst newspapers fanned the flames of any American resentment of Japanese immigrants on the West Coast by excited descriptions of the coming "yellow peril." San Francisco authorized segregated schools for Japanese children, and this aroused the Japanese government. Roosevelt persuaded San Francisco to desegregate its schools, and in 1907 reached an understanding with the Japanese government—known as the "Gentlemen's Agreement"—in which the Japanese agreed to keep out agricultural laborers.

Roosevelt still had a nagging worry about Japanese naval expansion. This probably prompted him to make a show of naval strength to the world. In any case, he dispatched the "Great White Fleet," composed of 16 battleships, most of them new, on a 45,000-mile voyage around the world. The fleet left in December, 1907 and reached home on its return voyage in February, 1909. At the invitation of the Japanese, the fleet put in at Yokohama and receiving a rousing welcome. Whether this influenced the Japanese or not, the Root-Takahira Agreement between the two governments was reached in 1908. Both agreed to respect the Open Door in China and to maintain the *status quo* in naval power in the Pacific.

3. Domestic Regulation

Most of the Progressive measures during Roosevelt's nearly two terms in office had to do with trust busting and railroad legislation. In the broadest sense, however, these and other measures were regulatory in character. Roosevelt offered the following justification for regulation of corporations in his first annual message to Congress:

> . . . Corporations engaged in interstate commerce should be regulated if they are found to exercise a license working to the public injury. It should be as much the aim of those who seek for social betterment to rid the business world of crimes of cunning as to rid the entire body politic of crimes of violence. Great corporations exist only because they are created and safeguarded by our institutions; and it is therefore our right and our duty to see that they work in harmony with these institutions.[165]

In 1903, Congress passed the Expedition Act for the purpose of expediting (speeding up) antitrust suits in Federal courts. Circuit courts were required to give such suits precedence on the dockets at the request of the attorney general. The same year a Department of Commerce and Labor was created with cabinet rank. It included a Bureau of Corporations which was to investigate and report on corporations engaged in interstate commerce (except for common carriers). This last signified a heightened interest in the doings of corporations by the government. The creation of the department indicated a recognition of economic interest groups, since a Department of Agriculture had been set up several years earlier. Commerce and Labor were made separate departments a few years later.

It was not until 1906, however, that Roosevelt's reformist bent, which he had made clear in the election campaign of 1904, resulted in several pieces of new legislation. The Hepburn Act of 1906 greatly increased the powers of the Interstate Commerce Commission. It increased the number of the members of the commission and authorized the commission to set "just and reasonable" maximum rail rates. Any rates prescribed were to go into effect, though the railroad could appeal to the courts. That way, however, the burden of proof would be on the railroad, not the commission. The act also extended the coverage of the commission to pipelines and other sorts of property auxiliary to transportation. It restricted railroads in hauling goods they produced or in the granting of free passes. Senator Robert M. La Follette of Wisconsin, a radical Progressive, had sought to include the requirement for physical valuation of railroad property as a basis for fixing rates in the bill. This simplistic idea continued to be pushed until it was eventually authorized at a later time, but it never amounted to anything. Not only did the physical valuation of property pose formidable difficulties, but it would only have resulted in disaster to the railroads if it had ever been acted upon.

During the same session, Congress passed the Pure Food and Drug Act and the Meat Inspection Act. These were the first national acts passed with the intent of regulating the quality of goods sold in interstate commerce. Although there is not one scintilla of evidence that the men at the constitutional convention had in mind authorizing such regulation, it has never been successfully challenged. Impetus to the passage of this legislation came primarily from the muckraking novel, *The Jungle*, written by Upton

Robert M. La Follette (1855–1925)

La Follette was a four-term Senator from Wisconsin and a leader in the Progressive movement. He was born in Wisconsin, graduated from the state university, studied law, and was admitted to the bar. Most of his working career, however, was devoted to politics. He was elected to the House of Representatives in 1885, where he served for 3 terms. In 1901, he was elected governor of Wisconsin, was re-elected for the succeeding two terms, and came to national attention as a reformer in that office. When he entered the Senate, he quickly became one of the most outspoken of the Insurgents in the Republican Party. Indeed, he contributed much to the dividing of the Republicans in the election of 1912 and, unintentionally to the conservative character of the Republican Party generally thereafter. La Follette sought the Republican nomination for President in 1924; when he failed badly to get that, he ran on the Progressive ticket, but was defeated.

Sinclair. Sinclair gave free rein to his imagination in depicting the unsanitary conditions in the meat-packing industry. The Meat Inspection Act provided for the enforcement of sanitary regulations in packing plants, and for Federal inspection of meat to be sold in interstate commerce. The Pure Food and Drug Act prohibited the shipment of adulterated or mislabeled food and drugs in interstate commerce.

The Immunity of Witnesses Act, passed on the same day, required corporation officers to testify or give information about the operation of their corporations. This reinforced a spreading idea that all sorts of information about corporations was really public information.

A banking panic occurred in 1907, and in its wake an act was passed with great portent for the future. Heavy demands for currency produced several bank closings in New York and raised the prospect of spreading panic and depression. While this did not happen, it did set the stage for legislative action. The basic cause of the panic, as well as most of those which preceded it in the 19th century, was fractional reserve banking. This practice enabled banks to keep only a fraction of the cash reserves necessary to meet their demand obligations. When enough of their customers demanded cash, banks would have to close their doors (go "bankrupt"), and the panic might spread closing more banks. Since fractional reserve and credit expansion were the root causes, it might be supposed that legislators would address themselves to those problems. That did not (and has not) happened, however. Instead, the lawmakers usually accepted the monetarist argument, and acted on the view that the problem was a shortage of currency.

Thus, Congress passed the Aldrich-Vreeland Act in 1908 to increase the currency supply. It authorized national banks to issue currency on the basis of business notes (commercial paper) and bonds issued by states, counties, and cities. The act was considered to be a temporary measure and was to run for only 6 years. However, it provided for a National Monetary Commission, and Senator Nelson W. Aldrich was picked to head it. The report of this commission in 1912 served as the basis for the Federal Reserve Act of 1913.

4. Conservation

Actually, the Roosevelt measures that were most clearly socialistic in tendency were those having to do with increasing government ownership of property in the name of conservation. Just as Progressives associated the notion of expanded government power with progress so they associated government ownership and control over land with conservation. To Progressives, when they were in a propagandistic mood, private owners wasted, exploited, and despoiled the land, whereas government would conserve it. Those who think in this way have both tunnel vision and an atrophied view of economy. In fact, governments can misuse and abuse lands as much as private owners. Nothing can quite equal the devastation of war, and wars are usually fought by governments. But even in more peaceful pursuits governments can greatly disturb natural configurations, as in building roads, for example. Where economy is concerned, there are three elements involved: land, labor, and capital. The decision on the mix of these is often made in terms of which is more plentiful and less expensive. Undoubtedly, governments may be in a better position to use labor and capital freely and save land than are most private owners, but that hardly proves that they are less wasteful.

In any case, Roosevelt threw himself enthusiastically behind the move to reverse the long-established trend of the government to sell and otherwise dispose of lands to which it held title. Throughout most of the 19th century, the federal government was bent on reducing its domain, and through these efforts attained much of its aim. The reversal began in 1891, when 47 million acres were set aside for national forests. The process of setting aside land was greatly accelerated under Roosevelt. His invaluable aide in this undertaking was Gifford Pinchot, who had been trained in forestry in European universities, and undoubtedly imbibed ideas about the forests being held in common. Mostly by executive order, Roosevelt created five additional national parks, and after the passage of the National Monuments Act in 1906, proclaimed 16 national monuments. In 1907, when Western

Gifford Pinchot (1865–1947)

Courtesy Library of Congress

Pinchot was born in Connecticut, graduated from Yale, and studied forestry in France, Switzerland, Germany, and Austria. He is credited with doing the first extensive systematic forestry on the Biltmore estate near Asheville, North Carolina. His background made him a likely candidate for a government position as the United States began setting aside forest preserves. Pinchot became Roosevelt's favorite conservationist, and the President appointed him to the Inland Waterways Commission and the National Conservation Commission. He soon ran into difficulty, however, during Taft's administration, and lost out in the Ballinger-Pinchot Affair. Later, he worked with forest preserves in Pennsylvania, and was twice chosen governor of Pennsylvania.

Congressmen attached a rider to an appropriations bill prohibiting him to set aside any further lands, he signed the bill because appropriations were essential. Before doing so, however, he added 125 million acres of land to national forests, reserved 4.7 million acres of phosphate beds, and set aside 68 million acres of land containing coal deposits. In addition, he reserved 2,565 sites for possible hydroelectric dams and vetoed a bill which would have allowed private power companies to develop the Muscle Shoals site on the Tennessee river in Alabama.

From the point of view of conservationism, Roosevelt's conferences and commissions on the subject may have been as important as the measures he took, for they spread the idea that the government should preserve the national domain from the spoilage of private property owners. Roosevelt set up an Inland Waterways Commission in 1907. Its purpose was to explore the inland waterways situation and suggest ways to prevent the spoiling of rivers by private development. In the light of its finding he called a White House Conference on Conservation, which met in May of 1908. The initial meeting was held in the East Room of the White House, and it was attended by a host of dignitaries: the members of the Cabinet, the justices of the Supreme Court, Democratic Party leaders, governors of 38 states and territories, and an assortment of prominent scientists, scholars, and other public officials. Roosevelt declared to the assembled audience that "The time has come for a change. As a people we have the right and duty . . . to protect ourselves and our children against the wasteful development of our natural resources."[166] The statement of the governors at the close of the conference was more than a little ominous for the future of private property and private enterprise, since it discussed the land and all its resources as if they were a proper concern of government. They said, in part, "We . . . declare the conviction that the great prosperity of our country rests upon the abundant resources of the land. . . . We look upon these resources as a heritage to be made use of . . . , but not to be wasted, deteriorated, or needless destroyed." They went on to assert that the conservation of these resources was a joint concern of the United States government and those of the states, and that the concern would result "in suitable action by the Congress" and "by the legislatures of the several States. . . ."[167] In short, theirs was a call for concerted action by the governments in the United States to act to conserve natural resources.

The Taft Administration

William Howard Taft was Roosevelt's hand-picked choice to succeed him. After all, Taft had been Roosevelt's right-hand man during much of the time he had been in the White House, and Roosevelt expected that what he had begun Taft would continue. Taft had played a leading role in establishing governments in the newly acquired colonies and then had served faithfully as Secretary of War. Even so, there were great differences both in temperament and outlook, though so far as could be told Taft was no less a Progressive than Roosevelt. But Roosevelt had a take-charge personality, advanced his own ideas vigorously, and visualized himself as setting the course of the nation. By contrast, Taft was taciturn, a chairman of the board, not a party whip, a mediator and judge, not an initiator. After all, Taft was a huge man whose voracious appetite showed in his girth, and who had to have an oversized bathtub installed in the White House to contain his bulk. Energetic he was not, though judicious he was, and his conception of the presidency was much more in keeping with what the Constitution prescribes than was that of Roosevelt.

It was not that Progressive measures did not continue during Taft's administration. They did. Far more antitrust suits were brought during this one term than during the nearly two of Roosevelt. The Interstate Commerce Commission's powers were strengthened and expanded by the Mann-Elkins Act in 1910. Telephone, telegraph, and cable companies were brought under its authority. The commission was given the power to suspend new rates railroads might introduce pending a court decision, and greater enforcement power over charges for long and short hauls. A Postal Savings system was established in the same year, and specified post offices could accept deposits and pay interest on them. This pleased Progressives, because it put the government into the savings bank business. Parcel post service was also initiated, by which the government would compete with the railroads in delivering parcels. The Mann Act was passed in 1910 (also known as the White Slavery act), prohibiting the transportation of women across state lines for immoral purposes. This was aimed at prostitution rings, a subject of lurid muckraking exposés.

Nor was Taft's foreign policy greatly different from that of Roosevelt. He sought to maintain the Open Door in China and continue American influence in the Caribbean. His Secretary of State, Philander C. Knox, used somewhat different tactics than had Roosevelt and his Secretary, Elihu Root. He attempted to get American banking interests involved more directly and to have government play a more supportive role. In China, when a foreign consortium was formed to build and operate railroads, Knox pressed to have American financiers participate. Bankers became involved in Haiti and in Nicaragua. These policies were dubbed "Dollar Diplomacy" by critics of it. In fact, they were not a great success. In China, American bankers were not nearly so enthusiastic as the State Department and eventually withdrew. The volatile situation in Nicaragua made it difficult for any government to stay in power or for American financial interests to operate. A pro-American government was installed in 1909, but it became so unpopular that Marines were sent in to quell an uprising in 1912. American military continued its presence in that country until well into the 1920s.

In fact, the Republican Party was divided, and that was not especially Taft's doing. A rift between Progressives and the "Old Guard" in Congress began to make itself felt during the last couple of years of Roosevelt's presidency. It widened during Taft's presidency until it had become a split by 1911. The Progressives undoubtedly wanted Taft to ramrod their programs through Congress, as they may have imagined Roosevelt would have done. Roosevelt thoughtfully left the country to go on an African safari in 1909. Taft had no intention of ramrodding programs of anybody through Congress. That was not his way. He worked within the system, and under the seniority system that prevails in Congress generally long-term members exercise considerable power over what is done. At the time, that meant that dominant influences were Speaker Joseph Cannon in the House and Nelson Aldrich in the Senate.

The debate over the Payne-Aldrich Tariff in 1909 highlighted the division within the Republican Party. The Republican platform of 1908 called for tariff revision, and shortly after his inauguration, President Taft called a special session of Congress to fulfill the promise. The Payne Tariff which was passed by the House contained a considerable revision downward. It faced rough going in the Senate, however. There, Senator Aldrich's Committee on Finance tacked 847 amendments to the bill, many of which raised the rates proposed in the Payne bill. Senator La Follette, leader of the Progressive branch of the Republicans, often called Insurgents, led an extended fight on the Senate floor but to little avail. The Payne-Aldrich Tariff became law much as it had been modified by the Committee on Finance. The Insurgents claimed that Taft had not supported them effectively in their effort. Taft, on the other hand, defended the new tariff as a good one. He explained that Republicans favored a protective tariff, not free trade, and advised those who favored a tariff for revenue only to join the Democrats.

The rift between the Insurgents and the President was widened farther by the Ballinger-Pinchot Affair. Richard Ballinger was Taft's Secretary of the Interior, and Gifford Pinchot, Chief Forester of the United States and a great favorite of Roosevelt, was removed from office by Taft. It came about in this way. A young investigator in the Interior Department charged that Ballinger was planning to turn over coal lands in Alaska to a Morgan-Guggenheim syndicate. He took his tale to Pinchot in the Agriculture Department, who sent him directly to the President with it. Taft accepted Ballinger's explanation and concurred in the dismissal of the young man. Pinchot took the matter to Congress, and the ensuing investigation found that Ballinger had done no wrong. However, Taft dismissed Pinchot for insubordination in going over his head to Congress, thus raising the ire of the conservationists. Indeed, the Congressional investigation had revealed that Ballinger was not an ardent conservationist, that instead he believed in the private development of resources. That was a scandal only in the fevered imagination of Progressive conservationists, but Taft's defense of him added more fuel to the fire of discord.

Roosevelt returned from his foreign tour in time to witness the primary campaigns before the election of 1910. What he saw disheartened him more than a little, for in many instances, the Progressives campaigned against the Old Guard. The fact that the Progressives (or Insurgents) often won the primaries did not lift his spirits much, for he thought they were too often "narrow fanatics, wild visionaries and self-seeking demagogues."[168] On the other hand, he had lost faith in Taft, as he wrote Henry Cabot Lodge: "For a year after Taft took office . . . , I would not let myself think ill of anything he did. I finally had to admit that he had gone wrong on certain points; and I then also had to admit to myself that deep down . . . I had all along known he was wrong. . . ."[169] This he kept to himself and close friends, however, for what he feared was happening was the break up of the Republican Party. Thus, he exercised his influence mainly in trying to hold the party together, while reaffirming his progressivism. Taft tried to use what influence he had, generally to get the regular Republicans elected to office. Neither had much success. The Democrats gained control of the House in the general election in 1910, and Republican Insurgents were dominant in the Senate, which remained Republican. The rift among Republicans was near to being an open rupture when Senator La Follette engineered the formation of a National Progressive Republican League in January, 1911. The Progressives aimed to gain control of the Republican Party if they could, block the nomination of Taft, and run La Follette for President.

Election of 1912

The election of 1912 was the electoral peak of the progressive movement. Progressives were unable to prevent the renomination of Taft, but with the possible exception of Taft, the presidential candidates were Progressive to socialist. At the extreme was the Socialist Party candidate, Eugene Debs, who had been getting an increasing number of votes in presidential elections. Roosevelt tried for the Republican nomination, but when he failed to get it, he accepted the nomination of the Progressive, or "Bull Moose," Party, a splinter off the Republicans. Woodrow Wilson was nominated by the Democrats.

The main contest during the ensuing campaign was between Wilson and Roosevelt. Both men had Four-Year Plans, Roosevelt's New Nationalism and Wilson's New Freedom. Both men, too, declared themselves to be progressives, but there were differences both in emphasis and how they proposed to achieve their goals. Perhaps the most important difference was in how they proposed to deal with businesses, especially with the large interstate businesses, often referred to as trusts. Roosevelt maintained that trust busting was not really the solution. It would only result in destroying a major source of prosperity. On the contrary, Roosevelt said, "We wish to control big business so as to secure among other things good wages for the wage-workers and reasonable prices for the consumers. . . . What is needed is the application to all industrial concerns . . . in interstate commerce in which there is either monopoly or control of the market of the principles on which we have gone in regulating transportation. . . . [A] national industrial commission should be created which should have complete power to regulate and control all the great industrial concerns engaged in interstate business—which practically means all of them in this country."[170]

Wilson contrasted his program with that of Roosevelt. Indeed, he sounded much more like a Jacksonian than a Progressive in his attack on

Woodrow Wilson (1856–1924)

Courtesy New York Historical Society

Wilson was the 28th President of the United States. He was born in Virginia, spent his early years in Georgia and South Carolina, was the son of a Presbyterian minister, and, as befitted one of that background, graduated from Princeton University. He went on to the study of the law, was admitted to the bar, but did not like the practice of it. He was drawn, instead, to political studies, entered graduate school at Johns Hopkins, from which he received a Ph.D. in history and government. Wilson was an excellent writer, more popular than scholarly, and wrote several books on history and government. He became a professor at Princeton and, in the course of time, became president of the university. His speeches and other activities brought him to the attention of Democrats in New Jersey, and he was elected governor in 1910. This set the stage for his nomination and election to the presidency in 1912. He was re-elected in 1916 in a campaign which pitted him against the Republican Charles E. Hughes, but he was badly crippled by strokes before completing his second term.

Roosevelt's plan. He declared that Roosevelt had abandoned the idea of breaking up the trusts and was on his way to empowering them. Roosevelt would, Wilson argued, regulate the trusts with his commission and look to them to provide for the well-being of Americans. In sum, in Roosevelt's vision, the trusts would become philanthropic institutions to take care of the people. Wilson declared, "I do not want to live under a philanthropy. I do not want to be taken care of by the government, either directly, or by any instruments through which the government is acting. I want only to have right and justice prevail . . . , and I will undertake to take care of myself.''[171] What he proposed, then, was to remove the tariffs by which the businesses had grown large, restore competition to the field, and, where necessary, break up the trusts. It sounded more than a little like Andrew Jackson, if not Grover Cleveland. It would turn out, however, that Wilson was much more akin to the Progressives than to his Democratic forebears.

Wilson won a landslide victory in the electoral vote. He got 435 to 88 for Roosevelt and 8 for Taft. He got only a minority of the popular vote, however: the total votes for his opponents 8,742,307, while Wilson got only 6,286,214. Roosevelt came in second with slightly more than 4 million votes. The Democrats gained control of both the House and the Senate. The large vote that Roosevelt received was probably more a tribute to his personal popularity than to his progressivism. The main result of his third-party candidacy was to lead the more radical reform elements out of the Republican Party, leaving the more conservative elements in firmer control than ever. The Republican Party, purged of its radical impetus, returned to power in the 1920s.

Wilson's New Freedom

Woodrow Wilson brought more than a Four-Year Plan with him to the White House. He brought a tenacious determination to push the legislation he wanted through Congress. We have become accustomed in the 20th century to seeing Presidents press their programs upon Congress and having actual bills originate in the executive branch. Not only was that not customary in the 19th century, but earlier Presidents conscientiously avoided exercising any direct influence upon legislation, even if their heads of departments were not always so restrained. Wilson, on the other hand, had no compunction about using whatever means were at his disposal to get Congress to do his will. Indeed, he had earlier believed our presidential system was flawed, that the parliamentary system was much better, and that the powers of the government were too separated to get effective action. Theodore Roosevelt's example, however, convinced him that a determined President could lead, and he came to the office primed to exercise whatever influence or powers he could summon. Wilson had made the observation in 1907 that the President "is . . . the political leader of the nation, or has it in his choice to be. The nation as a whole has chosen him, and is conscious that it has no other political spokesman. He is the only national voice in affairs. Let him once win the admiration and confidence of the country, and no other single force can withstand him, no combination of forces will easily overpower him.''[172]

In any case, President Wilson played a quite active role in getting his program through Congress. He was able to do this not only because of his tenacity but also because Democrats in Congress were surely glad to have a President of their own in office. He employed a number of practices, either new or revived, to exert his influence. He revived the early practice, abandoned by Thomas Jefferson and his successors, by delivering his annual message to a joint session of Congress in person. Thus, it became again the State of the Union Address. In addition, Wilson went before Congress on a number of other occasions to make appeals, met frequently with Congressional leaders or committees, wrote letters to particular members, and took care not to divert or divide Congress with other issues when one of his programs was under consideration. If he was not prime minister in name, he adopted many of their ways in practice.

Another practice which Wilson followed was extensive reliance upon intellectuals. That was not especially strange, since he qualified as an intellectual himself, even a reformist intellectual and visionary. He was an historian, a political scientist in effect, a former college professor and president. While Roosevelt had used the intellectual services of Brooks Adams, it was not his way to depend upon a "Brain Trust," as the collection of intellectuals assembled by Franklin D. Roosevelt was called. To Wilson, such a practice came more naturally. He relied extensively upon Louis Brandeis for advice on ideological as well as more practical problems.

The in-house intellectual of the Wilson administration, however, was Colonel Edward M. House. Whatever the Colonel's qualifications to be an intellectual, he had much experience as an adviser without portfolio before he came to the White House. He was a Texan, though Cornell was his university. House was involved in the campaigns of several Texas governors, and during the period 1894–1904 he exercised a decisive influence over Texas politics. This was always exercised behind the scenes, he never ran for office, and did not go after high appointive positions. Wilson offered him cabinet positions, but he refused, apparently preferring influence to direct power. As one writer observes, "Nearly all accounts agree that Colonel House dominated the decisions on appointments. Wilson frankly didn't want to be bothered."[173] He had a hand in the passage of the Federal Reserve Act as well as playing a prominent role in foreign affairs during Wilson's presidency.

It is more than a little curious that in the same year he became involved with Wilson's campaign, House published anonymously a sort of utopian novel. It is about a man who establishes a dictatorship in America and brings about sweeping reforms. Among these reforms were a graduated income tax, compulsory incorporation act, flexible currency system, an old age pension and labor insurance, a cooperative marketing system, Federal employment bureau, and the like. "This fantasy could be laughed off as the curious dream of Colonel House were it not that so many of these reforms strikingly resemble what the Wilson, and later the New Deal administrations either accomplished or proposed."[174] The ideas were not original with Colonel House, of course, but this advocate had the ear of a President. Among others who had intellectual influence on Wilson were George L. Record, George Creel, and Bernard Baruch.

1. Domestic Intervention

The extent to which Wilson was a Progressive was in doubt when he came to the White House. That he was a reformer was not in question; he had demonstrated this penchant both as head of Princeton and as governor of New Jersey. We know already, too, that he believed in strong presidential leadership, and he affirmed during the campaign his belief in a much more vigorous role for government. But did he intend mainly to remove the privileges on which he believed the "trusts" had been built and allow competition to solve most of the economic difficulties? In short, was he primarily a 19th-century liberal whose efforts would be devoted to reducing the role of government in the economy while making the government more popular? Or, was he a 20th-century Progressive, bent on using the power of the central government to control the economy and remake American society, to greater or lesser degree? Even at this remove, the best answer may be that he was both and neither. There is considerable evidence that he was drawn toward solutions built upon the traditional Democratic programs—which were liberal in tendency. On the other hand, he declared himself to be a Progressive, and he was certainly drawn toward some of their programs. He was a transitional figure in American politics, clinging to past policies of the Democrats yet bending toward the programs which viewed broadly have been a part of the gradual movement toward socialism.

The first legislation that Wilson shepherded through Congress was very much in accord with long-term Democratic aims, going back all the way to the early 19th century. It was the Underwood-Simmons Tariff Act, which reduced rates and made some bows in the direction of free trade. Wilson had maintained that the protective tariff had been a major source of overgrown and dominant businesses (monopolies, he tended to call them). He called a special session of Congress immediately after his inauguration to revise the tariff. The measure, finally passed in October, 1913, reduced rates from an average of 41 per cent to 25 per cent. Also, it placed raw wool, sugar, iron, and steel—all important products—on the free list. Even with both houses Democratic, with Congress devoting virtually its whole attention to the measure, with the President behind it, it took several months to pass the measure. The House acted rather quickly on a bill by Oscar W. Underwood of Alabama. But it took much longer to get a measure through the Senate, which then had to be worked over and sent through both houses again.

Although Progressives generally favored tariff reduction, this was in the main a measure in keeping with the Democratic impetus. But the revenue measure attached to the Underwood-Simmons Tariff was decidedly a Progressive step. An estimated $100 million in taxes would be lost by goods placed on the free list or through tariff reductions. To make up for this a graduated income tax was included. The 16th Amendment had just been ratified authorizing a tax on incomes (or removing the constitutional obstacles to one). It did not mention a graduated or "progressive" tax rate, but Progressives were champing at the bit to pass one. Indeed, the measure as it came from the House was too mild for the more radical of the Progressive Senators, such as La Follette, George W. Norris of Nebraska, and James K. Vardaman of Mississippi. La Follette wanted the highest rate at 10 per cent, and Norris wanted a steeply graduated inheritance tax. When Furnifold M. Simmons, Chairman of the Senate Finance Committee, proposed a compromise figure for the highest tax rate on incomes, Wilson supported him, observing that it was wiser to "begin upon somewhat moderate lines." This remark suggests that Wilson was somewhat of a gradualist himself. At any rate, the first income tax ranged from 1 per cent on income from $20 to $50 thousand to 6 per cent on incomes over $500,000.

It was not exactly clear whether the Federal Reserve Act was a pro-banking act, a Populist act, or a Progressive act. It was, in fact, a compromise measure whose long-term significance may have been little understood at the time. It was conceived as a device both to expand and contract the currency and credit and to disperse the control over them. Wilson's biographer, Arthur S. Link, says that Wilson had no very definite ideas about money and banking or any specific program for dealing with them. However, pressure had been mounting for some sort of reorganization of the banking system, and it had become an issue in the campaign of 1912. The Monetary Commission under the chairmanship of Senator Aldrich had submitted its recommendations in 1912. The thrust of these was that the United States needed a central bank to coordinate the clearing of checks, standardize the reserve requirements, and provide a more flexible credit and currency. In the same year as the recommendations were released, a subcommittee in the House of Representatives, headed by Congressman Arsene P. Pujo, was appointed to investigate banking and currency and make its legislative recommendations.

The Pujo Committee report was made in 1913. It was a fitting climax to years of muckraking about concentrated wealth, Wall Street banker domination, and what Marxists liked to describe as finance capitalism. The committee had documented what must have been generally well known, that many of the great banking and financial institutions in the country were concentrated in New York City. The committee went on to try to prove that there was a "money trust," which extended outward from New York to the other great banking and financial centers in such cities as Boston and

J. Pierpont ("J.P.") Morgan (1837–1913)

Morgan was a financier and banker, born in Connecticut, educated at the English High School in Boston and at the University of Göttingen in Germany. He was the son of a financier, J.S. Morgan, who not only had American connections but also founded an important financial branch in London. After gaining experience in a number of financial firms, Morgan put together his own, J.P. Morgan and Company. It was related to major financial bases in Philadelphia, London, and Paris, and under Morgan's tutelage became one of the leading and most influential houses in the world. Indeed, its location in New York City signified that the United States was reaching a point of financial leadership in the world, a fact that became clearly evident during World War I.

Courtesy Library of Congress

J.P. Morgan and Company organized United States Steel and played a major role in reorganizing several major railroads. Morgan's prominent place in finance was demonstrated in the 1890s when the United States government turned to him for $60 million to bring its gold reserve up to requirements. In the early years of the 20th century, Morgan became the symbol of "Wall Street" and the alleged domination of the country by "trusts." Indeed, the Pujo Committee described the situation in which his company occupied the central position in a "money trust." It should be said that Morgan demonstrated his public spiritedness on a number of occasions and gave much to charitable activities.

Chicago and thence to financial institutions throughout the country. Moreover, to quote from the report: "that there is an established and well-defined identity and community of interest between a few leaders of finance, created and held together through stock ownership, interlocking directorates, partnership and joint account transactions, and other forms of domination over banks, trust companies, railroads, and public-service and industrial corporations, which has resulted in great and rapidly growing concentration of the control of money and credit in the hands of these few men. . . ."[175] Indeed, according to the scenario which Samuel Untermyer, the counsel for the Pujo Committee, tried to construct, at the peak of this pyramid of financial power sat one man, J. Pierpont Morgan, or at least J.P. Morgan & Co. Morgan could, the committee tried to show, make or break companies, drive out competitors, and exercise control over the economy through alliances with other men and interlocking directorates. When questioned before the Pujo Committee, Morgan denied that he had any such power over credit, or that if he had, he could gain or keep it if he exercised it in any arbitrary way. Nonetheless, the report emphasized that in the sense it would use the word a "money trust" did indeed exist.

Confronted with this centralized control over finance, whether fantasy or reality, the New Freedom approach would presumably be to break it up somehow, to "bust" the "money trust." That is not what the Federal Reserve Act did, however. Instead, it left the financial institutions intact and created the Federal Reserve system which overlaid the banking system with yet another one. Granted, it authorized 12 Federal Reserve banks to be located in 12 Federal Reserve districts into which the country was divided. But instead of making each of the banks independent, it linked all of them under a Federal Reserve Board. Each bank was to be theoretically owned by member banks, and all national banks were required to be members and state banks could join. But the Federal Reserve system was a creature of the federal government and ultimately under its control. To those who would consider a private system, Wilson said in a speech to Congress, "The control of the system of banking and of issue which our new laws are to set up must be public, not private, must be vested in the Government itself, so that the banks may be the instruments, not the masters, of business. . . ."[176] So it was, though the overall Reserve Board was an independent one, the members were politically appointed. In effect, the act had established a central banking system with powers over credit and currency which were greater than any J.P. Morgan could have held.

While the Federal Reserve served a number of functions, such as a clearing house for checks and holding a portion of the reserves of member banks, its most basic, and controversial, function has been its control over money supply and credit. Federal Reserve banks issue notes which serve as currency. These bank notes are printed by the United States Treasury but are issued by the banks. Originally the banks had to have a 40 per cent gold reserve against their outstanding bank notes and a 100 per cent reserve of credit instruments. They could, therefore, monetize debt, though this was limited by the gold reserve requirement. They have been a major source of inflation over the years. They have a variety of controls over credit, including the setting of reserve requirements for member banks, by rediscounting commercial loans, and by raising or lowering rediscount rates. They have provided a major source of credit for the federal government over the years.

The Federal Reserve Act resembled much more a Rooseveltian sort of act than a New Freedom one. It regulated banks, was controlled by an independent board, and it definitely did not break them up or reduce government privileges. The Federal Trade Commission Act of 1914, moreover, was clearly in accord with the New Nationalism, not the New Freedom. Wilson had the idea at first of prohibiting those acts which were supposed to lead to the formation of "trusts" or monopolistic businesses. Indeed, some attempts were made at listing the acts. This approach was abandoned when it became clear the the list would be extremely long, incomplete, and almost certainly bring into question the very practices which constitute effective competition. In short, Wilson abandoned the idea that what he wanted to achieve could be done by the regular processes of law and turned to the commission approach, where an appearance of legality might be sustained by assembling the facts which could be alleged to be damaging (if large businesses were damaging). It is interesting that Louis Brandeis steered him in this direction, for Brandeis was the leading exponent of the legal brief in which facts largely took the place of law as the basis of court decisions.

At any rate, the Federal Trade Commission Act authorized a commission made up of 5 members. Its basic task was to enforce "fair trade practices" among interstate businesses (except banks and common carriers). The most striking sentence is the one which declares "That unfair methods of competition in commerce are hereby declared unlawful." Moreover, "The commission is hereby empowered to prevent persons, partnerships, or corporations . . . from using unfair methods of competition in commerce."[177] What constitutes "unfair methods"? The act does not say. This was more than a little like drawing up a referee's manual for football officials which prohibits players to use unfair tactics and enjoins officials to prevent unfair tactics, but does not specify them. The commission was empowered to make investigations, issue charges against companies, hold hearings in which companies would be permitted to answer charges. If companies were found by the commission to be engaged in unfair practices, the commission could issue cease and desist orders, which were subject to judicial review. Companies were required to provide the commission information by way of annual and special reports.

The Clayton Antitrust Act, passed in 1914, also was an attempt to strengthen the earlier Sherman Act. It suffered from some of the same defects, however. While antitrust laws have generally been pushed in the name of maintaining competition, their thrust has been to contain and restrain competition. For example, the Clayton Act prohibited businesses "to discriminate in price between different purchasers of commodities . . . where the effect of such discrimination may be to substantially lessen competition or tend to create a monopoly. . . ."[178] Such discriminations might, of course, both increase competition (be actual means of competing) and at the same time drive some competitor out of business. The act did try to specify what it considered to be abuses in price discrimination. It also attempted to prevent interlocking directorates in banking where the bank had more than $5 million in assets or in other types of corporations which had more than $1 million in capital. This was mainly an attempt to deal with the sorts of situations described in the Pujo Committee report.

The Clayton Act also made a stab at legitimizing labor unions and agricultural organizations and reducing the incidence of court injunctions against such organizations. In short, while attempting to stiffen the antitrust acts as applied to businesses, this act tried to reduce the application to labor unions. Section 6 of the act begins with a curious dependent clause: "That the labor of a human being is not a commodity or article of commerce." This strange congressional venture into metaphysics was not followed by any elabortion or explanation of its application. Since labor is bought and sold in the market, and, since Congress made no attempt to prohibit this traffic, it would not appear to make any difference what generic name is applied to it. Presumably, the author(s) of the sentence intended to imply that different rules for deciding upon price applied to labor than to commodities and articles of commerce. Undoubtedly, it was some sort of slap at the market and a roundabout attempt to justify union activities. At any rate, the act did restrict injunctions to those cases where there was a showing that otherwise irreparable damage might be done. Samuel Gompers proclaimed the Clayton Act to be organized labor's "Magna Carta," but it did not greatly alter existing law, and courts continued to issue injunctions much as they had in the past.

Several other acts help to show the interventionist tendency of the New Freedom, or whatever it should be called, during Wilson's administrations. The Adamson Act, passed in 1916, established an 8-hour day for railroad workers on interstate lines and required payment of time-and-a-half for overtime. This was the first such act by the federal government imposing payment and time rules on privately owned industries. A Federal Farm Loan Act was passed in the same year, providing credit for farmers. This culminated a lengthy effort to set up a governmentally supported long-term credit system for farmers. Confronted with an earlier bill for rural credit, Wilson declared, "I have a very deep conviction that it is unwise and unjustifiable to extend the credit of the Government to a single class of the community."[179] He had overcome his qualms by 1916, for that was hardly the first piece of class legislation passed. The Transportation Act of 1920 was undoubtedly the most far-reaching regulatory act ever passed to that point in American history. While it restored railroads (which had been taken over by the government during the war) to their owners, it placed a dictatorial control of them in the hands of the Interstate Commerce Commission.

The Progressive fervor had largely spent itself by 1920. But it left in its wake a considerable body of legislation, commissions, boards, constitutional amendments and court rulings, some of which have an impact to the present day. The Progressives succeeded in establishing an anti-capitalist mentality with the view that capital must be held in check and that business activity must be carefully monitored and controlled. The New Freedom, as it turned out, did not differ greatly from the New Nationalism or Square Deal, and it looked much more like a not so gradual movement toward socialism.

2. Foreign Intervention

President Wilson was, if anything, more given to foreign intervention than to domestic intervention in the economy. He started out by intervening in Latin American countries, but before he was finished he was vigorously involved in redrawing the boundary lines of Europe and providing a covenant for the League of Nations. The latter intervention, however, was largely an aftermath of World War I and will be discussed elsewhere.

Of course, Wilson justified his intervention in Central American and Caribbean countries on different grounds than those of his two predecessors in the presidency. Democratic leaders, especially William Jennings Bryan, had been critical of territorial expansion, of the Roosevelt intervention in Panama, and of Taft's "Dollar Diplomacy." Wilson rejected "Dollar Diplomacy." But both he and his Secretary of State at the outset, William Jennings Bryan, saw it as their task to set errant countries straight, both in their domestic political arrangements and in their relations with other nations. On one occasion, Wilson assured a British diplomat that he would "teach the South American republics to elect good men" and establish governments "under which all contracts and business and concessions will be safer than they have been." Wilson tended to justify his interventions on democratic grounds or grounds of establishing justice. He was doing so, he inclined to maintain, not to advance the particular interests of the United States but to do what was good and right for all concerned. But whatever their reasons, as one historian has said, Wilson and Bryan compiled "a record of wholesale diplomatic and military interference in the affairs of neighboring states unparalleled at any time in the annals of American diplomacy."[180]

The most dramatic interventions were in Haiti, Santo Domingo, and

Mexico. Americans had been financially involved in Haiti for a number of years. Haiti was deeply in debt to foreigners and was making no headway in meeting its obligations. A revolution early in March, 1915 brought a new government to power, but it was short-lived, for a new revolution broke out in July, the government overturned and its head assassinated. President Wilson sent in the Marines late in July, and imposed a military occupation on Haiti. A new president was elected, and a treaty was signed between the countries which made Haiti a protectorate, in effect, of the United States.

Recurrent revolutions in Santo Domingo had brought the country to such conditions by 1914 that Wilson was moved to take a stronger hand there. He managed to get an agreement among the warring forces to stop fighting and to elect a provisional president. However, the country would not permit the United States to make it a protectorate. When a new revolution broke out in 1916, Wilson sent marine and other naval forces into the country. They took over the government temporarily. When native leaders refused to accept a treaty which would have made the country a protectorate, the naval commander established a military government, which ruled for the next six years. The country did have peace for the next few years; many conditions improved; but they hardly had democracy.

The intervention in Mexico did not have such clear-cut results, and the situation was anything but simple. Mexico had been ruled for about 30 years by Porfirio Diaz, until he fled the country in 1911 because of mounting difficulties. Mexico's rich endowments, especially in oil, had drawn numerous foreign investors, including large investments from the United States during Diaz's rule. Revolution came in 1911, and it was followed by a series of revolts and changes of government. The man who became President in 1911 was murdered in early 1913, and General Huerta became the head of the government only a few weeks before Wilson's inauguration. The turmoil that had been going on in Mexico and the ongoing threat to American lives and property in that country gave rise to demands for intervention. At first, Wilson rejected intervention, but he refused to recognize the government of Huerta because of the way it had come to power. European countries did, however, begin to give formal recognition to the Huerta government. Moreover, Huerta did restore order for a while, and the property of foreigners was generally protected.

When a new Mexican revolutionary, Venustiano Carranza, began to make headway against the forces of Huerta, Wilson began to change his posture and to think in terms of driving Huerta from office. He lifted the embargo on arms so that they could flow to Carranza and his military chieftain, Francisco ("Pancho") Villa. In April, 1914, Wilson ordered naval units to seize the Mexican port of Vera Cruz to prevent a German arms shipment to Huerta from being unloaded. The Huerta government fell in the middle of the year, and Carranza became president. The revolutionary thrust which got underway under Carranza has continued to plague Mexico over the years.

However, the triumph of Carranza whom Wilson had helped to bring to power did not bring the troubles in Mexico to an end. "Pancho" Villa was not pacified by the success of Carranza, and he continued his villainous ways in northern Mexico. His followers killed 16 American citizens in cold blood in 1916, and in March, 1916, he entered the United States, attacked the town of Columbus, New Mexico, leaving 17 Americans dead. General John J. Pershing led an army into Mexico in an attempt to round up Villa. Although Pershing's forces went fairly deep into Mexico and the Carranza government became more and more impatient, they did not succeed in capturing Villa. With war impending in Europe, Pershing's force was withdrawn from Mexico in early 1917. Shortly afterward, the Mexicans adopted a new constitution, Cararanza was elected president, and the United States gave full recognition to the government.

The Progressive Amendments

Four amendments were added to the Constitution between 1913 and 1919, all a result of the Progressive impetus. The 16th Amendment, which empowered Congress to tax incomes, was declared ratified in 1913. An income tax had been passed in 1894, but it had been found unconstitutional by the courts. There were repeated efforts after that to enact such a tax. The constitutional obstacle was that it was quite difficult to see how an income tax could be anything but a direct tax, and the Constitution prescribes that direct taxes are to be apportioned among the states on a population basis. At the special session of Congress in 1909, Progressives proposed a graduated income tax as an amendment to the tariff bill. It had widespread support both from Republican Insurgents and many Democrats. To forestall the effort, conservatives proposed a constitutional amendment authorizing a tax on incomes, in the hope that it would not be ratified, no doubt. Both houses of Congress approved it by the necessary majorities, and its ratification by the states was completed in 1913. Although the amendment does not mention graduation of taxes and there is not elsewhere in the Constitution any presumption in favor of it, the taxes imposed under it from the outset have been graduated. The 16th Amendment set the stage for a large-scale redistribution of the wealth, not necessarily from the rich to the poor but most often from the productive to the subsidized and unproductive.

Reformers from Populists to Progressives favored both a graduated income tax and direct election of Senators. The 17th Amendment, proposed in 1911 and ratified in 1913, provided for the direct election of Senators. No other amendment to the Constitution has done so much to unsettle the structure of the government conceived by the Founders. Until the 17th Amendment went into effect Senators were elected by state legislatures. The Founders understood that the Senate was to represent state governments, and confided great powers to it with that understanding. Most important, it

THE PROGRESSIVE AMENDMENTS

Article XVI

[Declared Ratified February 25, 1913]

The Congress shall have power to lay and collect taxes on incomes, from whatever source derived, without apportionment among the several States, and without regard to any census or enumeration.

Article XVII

[Declared Ratified May 31, 1913]

The Senate of the United States shall be composed of two Senators from each State, elected by the people thereof, for six years; and each Senator shall have one vote. The electors in each State shall have the qualifications requisite for electors of the most numerous branch of the State legislatures.

When vacancies happen in the representation of any State in the Senate, the executive authority of such State shall issue writs of election to fill such vacancies: *Provided*, That the legislature of any State may empower the executive thereof to make temporary appointments until the people fill the vacancies by election as the legislature may direct.

This amendment shall not be so construed as to affect the election or term of any Senator chosen before it becomes valid as part of the Constitution.

Article XVIII

[Declared Ratified January 29, 1919]

Section 1.   After one year from the ratification of this article the manufacture, sale, or transportation of intoxicating liquors within, the transportation thereof into, or the exportation thereof from the United States and all territory subject to the jurisdiction there of for beverage purposes is hereby prohibited.

Section 2.   The Congress and the several States shall have concurrent power to enforce this article by appropriate legislation.

Section 3.   This article shall be inoperative unless it shall have been ratified as an amendment to the Constitution by the legislatures of the several States, as provided in the Constitution, within seven years from the date of the submission hereof to the States by the Congress.

Article XIX

[Declared Ratified in 1920]

The right of citizens of the United States to vote shall not be denied or abridged by the United States or by any State on account of sex.

Congress shall have power to enforce this article by appropriate legislation.

had the power to ratify treaties and approve the appointments of the President, matters which would often be of great concern to state governments. A movement had been underway for some time to have the members of the Senate elected by popular vote. Several times constitutional amendments to that effect had passed the House, only to be defeated in the Senate. Those who believed that the United States was, or ought to be, a democracy favored it, and the Progressives pushed it vigorously. Popular support was gained by picturing Senators as bloated millionaires placed in their high position by the manipulation of state legislatures by the "trusts." What probably turned the tide for the amendment, however, was that a number of states had senatorial primaries, and legislatures increasingly simply ratified the will of the people. At any rate, state governments lost their main check on the federal government, and that has borne some strange fruit in the 20th century.

The 18th Amendment, prohibiting the manufacture or sale of intoxicating liquors, passed Congress in 1917, and was ratified in the course of 1919. The passage in Congress was preceded by a few months by a war food and fuel act which prohibited the use of food in the manufacture of liquor. This was understood as a war measure, but sentiment quickly reached a point for taking permanent action. Prohibition had been picking up in momentum in the years before the war, as indicated in an earlier chapter, and the Anti-Saloon League had been pressing the case ever more vigorously. It was the triumph of the reformist spirit, however, that made such a drastic act acceptable. Populism and Progressivism were undergirded by a belief in the possibility and desirability of making over society by regulation and law. The war mood provided the setting to act decisively. The anti-business mentality, supporting, as it did, the assault on property, made it much easier to ride roughshod over property rights. After all, the manufacture and sale of alcoholic beverages is a business. The passage of the amendment, and its subsequent enforcement by the Volstead Act, deprived a whole mass of owners of their businesses and property.

The 19th Amendment, ratified in 1919, provided that women should not be denied the right to vote on account of their sex. In one swoop, the number of potential voters in the country was doubled. Thus, the measure was in its animus populistic or democratic and equalitarian. It placed women on an equal plane with men politically. The full impact of this change is still working itself out in the lives of Americans. No great change in the quality of character of those elected to office has been discerned. If it be true, and there is much evidence for it, that women are generally much more concerned with security than men, it would be plausible to suppose that women's influence would be in that direction. Certainly, during the New Deal and afterward, there has been increasing emphasis upon politically provided security. However that may be, the continued thrust toward equality since then has greatly altered the status of the sexes and has reached through to threaten the ancient institutions of marriage and the family.

Chapter 8
World War I and the Disruption of Europe

While our enemies . . . have proclaimed war without mercy until our utter destruction, we are conducting war in self-defense. . . .We have been obliged to adopt submarine warfare to meet the declared intentions of our enemies. . . .
—German Note to the United States, 1915

The present German submarine warfare against commerce is a warfare against mankind. It is a war against all nations. American ships have been sunk. American lives taken. . . .There has been no discrimination. The challenge is to all mankind.
—Woodrow Wilson, 1917

. . . The independence of the United States is not only more precious to ourselves but to the world than any single posses-sion . . . You may call me selfish, if you will, conservative or reactionary . . . , but an American I was born, an American I have remained all my life. . . . I have never had but one allegiance—I can not divide it now. . . .
—Henry Cabot Lodge, 1919

Chronology

1882—Triple Alliance formed.

1904–1907—Triple Entente formed.

1914—

June—Assassination of Archduke Franz Ferdinand of Austria.
July 28—Austria-Hungary declares war on Serbia.
August 1—Germany declares war on Russia—WWI begins.
August 4—Wilson's Proclamation of Neutrality.

1915—Sinking of the *Lusitania*.

1916—

March—*Sussex* Affair.
May—Germany restricts submarine warfare.

1917—

February 1—Germany resumes unrestricted submarine warfare.
February 3—United States breaks relations with Germany.
March 1—Publication of Zimmermann Note.
April 6—United States declares war on Germany.
June—American troops arrive in France.
December—United States declares war on Austria-Hungary.

1918—

August—Allies launch Somme Offensive.
September—Meuse-Argonne Offensive.
November—Armistice ending hostilities.

1919—

January—Peace negotiations begin at Paris.
June—Germany accepts Treaty of Versailles.
November—Senate rejects League of Nations.

1920—Congress ends war with Joint Resolution.

World War I had a tremendous impact on Western Civilization. Indeed, it was not only shocking to Western sensibilities but it was also not easily assimilated into the prevailing outlook. Ultimately, it was the most definite dividing line, other than the calendar, between the 19th and 20th centuries. The belief in progress was widespread, and it entailed the view that civilization was expanding and barbarism on the retreat. As men became more and more civilized, many believed that bloodshed and war would be relegated to the brute past. An undergirding utopianism gave support to this view. Nations would settle their disputes by mediation and arbitration, and a concert of the more peaceful and civilized nations would see to it that nations observed their pledges. Just about everything connected with World War I cast doubt upon those assumptions.

The duration and devastation of the war, as well as its extent, had a numbing impact. When the war broke out, some who believed themselves experts declared that it simply could not last more than a few months. No nation could afford the costs of munitions for longer than a short period. Yet it went on month after month and year after year, reaching outward to draw in more people and embracing the total effort of nations. The loss of lives in the armed forces was unprecedented: nearly 10 million killed on the battlefields, and perhaps three times that many wounded more or less seriously. About 16 per cent of the male populations of Germany and France were lost. And in the wake of the war came an influenza epidemic, spreading to much of the world including the United States, in which perhaps three times the number of those killed in the war died. The financial costs of the war had been astounding. England spent more than all the capital invested in industrial businesses in the United Kingdom. France spent 30 per cent of the wealth of the country. As for property destruction, it was almost incalculable: in Northern France alone 300,000 houses and 8,000 factories and mines were gutted or destroyed, and some 8 million acres of land was so ravaged that it would be lost to cultivation indefinitely.

World War I came close, too, to being a total war. The Civil War in the United States had moved in the direction of total war in its last two years. Most of the European countries had adopted military conscription before the war came, and those which had not turned to it in the course of the war. Thus, large portions of the male populations of countries were drafted into service. Many of these were subjected to the debilitating experience of prolonged trench warfare, which one historian has described in this way: ''Stretching for some 450 miles, the western front was a lunar expanse scarred with trenches, with their smell of stagnant mud, latrine buckets, rotting sandbags, disinfectant, lime, and stale sweat, stretching amidst muddy fields and tangles of barbed wire, flooded in rain, freezing in winter, ceaselessly shelled and sniped and raided, treeless, birdless, and with no wildlife besides rats, lice, and fleas, where the thick square ration bisquits were often used for fuel, where soldiers were expected to last four or five months, sergeants and junior officers half that time, and where men who considered themselves under suspended sentence of death prayed for the flesh wounds that would save their lives.''[181] World War I was not a total war simply because it engaged the total lives of so many men but also because it tended to engulf whole populations and their resources in the struggle: through the production of war materials, by way of taxation, through propaganda, and also by bombings, shellings, the assaults upon shipping, and in numerous other ways.

In the course of the war, or in its wake, the governmental systems of major empires collapsed or were dissolved. Thus, the war, or the ensuing peace settlements, were revolutionary in their impact. The order that had prevailed in Europe no longer held sway. Revolution was total, in its intention, in Russia, but it was only less so, immediately or within a few years, in many other countries. Monarchy survived in a few countries, but it lost most, if not all, its authority in those lands. With the dissolution of monarchy went most of the ancient framework of hierarchy, and the abrupt efforts to replace it with democracy and equality left the authority of such ancient institutions as family, church, and school greatly weakened.

The United States was not immediately so greatly affected by the shattering of the old order in Europe. Not only was the United States remote from Europe geographically and involved in the war directly only for its last year and a half, but also republican government and institutions were long established here. Moreover, the number of men lost in battle was small compared with those of most European countries, and the United States was spared the physical destruction. The war shook much of Europe to the core;

its impact on the United States was more indirect though none the less important.

War Comes to Europe

War came swiftly to Europe in late July and early August of 1914, almost as a great storm may descend upon a region after weeks or even months of fair and dry weather, interrupted only occasionally by fleecy clouds and a brief shower. There had not been a major war in Europe for nearly 50 years, and threats of war usually brought diplomats to conference tables to mediate disputes. Then, as if out of the blue, war came over a period of 6 days, a war that would engulf most of Europe and extend to much of the rest of the world. On July 28, the Austro-Hungarian Empire declared war on a small Balkan country, Serbia. Russia began to mobilize for war, and Germany declared war on Russia on August 1. France entered the fray on August 3. Germany invaded neutral Belgium on the way to France, and the British Empire went to war on August 4. Although the two sides have been known by a variety of names, American historians have usually called them the Allies and the Central Powers. The core of the Allies was France, Russia and Great Britain, but they also counted in their ranks, sooner or later, Japan, Italy, the United States, China, Brazil, and a host of smaller countries. The core of the Central Powers was Germany and the Austro-Hungarian Empire, but Turkey and Bulgaria eventually joined their side. Most of the fighting took place in Europe, mainly in France, Belgium, and Eastern Europe, but the empires and systems of alliances made the war worldwide in scope.

Of course, these countries did not plunge into war quite by accident; although it got underway swiftly, the stage had been set for it over a period of more than 20 years. Systems of alliances and entanglements preceded the war, especially the Triple Alliance and Triple Entente. The Triple Alliance of Germany, Austria-Hungary, and Italy went back to 1882. The Triple Entente took shape in the early years of the 20th century, but except possibly for the alliance between Germany and Austria, none of these committed the countries to go to war. Italy did not even come in on the side of the Central Powers. Moreover, most of the countries involved had assorted treaty and other kinds of agreements cutting across the basic alliances or involving other countries. Certainly neither the Triple Alliance nor Triple Entente envisioned the particular world war that developed.

There were other developments that more clearly set the stage for the war. A major one was the New Colonialism of the late 19th and early 20th centuries. Underlying this development were some of the same practices that had given rise to the old colonialism. The most notable of these was the protective tariff, though some of the other mercantilistic practices naturally accompanied it. Country after country adopted high protective tariffs in the latter part of the 19th century. This set off a quest for colonies, which would provide both a market and raw materials for the country which possessed them. Germany was a major new entry in the field, but Russia was also expansive, and a united Italy began to take an interest in colonies. To back up the effort, Germany, particularly, enlarged its navy, and countries began an armaments race.

But the catalyzing events occurred in the Balkans. Before discussing those briefly, however, it should be noted that even as empires were expanding, anti-imperial feelings and movements were afoot in Europe, especially. There were three empires in Central and Eastern Europe in 1914, and the remnants of a fourth. The German Empire, ruled by Kaiser Wilhelm II, was an empire more in name than in the makeup of its population. They were mostly German in language and background, but it had nonetheless been forged from a number of kingdoms and provinces during the past half century or so. The Russian Empire, ruled by Czar Nicholas II, was both European and Asiatic. Pan-slavism—the uniting of all Slavic people under one rule—had been a strong current in Russia, since Russia would be the obvious instrument of it. The Austro-Hungarian Empire contained many peoples—Poles, Czechs, Ruthenians, and the like—who were neither Austrian nor Hungarian, and the nationalists among these were thirsting for independence. Then there were the remnants of the Ottoman Empire in Southeastern Europe, though it was restricted mostly to Turkey when World War I broke out. The empire had been disintegrating for decades, and in its wake several small countries had been formed in the Balkans: e.g., Serbia, Romania, Bulgaria, and others. Austria had annexed Bosnia-Herzegovina from the Ottoman Empire, and was concerned about Serbia. Russia took an interest in Serbia, as protector of the Slavs, while Serbia posed at least a potential threat to Austria in encouraging independence among her neighbors in the Empire.

When the Archduke Franz Ferdinand, heir to the Austrian throne, was assassinated at Sarajevo in Bosnia, war loomed ahead. The assassination was plotted in Serbia and Austria blamed that country for the act. Austria made demands on Serbia which reduced its independence. Germany promised Austria full support. Serbia agreed to most of the Austrian demands, but when they objected to an aspect of one demand, Austria went to war against Serbia. When Russia mobilized, Germany went to war against them, and in short order most of Europe was involved.

The German plan called for a swift end to the war in the West and then joining with the Austrians to crush Russia. It did not work out that way. The Germans did succeed at first, by wheeling around the French defenses through neutral Belgium. They almost reached Paris before the French rallied to stop them. After that, however, only the most limited movement of the armies was possible, and it turned into trench warfare for nearly four years. The day of the dashing cavalry was at an end, though cavalry forces were still assembled, and massed troops assaulting in broad daylight on open plains was suicidal. Defensive weapons had gained the upper hand. The main weapon which had turned the tide was the machine gun. The machine gun, which could now fire hundreds of rounds of deadly ammunition per minute, was the nearly perfect defense weapon. Machine gunners, dug in, could repulse any number of troops, afoot or on horseback, on the attack. Repeater rifles and vastly improved artillery could add to the devastation. The slaughter of men in massed assaults during World War I provided evidence of the damage. Hundreds of thousands of men lost their lives in major battles, in which neither of the opposing armies could be dislodged. The use of poison gas during the war added to the toll of the dead and wounded without greatly altering the advantage on either side.

The counterpoint for the offense to the machine gun and other rapid firing weapons was to be the tank. No effective tank, however, had been built when World War I broke out. In September, 1916, the British used tanks for the first time in battle. They were too few in number, too slow, and too undependable to make any impact. The French also developed tanks, and before the end of the war these and improved British models had begun to help in restoring some balance between offense and defense. After the United States entered the war, a large-scale tank building program was undertaken in conjunction with the British, but the resulting tanks did not reach the battlefields before the Armistice ended the conflict. The Germans did not succeed in developing an effective tank, and, indeed, concentrated little effort on their projects. This gave some advantage toward the end of the war to the Allies. Artillery was utilized on a massive scale to prepare the way for infantry attacks. Before the Battle of the Somme in 1916, the Allies ranged 2,000 cannon behind a ten-mile front and bombarded enemy lines for 7 days and nights before advancing. Even so, the enemy could move back a few miles, dig in again, and stop an advance. Artillery pieces took too long to move to launch sustained attacks that might rout an enemy. Again, mobile artillery, especially by way of armored tanks, was the technological solution, but these were only available in any quantity near the end of the war.

Airplanes, dirigibles, and blimps were also used to some extent during World War I. Airplanes were too primitive, too few, and information too limited and difficult to convey for them to be very effectively used during the war. Once aircraft had left the ground, no ground to aircraft control could be exercised, in the absence of radio communication, and all communication had to be by sighting. While aircraft hardly had a dramatic impact on the outcome of the war, the lighter than air ships—dirigibles and blimps—were of some use in submarine surveillance. More significant, airplanes and dirigibles were used to bomb both enemy war plants behind the lines and civilian populations to some extent. The most dramatic use of these was by the Germans, who used rigid lighter than air ships, Zeppelins, they called them, to raid England, and especially London. In the course of the war, a total of 208 Zeppelins at various times dropped over 5,000 bombs on England. These, plus less effective raids by airplanes, killed 1,316 people and injured over twice that many. This extended warfare to civilians on a considerable scale.

The other major technological innovation was the submarine, developed and used extensively by the Germans. The great advantage of the submarine lay either in the surprise attack, by launching torpedoes while submerged or against unarmed merchant and passenger ships. Once it surfaced, it could be easily defeated by an armed vessel. If the submarine was to be effectively used, the rules regarding neutrals, neutral shipping, and blockades had to change. Submarines had little passenger room for survivors, could not warn armed vessels, and blockading vessels could not operate with any safety in the vicinity of ports. Their use by the Germans was a major factor in drawing the United States into World War I.

American Neutrality

Immediately after war broke out in Europe, President Wilson proclaimed the neutrality of the United States. On August 19, 1914, he went further by urging Americans to ''be impartial in thought as well as in action,'' to ''put a curb upon our sentiments as well as upon every transaction that might be construed as a preference of one party to the struggle before another.''[182] He pointed out that Americans had been drawn from many lands, and especially from those which were now at war with one another. That being the case, he thought that to take sides in the conflict would hopelessly divide the country. Many Americans agreed with him at this point in believing that it was a European war, and that in accord with long-established principles this country should not become involved.

That was easier said than done, however. Ties with Britain had become closer in recent decades. The long friendship with France had hardly been tested for more than a century. Granted, American relations with Russia had been somewhat tense in recent years, the case against Germany was more immediate. The brutal invasion of neutral Belgium by Germany, and the direct threat to the existence of France awakened sympathy for the cause of the Allies. British propaganda activities had some effect in enlisting American sympathies for the Allies as well. Above all, though, it was German submarine warfare that provided the provocation for going to war.

Before turning to the problems of neutral shipping and submarine warfare, however, it might be well to note that American financial interests, manufacturers, and prosperity involved America to some extent with the fate of the Allies. William Jennings Bryan, Secretary of State at the outset, was thoroughly convinced about the desirability of the United States remaining completely neutral. His initial position was that the United States government would oppose privately floated loans to belligerents. However, when the French approached the House of Morgan early in 1915 for arranging a loan, the State Department relented. Moreover, when an Anglo-French Commission came to the United States in September, 1915 to arrange a $500,000,000 loan no official objection was raised. Following that, nearly $2 billion more was loaned by American bankers to the Allies before the United States entered the war.

This was one outward sign that American prosperity was being linked to the Allied cause. There were others. When the war broke out, there was a recession in the ensuing months, due to disruptions in European trade and withdrawal of investments. As the British blockade of the Central Powers began to become effective, most of the trade with them ceased. American trade with Germany fell from slightly over $169 million in 1914 to slightly over $1 million by 1916. On the other hand, it was far more than made up for in the trade with the Allies, which rose from over $824 million in 1914 to more than $3.2 billion in 1916. The United States was becoming an arsenal and storehouse of food and raw materials for the Allies. In matters of diplomacy, too, once Bryan had resigned in 1915, the most important persons were or tended to be pro-British. Walter Hines Page, the American ambassador to Britain, was a funnel of British flavored information to the State Department. The new Secretary of State, Robert Lansing, was no obstacle to actions that threw the weight of the United States on the side of the Allies. And Colonel House, who was at the forefront of negotiations, leaned in the same direction.

But the questions that eventually became crucial had to do with the rights of neutrals, and they generally involved maritime and naval issues. One of the vested problems of international law (aside from the extent to which there is such a body of law) is the extent of the rights of neutrals and belligerents in times of war. The extreme neutral position would be that citizens of neutral nations might go about their affairs as if there were no war. The position of belligerents might be that neutrals can do only such things as are beneficial to them and that they could otherwise interfere as they pleased with their goings and comings on the high seas. The thrust of international law has been to protect the rights of neutrals in trade and maritime activities and to restrict belligerents to punitive actions where definite aid is going to the military forces of the enemy. No doubt about it, international law usually works best when there is little occasion to invoke it, i.e., in times of peace, and when no great powers are directly involved. When much of the world is at war, when the fate of great nations is at stake, and when the thrust is toward total war, international law is bound to have tough sledding. The United States was, almost from the outset, at odds with both Britain and Germany over the rights of neutrals. With the British, they had to do mainly with the shipment of goods; with Germany, it had to do mostly with the safety of American passengers on unarmed Allied vessels.

Robert Lansing (1864–1928)

Courtesy Library of Congress

Lansing was a lawyer, diplomat, practiced international law, and served as Secretary of State under President Wilson. He was born in Watertown, New York, graduated from Amherst, and practiced law for many years in his hometown. Nationally, he served as counsel to the Bering Sea Commission, Alaskan Boundary Commission, and as American counsel before the Hague tribunal. His familiarity with international law led to appointment as counselor to the Department of State in 1914. When war came, Lansing was soon deeply involved in questions of the rights of neutrals at sea. When Bryan resigned in 1915, Lansing became Secretary of State, remaining in that position until early 1920. He played a larger role in directing the course of American neutrality than in the peace negotiations after the war because Wilson had become his own chief diplomat in those.

The earliest difficulties were with the British. Although Germany had been building up its navy in the years before World War I, it was far from being a match for the British fleet. Within several months of the outbreak of war, the German navy had either been defeated or largely driven from the high seas. The British proclaimed a blockade of the German coast and maintained it, not by blockading ports, but by patrolling the entries to the North Sea. Not only was this contrary to international law, but also the British defined contraband merchandise so as to deny to neutrals the right to ship most goods to Germany. The British could argue that the threat of submarines and the danger of mines made it impractical to blockade ports in the traditional way. In any case, the United States lodged protests against the British methods, but they were not vigorously pressed in any way that might threaten friendly relations between the two countries. In effect, the United States accepted, with only mild protests, the cutting off by the British of shipments to Germany.

The Germans retaliated against what they described as the inhuman British blockade by establishing a broad war zone around the British Isles in February, 1915, within which all enemy ships were subject to sinking by submarines on sight, without provision for rescue of survivors. Neutral vessels were told that if they entered the war zone they did so at their own risk. The United States protested vigorously, but the German government did not relent. Instead, the German ambassador urged the State Department to warn Americans not to travel on belligerent ships. The United States maintained that it was the right of Americans to travel on passenger ships. In late March, an American was killed when a German torpedo hit a British liner in the Irish Sea.

The most dramatic incident, however, was the sinking of the *Lusitania*, a large British passenger ship, off the Irish coast on May 7, 1915. It had sailed from New York on May 1 with a goodly number of Americans aboard, though the German embassy had warned that they would sail into the war zone at their own risk. The United States sent a strongly worded protest to the Germans, demanding that they abandon unrestricted submarine warfare, disavow the sinking of the ship, and make reparations for the lives of Americans lost (124 of them in all). The Germans replied that the vessel was armed and was carrying munitions. Actually, the ship was unarmed, but it did have military rifles and ammunition in the cargo hold. When Wilson drafted an even sterner message to the Germans, Bryan resigned rather than send it. The note was sent but without any formal result. In July, the United States sent a third note to the Germans, which was virtually an ultimatum. Meanwhile, the German government had privately warned submarine commanders not to sink passenger ships without warning. The sinking of the British steamer *Arabic* in August, in which two Americans lost their lives, led to a pledge, called the *Arabic* pledge, that German submarines would sink no more liners without warning and making provision for the safety of noncombatants, provided the ships made no resistance. That ended, for the time being, the dispute over submarine warfare.

No decisive changes occurred during 1916 in the relation between the United States and the warring powers. The tensions remained, though they shifted back and forth between Britain and Germany more than the preceding year. It was a presidential election year, and Wilson struggled to keep the Democratic Party behind him as he continued to defend neutral rights under pressure from the belligerents. At the beginning of the year, Wilson had some hope of ending the war by his mediation. Both the Allies and the Central Powers indicated some interest in a mediated peace. Colonel House went to Europe to try to discover the terms which might be agreeable to the warring powers. Not much came of the talks. The British and French were planning major military campaigns for the summer, which they hoped might defeat the Germans. It became clear, too, that the terms they sought would not be agreeable to Germany. However, in the discussions between House and Sir Edward Grey, the British foreign minister, the idea of an association, or league, of nations to maintain the peace did begin to take shape.

In March, 1916, the issue of German submarine warfare came to the fore once again. A German submarine torpedoed an unarmed French passenger ship, the *Sussex*, in the English Channel, injuring several Americans aboard it. The United States held that this was a violation of the *Arabic* pledge, and the government sent an ultimatum to Germany that if that country did not abandon its methods of submarine warfare the United States would break diplomatic relations. Germany agreed to the American demands, but attached the condition that the United States should make the Allies abide by the rules of international law in imposing their blockade. Wilson accepted what became known as the *Sussex* Pledge, but rejected the condition. Even so, Germany restricted its submarine warfare until early the next year.

In the summer and autumn of 1916 the Germans tried to tighten the blockade by bringing neutral shipping under their control. In effect, they sought to make American shipowners conform to their requirements, in return for coaling at British ports. In addition, they issued a "blacklist" of American firms suspected of trading with the Central Powers. They sought to use the United States as if it were a part of their war effort. Wilson protested vigorously, but to little avail. His own party would not tolerate a very aggressive attitude toward the belligerent powers.

Charles Evans Hughes was the Republican nominee for President in 1916, and Theodore Roosevelt, back in the Republican Party, hit the campaign trail. While Hughes was not very outspoken, Roosevelt accused Wilson of not defending American rights with much zeal. In fact, Wilson took a stance that the Democrats were the party of peace and progress, and he aimed his campaign toward the progressive element in all parties. Progressives generally were opposed to becoming involved in the European war, and Socialists were adamantly opposed to the war. In consequence, many of the Progressives who had not abandoned the Republican Party after 1912, voted Democratic in 1916. Large numbers of Socialists voted Democratic as well. The Democratic slogan, "He kept us out of war," coupled with the continuing emphasis on reform, drew most of the reformist element toward the Democratic Party. Though the election was close, Wilson won by carrying the South, the Southwest, and the western states generally.

Wilson may have kept the United States out of the war up until the time of his re-election, but neither he nor his advisers believed that it would be possible to do if the war continued. The British blockade left less and less choice for neutrals, and the situation was ripe for resumption of all-out German submarine warfare. The German government had approached the United States before the election about starting peace negotiations. Wilson indicated that he could do nothing until after the elections. Before he did act, the Germans announced early in December that they were ready to negotiate peace terms. The Allies refused because Germany had not announced its terms. Wilson then called upon both sides to state their aims. The Germans made no statement, and the terms set forth by the Allies went far beyond anything the Germans would conceivably accept.

The failure of the German peace overtures galvanized their determination to make an all-out effort to win the war. On January 31, 1917, the German ambassador notified Secretary of State Lansing that unrestricted submarine warfare would be resumed on February 1. Two days later, the United States broke diplomatic relations with Germany. Shortly thereafter, Wilson asked Congress to authorize the arming of merchant ships and placing naval forces on them. As Congress was debating this move, the British turned over a message from the German Foreign Secretary, Alfred Zimmermann, to the German ambassador in Mexico. It proposed to the Mexicans that if war broke out between the United States and Germany, Mexico should come into the war on the German side. Germany would give full support, then, to the Mexican reconquest of Texas, New Mexico, and Arizona. Resentment of Germany rose to a new pitch, and Wilson proceeded with the arming of merchantmen. Over the next weeks, several merchant ships were torpedoed and sunk by German submarines. Clearly, Germany was making war on American shipping—a fact which must be acted on or accepted. One other event occurred in early March which seemed to clear the way for war. A revolt in Russia led to the abdication of the Czar and brought into power a provisional government committed to democratic changes as well as social reform. No doubt, Wilson would have felt uncomfortable joining hands with the autocratic government of the Russian Empire, especially since he described the goal as making the "world safe for democracy."

The declaration of war now awaited only a message to Congress from President Wilson. Most likely, Wilson did not want war, though the posture toward German submarine warfare had set the stage for events that were now unfolding. He was reported to have told a friend on the eve of his request for a declaration of war that "Once lead this people into war and they'll forget there ever was such a thing as tolerance. To fight you must be brutal and ruthless, and the spirit of ruthless brutality will enter into the very fibre of our national life, infecting Congress, the courts, the policeman on the beat, the man in the street."[183] But if Wilson was reluctant to go to war, he was more than eager to participate in making the peace. Nor was this prospect something born of United States active participation in the war. As early as 1916, he had begun to see himself in the peacemaking role. His reformist zeal was moving out on the world stage, and victory for the allies in the war might offer the prospect of remaking Europe. The surest way to be a participant in the peace conferences was to become involved in the war.

At any rate, April 2, 1917, Wilson went before Congress to ask for war. There were two main themes in his address. One was to lay the blame for the war on the German government, which, he said, had set upon a reckless course in the use of the submarine which was destructive of the rights of nations and inhumane in its employment. The other theme was to declare the idealistic aims of the United States in entering the war.

"Our object," Wilson said, "is to vindicate the principles of peace and justice in the life of the world as against selfish and autocratic power. . . .

The world must be made safe for democracy. . . . We have no selfish ends to serve. We desire no conquest, no dominion. We seek no indemnities for ourselves, no material compensation for the sacrifices we shall freely make. . . .'' The "right," he continued, "is more precious than peace, and we shall fight for the things which we have always carried nearest our hearts,—for democracy, for the right to those who submit to authority to have a voice in their own Governments, for the rights and liberties of small nations, for a universal dominion of right by such a concert of free peoples as shall bring peace and safety to all nations and make the world at last free.''[184] That Wilson's vision was utopian, there should be no doubt; that it reeked with national self-righteousness may not have been so apparent; that it assumed such a commonality of purpose among diverse peoples as is unlikely to occur would be proved by events.

Congress voted for war, but that was no indication that many of its members shared Wilson's vision for peace. The vote for the war resolution was 82-6, despite passionate opposition from some of the Progressives. The vote in the House was 373-50; it came on April 6. Opposition to the war was most vocal among Socialists, but they had no power.

United States in World War I

So far as the fighting against Germany was concerned, the United States was at war from April 6, 1917 to November 11, 1918, a period of little more than one year and seven months. Moreover, American troops in significant numbers did not arrive in France until well into 1918. Futhermore, it was not generally believed by American leaders at the outset that the United States would be called upon to play a large military role. Wilson indicated in his address before Congress on April 2 that it might be necessary to add 500,000 men to the army. That estimate fell short by 3½ million of those who were eventually called into the armed services. General John J. ("Black Jack") Pershing, who would head the American Expeditionary Force in France, gave a very discouraging report on the situation when he went to France shortly after the declaration of war. The French and British, he said, were running out of manpower, money, and materials. They would need major reinforcements if they were to withstand the German onslaught and have any hope for victory. Another development also made the increased American role more essential. The Bolshevik (Communist) Revolution began in Russia in November, 1917, and Russia pulled out of the war shortly thereafter. That enabled the Central Powers to concentrate their efforts to the west and south.

1. Mobilizing for War

The United States undertook a full-scale mobilizing for war. The expansion of the Army had already begun before war was declared, and increases

John J. Pershing (1860–1948)

Courtesy Library of Congress

Pershing was a professional soldier and commander of the American Expeditionary Forces in France during World War I. He taught school to gather the means to go to college, but was later admitted to and graduated from West Point. After he received his commission, Pershing fought in the last of the Indian wars and served in a variety of posts. He was sent to Cuba during the Spanish-American War, and afterward spent several years in the Far East—the Philippines, Japan, and Manchuria. Wilson chose him to be commander of American forces in Europe during World War I, and he led his armies to victory on the battlefields in France. He was famed for his toughness and decisiveness, both in maintaining the integrity of American forces in France and in the drive to defeat the Germans. In 1919, he was made General of the Armies, the first general so honored since George Washington, and finished his tour of service as chief of staff of the Army.

were being made in naval strength. Now, however, once it became clear that whatever the United States could contribute would be needed, a concerted effort was made to arm as swiftly as possible and bring the weight of American production to bear on the war effort. Indeed, Wilson had already conceived something of the dimensions of the effort when he made his war address. He declared that "It will involve the organization and mobilization of all the material resources of the country to supply the materials of war. . . ."[185] The government attempted to direct and control the economy and much of the lives of Americans.

Since the effort to do this had an impact that went far beyond the war, it may be well to point out some of its broader significance before detailing the controls. Both in the United States and in European countries, many intellectuals were greatly impressed at what could be accomplished, or what they thought was accomplished, by government direction and control over the economy, impressed, that is, by the vast production of goods, by the coordination of effort, by the aura of prosperity, and so on. The British referred to the phenomenon as war socialism, and the phrase is quite apt.

After all, the purpose of socialism is to control and direct an economy toward a common goal, and that was what the war effort was supposed to be about. Why could government not do the same sort of thing in peacetime, not to win wars, of course, but to get rid of poverty, provide plenty, and remove the inequities among peoples? A good many of the New Dealers would be fascinated with this possibility in the 1930s.

Some salient points were often ignored or glossed over in this line of reasoning. For one, making war is something quite different from the day to day business of making a living and living lives. There is a common enemy in time of war, one on which attention can be focused, and which force can overcome. There is no common enemy in economic and social activity (except in the heated imagination of demagogues), and force, certainly that coming from weapons, cannot ordinarily be used to overcome such obstacles as stand in the way of it. Moreover, war is essentially a destructive undertaking, not a productive one; the basic production is of what government orders and no one wants used on them. By contrast, production for use is a market function, or depends ultimately on decisions made in the market.

For another thing, the central planning and government control and direction of the economy during World War I was an extension of the concept of total war to the whole society. It contained the seeds of totalitarianism, the extension of the power of government into all areas of the lives of the people. Central planning and carrying it out requires concentration of power in the executive, and becomes dictatorial. All this is the opposite of limited government and individual liberty. Moreover, "war socialism" was not simply a reflex of the requirements of war under 20th century industrial conditions. The bent toward government intervention in the economy which preceded the war in other lands as well as the United States had set the stage for controls during the war. World War I had many of the aspects of the death throes of a civilization, of government power breaking loose from its moorings and running rampant with modern weapons of destruction. (That World War II would be much more barbaric in most respects does not alter that judgment.)

Even before the United States entered World War I, the British had taken the road toward concentration of power in the executive and the exercise of great powers over the lives of Englishmen. A central figure in this movement was David Lloyd George, who became Prime Minister in 1916. The British government had not only been bent toward intervention in the economy but also the removal of ancient checks on the exercise of power by the House of Commons, the more democratic branch of the government. Lloyd George had supported these developments. As to his beliefs, one writer has described their tendencies this way: "If his convictions had been otherwise than emotional, he would have been a Socialist. . . . He wanted the poor to inherit the earth, particularly if it was the earth of rich English landlords."[186] Indeed, Lloyd George was a socialist, in all but name.

As Prime Minister, he quickly concentrated all power in his hands. "Lloyd George's accession to power in December 1916 was more than a change of government. It was a revolution British-style. . . . The backbenchers and the newspapers combined . . . and made Lloyd George dictator for the duration of the war."[187] The traditional cabinet was subordinated to the "war cabinet," made up of five members who executed the will of Lloyd George. The government directed the war effort, and much more. Military conscription was instituted; the merchant marine was appropriated, the mines were taken over. All sorts of controls were introduced: price controls, rent controls, rationing, government allotment of materials, manipulation of the money supply, steeply graduated income taxes, and so on. Much of the compulsion no doubt stemmed from the fact that those in power wanted to do it that way, were already inclined to think in terms of using government power, rather than simply responding to a need. When the British government imposed military conscription, for example, "The army had more men than it could equip, and voluntary recruitment would more than fill the gap. . . . Auckland Geddes, who was in the best position to know, later pronounced this verdict: 'The imposition of military conscription added little if anything to the effective sum of our war efforts.'"[188]

When the United States entered the war, the Wilson administration had not only the example of the British but also their own determination to muster the resources of the country and focus them on the war effort. One of the early measures passed was the Selective Service Act on May 18, 1917. It called for the registration of all men between the ages of 21 and 30. Undoubtedly, large numbers of men would have volunteered for the Army if they could have joined local organizations under leaders of their choosing, but Wilson would have none of that. In past wars, this device had been widely used for raising armies. But the government wanted to control the numbers who came in at any particular time, to defer the service for those whose civilian work might be essential, and to have the whole process under national command. All those registered were subject to be drafted, and nearly 3 million were eventually called into service. The Navy relied on volunteers, and some did volunteer for the Army, but they were assigned to their units by the military.

The financing of the war effort was carried out in a way to achieve a considerable redistribution of wealth in the country. The main device for this was the income tax, though other programs had a redistributionist bias against the wealthy and in favor of wage earners and to some extent farmers. Government expenditures in the course of the war and for the period of demobilization after it came to around $35 billion. This figure includes government loans to the Allies. These figures were more than ten times usual government expenditures. A portion of this was raised by taxes (less than a third), the remainder by borrowing.

In October, 1917, Congress passed a bill which raised income taxes to new heights and was steeply graduated. The basic tax rate was raised from 2 to 4 per cent, and the exemption was reduced to $1,000 for single persons and $2,000 for married couples. The graduated portion of the tax was added to the basic tax; it was called a surtax, and the maximum was increased from 13 to 63 per cent. The corporate income tax was increased from 2 to 6 per cent, and an "excess profits" tax was introduced, with rates ranging from 20 to 60 per cent. And the inheritance tax on wealthy estates was raised to a maximum of 25 per cent. While the base of the tax was broadened somewhat, the intention of these new and higher taxes was to tax the prosperous and wealthy much more heavily than the general population. Since the larger portion of the government payments would be made to Americans, the effect would be redistributionist.

On the face of it, the borrowing was supposed to be accomplished in such a way as not to enrich bankers and investment firms or to increase the money supply (be inflationary). Liberty bonds were sold to the general public in a series of patriotic loan drives. These were quite successful in raising funds, but much less so in preventing either monetary or price inflation. In fact, there was both a major credit expansion and monetary increase during the course of the war. Outstanding bank loans increased from nearly $18 billion to over $25 billion from 1916 to 1919, and the amount of Federal Reserve notes (currency) increased from $150 million to $2.5 billion. Prices rose to reflect in some measure the increases in the money supply. Government policies in general and the Federal Reserve policies in particular helped to fuel the inflation. Not only did the Federal Reserve increase greatly the currency in circulation but it cut the reserve requirements of member banks by one-half, thus greatly increasing their lending capacity. The Liberty bonds could be used as security for loans, thus contributing to the credit expansion. The Federal Reserve was shifting toward its long-term role of fostering government borrowing by aiding credit expansion.

Government policy during the war favored the organization of labor. Not only was Samuel Gompers invited to sit in the highest councils of the government but unionization was more or less encouraged. The War Labor Board, on which 5 out of 12 members were unionists, insisted that workers had a right to join a union and that no worker should be fired for union activities. Between 1915–1920 union membership increased from 2,582,600 to 5,047,800. As one historian has said, "it was the government that opened the doors to unionism in industries heretofore closed. . . . The government, by virtue of its war time power and prestige, gave the unions the all-important right to organize against a temporarily confounded and half-rebellious employing group. . . ."[189] While the wages of workers in general appear to have risen no more than enough to offset the rise in prices in general, workers in manufacturing, where war industries and unionization were concentrated did rise significantly. The annual wage of workers in factories was approximately $580 in 1914 and reached $980 in 1918.

A considerable number and variety of boards and commissions were created during the war to direct and encourage production and transportation of goods for the war and, in some instances, to discourage consumption at home. These boards generally operated outside the framework of regular government departments, were responsible to the President, and their constitutionality was doubtful, to say the least. One of the most powerful and important of these boards was the War Industries Board, created by the administration, not by act of Congress, and assigned the duty of coordinating and directing the production of military supplies. At the peak of its activities it was headed by Bernard Baruch. The powers of the board were extensive, as this brief summary suggests:

> The elastic powers conferred on Baruch as chairman of the War Industries Board made him a dictator over large areas of the war economy. His authority to establish priorities on all materials except agricultural commodities gave him life-and-death power over business. If a manufacturer refused to convert from the production of horseshoes to trench shovels, Baruch could cut off his supplies of iron and shut down his assembly lines. He could even commandeer the plant for the government and operate it. In cooperation with the price-fixing committee, he could exercise further leverage by setting the prices of raw materials at wholesale.[190]

Since Baruch tried to operate by negotiation with companies normally, since it was considered patriotic to comply with government requests, and since cost-plus contracts were used to induce manufacturers to produce what was wanted, direct force was not often applied.

The Food Administration was probably the second most important of these war organizations to mobilize the economy. The European Allies needed shipments of food badly, and of course the American military forces had to be clothed and fed. Herbert Hoover headed the Food Administration, and he proceeded along two lines to make the food available. One was to encourage increased production of the food most wanted. This was done mainly by setting a minimum price which government would pay for particular goods. This worked best in increasing production if the minimum was higher than the market price had been. For example, the price for hogs was set at 15½ cents per pound, considerably higher than the market price, and exports of pork were nearly doubled in the course of the war. The Food Administration had the power to license those dealing with the production and distribution of food, and those who failed to comply with its orders could have their license cancelled and would have to go out of the business.

The second line of the operation of the Food Administration was to discourage domestic consumption. This was done mainly by campaigns against the consumption of wheat products, pork, and sugar. A newspaper carried this instruction, for example: "Under the new food regulations, each member of the family is allotted not more than 6 pounds of flour per month. . . . Do not try to fudge and ask your grocer for more. It might cause serious trouble both for you and for him."[191] The same newspaper item noted that for the next four weeks people in that county should observe wheatless Mondays, meatless Tuesdays, meatless breakfasts and wheatless suppers on Thursdays, porkless Saturdays, and so on. So far as sugar was concerned, it should be used sparingly; only one spoonful to a cup of coffee. All these exhortations may have reduced consumption, especially since they were promulgated as government rules.

But these two organizations were only the tip of the iceberg of a whole array of bodies directing the economy during World War I. There was the War Labor Board, already mentioned. A Grain Corporation purchased all the grain for the Allies, the United States government, and the Red Cross. A Sugar Equalization Board bought entire crops of both the United States and Cuba and sold them to American refiners. A Railroad War Board was established in April, 1917 to coordinate rail shipments. As a result both of past government rail regulations and the activities of the board the whole system nearly came to a halt in trying to cope with the shipping needs of the country. In consequence, President Wilson took over the railroads in December, 1917, and the government continued to operate them until early 1920. A United States Shipping Board was set up in 1916, and after the United States entered the war it undertook a large-scale shipyard and shipbuilding program. Much of shipping was brought under the control of the Emergency Fleet Corporation. A War Trade Board had control of all foreign trade. A Bureau of War Risk Insurance provided marine insurance against the hazards of operating in dangerous waters. The War Finance Corporation provided credit for war industries. The Overman Act, passed in May, 1918, gave the President authority to organize this great assortment of executively controlled agencies at will. So extensive and unprecedented was this grant of power that one Senator ironically proposed that "If any power, constitutional or not, has been inadvertently omitted from this bill, it is hereby granted in full."[192]

Once the war came, then, Wilson abandoned quickly most of the remains of the 19th-century liberalism which had been the bulwark of Democratic policy at one time and turned with a passion to government control. The takeover of the railroads is especially instructive. The railroads had been the focus of much of the government regulation in the decade or so before the war. It was these very regulations, in many instances, that stood in the way of effective coordination of rail activity when war came. As a railroad historian has observed, the "poor condition of the rail lines in 1917 was no doubt partly the result of earlier excessive or mistaken regulation. . . ."[193]

Even the Interstate Commerce Commission's recommendations at the time indicated an awareness of how much government restrictions were hamstringing the railroads. It recommended that the government either take over and operate the railroads or "that all legal obstacles to the complete unification of the railways for that period be removed. . . ."[194] Once it had power over them, the government simply reversed or ignored its former policies toward the railroads. William G. McAdoo, who was in charge, proceeded to do all sorts of things that had been either prohibited or beyond the power of rail executives. Rail service was speedily coordinated; the railroads were treated as if they were part of a single system, all of which was prohibited by the antitrust laws. Freight was routed the shortest way to its destination. The government discriminated vigorously among shippers, giving war goods the preference. The Interstate Commerce Commission had denied the roads any rate increase for several years. Under the act by which they were taken over, the government could simply proclaim new rates, and it did increase rates by 25 per cent. Undoubtedly, much of this could have been accomplished under private ownership had the restrictions been removed.

Nor did the Wilson Administration limit itself to control over the economy. It made a concerted effort as well to mobilize opinion. Wilson set up a Committee of Public Information, headed by George Creel, to make a concerted propaganda effort for the war. The Committee provided pre-digested news for newspapers, published pamphlets which provided the "correct" interpretation of the war for history classes, and tried to keep information of troop movements and the like out of the newspapers. Four-minute men gave rousing speeches about the war wherever people assembled. Movies were made which popularized the war effort, and war songs expressed the patriotic fervor. (Much of this would have occurred without the Committee, most likely.) It also promoted Wilson's war aims abroad.

2. Winning the War

Whether the activities of all these boards, committees, commissions, and government corporations contributed or not, the United States Army and Navy did play an important role in ending the war in Europe. The Navy's contribution began almost at once and increased greatly during the course of American participation in the war. The great threat to shipping was the German submarines. After the Battle of Jutland in 1916, German warships did not venture out on the high seas. On the other hand, the submarines were taking a frightful toll on British shipping from February of 1917 into the spring and summer of that year. They sank 540,000 tons in February, 593,000 tons in March, and over 880,000 tons in April. At the rate they were going, the British merchant fleet and a good portion of the American would be at the bottom of the ocean within a few more months. "They will win, unless we can stop these losses," the British naval leader told Admiral

William S. Sims of the American Navy. "The British transport of troops and supplies is already strained to the utmost, and the maintenance of armies in the field is threatened."[195]

The best weapons against submarines were light warships, destroyers, depth charges and mines. The United States sent several destroyers to ply the waters around the British Isles immediately and continued to augment the supply of them over the next year or so. The loss of shipping to submarines had been halved before the end of 1917, and by the spring of 1918 had been cut to about a fourth of what it had been at the high point. The American merchant fleet also helped with the shipping to Europe. In 1918, the United States Navy took the lead in mining the Atlantic entrance to the North Sea, and, though this tremendous undertaking had not been completed by the end of the war, it added another dimension to the effort to contain submarine warfare.

The impact of the United States Army came much slower. The United States had only a small army at the outset, and only enough to send a token force to France in the course of 1917. Although large numbers of soldiers were drafted and others volunteered, it took much longer to train and arm them for the European war. Indeed, though production facilities were available or expanded to provide the smaller weapons, the war ended before Americans were producing in quantity either the heavy artillery or tanks used in the war. Heavy weapons had to be obtained from the Allies, for the United States could supply only about 15 percent of the artillery used by the army in France. As for tanks, only 64 six-ton vehicles had been produced by the end of the war. This country was more successful in producing a satisfactory airplane engine, and more than a thousand redesigned British bombers were made in America and shipped to France. As American troops began arriving in France, the other Allies wanted to integrate them into their armies as replacements. General Pershing insisted, however, that American forces would be kept together and fight under American command. His most telling argument for this was that French and British commanders were too worn and dispirited to undertake the offensive effectively.

The advantage shifted toward the Central Powers in early 1918. The Bolsheviks had taken Russian forces out of contention, and German forces could now be concentrated on the front in France. In addition, the Austrians had won a crushing victory in battle with the Italians in 1917. The Germans launched a massive offensive in France in March, 1918, an offensive which enabled them to come within 50 miles of Paris and bombard the city with long-range artillery. This offensive was not finally stalled until mid-summer. American forces were used for the first time extensively in slowing the offensive. Meanwhile, French Marshal Ferdinand Foch had been made supreme commander of Allied forces in France. As soon as the German offensive was stopped in July, he began a counter-offensive against the Germans which ended with the war.

On August 10, the American First Army, over a half million men strong, went into operation as a distinct unit under the command of General Pershing. It proceeded to reduce the St. Mihiel salient in September and then commenced the Meuse-Argonne offensive which continued until the Armistice ending the fighting. In October, a second American army was formed, and by the end of the war more than a million Americans were engaged in the conflict in France. American forces had succeeded in driving the Germans back to the Belgian border in their sector when the fighting came to a halt.

In early October both the German and Austrian governments approached the United States, more specifically President Wilson, with the proposal of an armistice. An armistice is a truce or, in current terms, a cease fire. What the main Central Powers were asking, then, was that hostilities cease and that diplomats of the involved countries work out the terms of the settlement. They approached Wilson both because they hoped he would be more favorably disposed and that he might serve as a buffer against the other Allies. Wilson proved tougher than they expected, however, for he began to impose terms on them. To the Kaiser's ministers, he said that he wished to deal with a government which represented the German people, and to the Austrians he indicated that the continued existence of the Austro-Hungarian Empire was in doubt. Austria left off negotiations with Wilson and made a separate armistice with Italy, with whom they were militarily engaged. Germany began to make some changes looking toward a constitutional monarchy. However, revolution intervened; the Kaiser abdicated on November 9, and monarchy ended both in that country and in Austria. Wilson had already informed the Germans that an armistice would, in effect, amount to surrender. Marshal Foch then proceeded to treat with the German commanders, and on November 11, an agreement was reached in which the Germans agreed to lay down their arms and demobilize their forces.

A Discordant Peace

Marshal Foch said of the peace treaty with Germany, "This is not peace; it is an armistice for twenty years."[196] His observation was right on the mark, for within 20 years, nearly to the day, Europe erupted once again in the more brutal, devastating, and total World War II. In fact, the treaties of peace with the defeated Central Powers so badly upset the power system in Europe and left festering wounds to the pride and status of these truncated countries that another war became, if not inevitable, at least highly likely. Ancient loyalties were broken, peoples herded into whatever boundaries the victorious great powers determined, and the balance of power upset. Americans can take what comfort they can from the fact that the Senate never ratified these treaties, that ultimately the United States did not impose them nor accept them as binding.

On the other hand, the United States did participate in the making of the treaties, at least President Wilson and his delegation did. Indeed, Wilson played the leading role in the Paris Peace Conference in 1919. It was a role for which he had been grooming himself even before the United States entered the war. He had a vision of himself as peacemaker apparently, and he certainly developed a vision for what the world should be like in order to not only obtain peace at the end of the war but perpetually. In truth, Wilson's vision for the world was utopian; his approach to maintaining the peace was collectivist; and at the end of the war he turned the reforming zeal and interventionist methods from domestic reform and straightening out Latin American countries to Europe and the rest of the world. Undoubtedly, he had, as one historian has said, "Great natural endowments, literary power, a burning moral fervor, deep religious convictions," and more than "a touch of the visionary . . . combined with unreal, academic habits of mind and a sensitive, humorless vanity."[197] In short, he was a reformist intellectual, under the sway of a vision of peace for the whole world, and determined to see it realized come what may.

The basic outlines of this vision had already begun to take shape before the United States declared war. He wanted a peace without vengeance and an association of nations to maintain it. He had said in a speech to the Senate in January, 1917 that when it came "it must be a peace without victory. . . . Victory would mean peace forced upon the loser, a victor's terms imposed upon the vanquished. . . . Only a peace between equals can last."[198] Such notions were much easier to accept when America had not yet gone to war, and as we shall see he did not hold on to them at the end of the war. A year later, however, when the United States was in the midst of the war, he fleshed out his peace aims in a speech before Congress. This speech contained what would thereafter be referred to as the Fourteen Points. Wilson's statements were at least in part in service to the Allied cause at the time. The Bolsheviks in Russia had published secret treaties made with the Allies which set forth their agreements about territorial aims. These hardly painted a pretty picture of the Allied cause, and Wilson's statements helped to counter these.

The Fourteen Points called for "Open covenants of peace, openly arrived at. . . .," in short, public rather than secret diplomacy, freedom of the seas, removal of trade barriers and equality of trade, the reduction of armaments, and an adjustment of colonial claims so as to take into consideration the aspirations of colonial peoples These things were treated in the first five points and were presumably to govern the settlements at the end of the war. The other nine dealt with territorial adjustments to be made in the course of the peace settlements. Later, Wilson added further particulars, or generalizations, as the case might be. For example, he declared "that peoples and provinces are not to be bartered about from sovereignty to sovereignty as if they were pawns in a game. . . ." Instead, "every territorial settlement . . . must be made in the interest and for the benefit of the populations concerned, and not as a part of any adjustment or compromise of claims amongst rival states. . . ."[199] He made it sound for all the world as if the gods were going to gather on Mount Olympus and bring justice and peace to the nations of the world. To top it off, Wilson included in his Armistice Day speech the announcement that "It will now be our fortunate duty to assist by example, by sober, friendly counsel, and by material aid in the establishment of a just democracy throughout the world."[200] The Fourteen Points and elaborations were the relics of 19th-century liberalism (freedom of the seas and trade) blended with utopian collectivism (association of nations) brought to a boil with incantations to democracy.

George Creel and his Committee on Public Information not only publicized the Fourteen Points in the United States but abroad as well. The Germans were inundated with leaflets describing them dropped from airplanes and shot across the lines separating the troops by heavy weapons. They were also given great publicity in Allied and neutral countries, and both the German and Austro-Hungarian governments indicated while the war was still going on that they accepted the first four of them. The other Allied governments indicated their endorsement of them in general terms. By the end of the war, Wilson had become an idol to many Europeans.

Wilson apparently had come to believe his own publicity, or at least the absolute desirability of his cause, and that he must personally bring about its realization. At any rate, he concluded that he would go personally to the peace conference in Paris, participate in the treaty negotiations, and see to it that his beloved League of Nations was formed. His personal participation was unprecedented. No President had ever left the country during his term of office before. Nor did Presidents participate directly in peace negotiations up to that time. Neither of these acts were direct violations of the Constitution, but direct participation in treaty making did not accord well with our system of government. Indeed, for all his studies in American history, Wilson never fully accepted the limitations of the presidential system. He tried to convert it instead into something closer to the parliamentary system. In that system, the prime minister may not only formulate programs but also actively push them in the legislature, for he is a member of it. In fact, the President is neither a member of the Senate nor can he play any direct role in securing passage of a treaty, which must be approved by the Senate before it can go into effect. Indeed, if the United States had adopted a parliamentary system, and if Wilson had been the prime minister earlier, he would have lost his position to the Republicans, who were a majority following the election of 1918.

To make matters worse, Wilson took no prominent Republicans with him to Paris; indeed, the members of his delegation were not sufficiently prominent to have much of an impact on the political situation at home. Moreover, since Wilson played a direct role in the negotiations himself he could hardly be less than fully committed to what had been done. This made compromise difficult at home, and would probably have done so for a man less determined to have it his way than Wilson.

At any rate, Wilson led the American delegation to Paris in January, 1919. The most crucial negotiations were between the Big Four, as they came to be called: President Wilson, Prime Minister David Lloyd George of Britain, and Premiers Georges Clemenceau of France and Vittorio Orlando of Italy. Wilson not only insisted that the negotiations be held in Paris rather than a neutral site in Geneva, but also that a charter for the League of Nations be taken up first. He was determined to incorporate it into the treaties, thus committing all those countries (at least those on the winning side) to the League in order to effect the peace treaties. A charter, known as the Covenant, for the League of Nations was rather hastily devised. Colonel House played a role in preparing a draft for it, and the project was helped along by Jan Christian Smuts of South Africa, who was an enthusiast for the idea.

The basic idea underlying the League was to form an association of nations to maintain the peace and promote international cooperation. Theodore Roosevelt had earlier proposed that membership be restricted to ''peace loving'' nations, but the League that emerged would be open ultimately to all nations. The basic premise of the League was collectivist to the core; it assumed that a concert of nations would work together to maintain the peace. Each nation would, presumably, forgo its particular national interest and join in the common enterprise. The idea of a balance of power would be abandoned, to be replaced by a concert of all other nations against any who would threaten the peace. What was supposed to make this work was that the peoples of the world want peace. It is probably true that people generally do want peace—on their own terms! Unfortunately, they often differ greatly on the terms that will keep them at peace. The best that the League could offer in such circumstances would be the promise that all other nations would band together and beat up any disturbers of the peace. The League was supposed to provide a mechanism for accomplishing this action.

Having presented a Covenant which could be worked into the peace treaties, Wilson returned to the United States in February to deal with legislative matters. In March, he returned to Paris to work on a treaty with Germany. The result was the Treaty of Versailles, which was imposed on an unwilling Germany. The Allies continued to impose the blockade on a disarmed Germany while the peace negotiations proceeded. German representatives were neither invited nor permitted to participate in the negotiations. It was a dictated, not a negotiated, peace, dictated largely by the Big Four. Wilson's fine rhetoric was largely abandoned in making the peace settlement. Clemenceau wanted, if not revenge (that too, no doubt), at least a weakened and impotent Germany. Lloyd George would be happy to have Germany out of the way as a rival either on the high seas or colonies. Orlando wanted, above all, a pre-eminent position for Italy on the Adriatic. Germany had no friends at that court, though Wilson sought no reparations for the United States and had little interest in the German colonies.

The Treaty of Versailles was a harsh and punitive settlement. Germany was made to accept the full guilt for bringing about the war, along with her allies. With German guilt thus established, the Allies then imposed heavy reparation payments to be made to the damaged European countries. Germany was to remain virtually disarmed in the future, with only a token army, no air force, a navy reduced to small vessels, and forbidden to develop a munitions industry. All German colonies and special trade privileges abroad were taken away. Territory in Germany itself was taken away, part turned over to France (including continued occupation of the Rhineland), to Poland, and to the new nation of Czechoslovakia. Even large ships in the commercial fleet were confiscated. The German government objected bitterly to the terms of the treaty. For example: "The idea of extracting the enormous indemnities stipulated in the draft of the peace treaty from what would be left of Germany according to the draft, is impossible. A Germany, in whose population any delight in work would be killed at the very outset by the despair of the present and the hopelessness of the future, cannot even be counted upon in the question of the payment of indemnities."[201] Most of these pleas fell on deaf ears, however. The victors took their spoils, highsounding pronouncements to the contrary notwithstanding.

The broader settlement in Europe dealt mainly with dividing up and apportioning out the territories of the broken up empires. Austria, lately the seat of a great empire, was reduced to a tiny country, to the metropolis of Vienna and some scenic country. Hungary was reduced to a small Balkan country. Wilson had originally proposed only some degree of autonomy for the subject peoples within the Austro-Hungarian Empire in his Fourteen Points, but the monarchy had fallen, and he had shifted to complete independence for most of them. A goodly portion on the European side of the Russian Empire had been cut away by the Treaty of Brest-Litovsk with Germany in early 1918. The Allies repudiated this treaty, but not for the purpose of restoring the territory to Russia, which was, in any case, now deeply involved in a civil war between the Reds and the Whites. Most of the Turkish Middle Eastern empire was cut away; the British and French became the dominant forces in that area.

Eastern Europe, aside from what remained in Russian Europe, became a land of small countries, some new, some the revival of older nations, and some expanded or reduced. Among the new countries were: Estonia, Latvia, Lithuania, Czechoslovakia, Yugoslavia, Finland, and Albania. Poland was revived and its borders expanded. Most of the Balkan countries, with the exception of Bulgaria, which had been on the wrong side, were given increased territory by the peace treaties. No clear principle emerged in this reviving of old countries, making of new ones, and enlarging or reducing of others. Large numbers of people were shifted from one country to another, often without so much as a by-your-leave or kinship with the dominant peoples in that country. Language and ethnic background may not have been entirely ignored, but they hardly were accommodated in many instances. Yugoslavia was built upon a Serbian base, but it included, besides the dominant Serbs, Montenegrins, Croatians, Bosnians, Herzegovinians, Slovenes, Italians, Germans, Hungarians, Greeks and Bulgarians. Though it was usually less dramatic than this, many of the other countries contained sizeable minorities, often at odds with the dominant populations.

Well before all the redrawing of the map of Europe had been agreed upon, Wilson returned to the United States in July, 1919. The prize with which he hoped he had returned was the Treaty of Versailles, containing the Covenant of the League of Nations. The League became the focus of the senatorial debate over ratification, which was already underway when Wilson returned. During the peace negotiations, Wilson had become increasingly stubborn, determined, and isolated—alone—, even from most of his own delegation, including Colonel House. He was determined to have his way, and that was to have his League of Nations without crippling amendments. There should be no doubt that he was set on a course which would have reversed long-established foreign policy of the United States. The government of the United States devoted a considerable portion of a third of our history to disentangling from Europe and establishing full-fledged American independence. In the Monroe Doctrine, the United States was committed not to become involved in European affairs. Now, however, Wilson was for going all the way toward involvement, including going to war if some member nation were threatened.

The Senate divided early into three factions on the question of becoming a member of the League. There were those dubbed "Irreconcilables," who did not wish to join the League under any circumstances. Another faction were those who sided with Senator Lodge, and professed to favor the League with reservations. The other faction was made up almost entirely of loyal Democrats, loyal to Wilson, that is, or the League idea. There were generally about 17 "Irreconcilables," 34 reservationists, and about 44 loyalists. Since the approval of treaties requires a favorable vote of two-thirds of the Senate, the only possibility for ratification lay in some compromise between the reservationists and loyalists. Wilson refused to make any significant compromise.

William E. Borah was probably the most eloquent of the "Irreconcilables." His position was that to join the League would take from Americans the right to govern their affairs, destroy their independence, and entangle them in the affairs of Europe. He said that when the United States joined the

League, the country would have "forfeited and surrendered, once and for all, the great policy of 'no entangling alliances' upon which the strength of the Republic has been founded for 150 years."[202] Senator Lodge maintained that he favored the League, but he could approve joining it only with major reservations. The United States must retain its independence of action, he held. "The United States is the world's best hope," he said, "but if you fetter her in the interests and quarrels of other nations, if you tangle her in the intrigues of Europe, you will destroy her power for good and endanger her very existence. . . ."[203]

Wilson remained adamant throughout, to no avail so far as getting the treaty ratified. He went on a speaking tour in the late summer of 1919 in an effort to rally the country behind the League. He suffered a stroke during the tour and was an invalid for the rest of his term. Two votes were taken on the League in the Senate, but on both occasions it failed to get the necessary majorities. Thus, the United States neither joined the League nor approved

Henry Cabot Lodge (1850–1924)

Lodge was a lawyer, historian, legislator, and long-time Republican Party leader and Senator. He was born in Massachusetts, graduated from Harvard, and attended law school there. Though he was admitted to the bar, the teaching and writing of history interested him more than the law, and he had hardly begun that career before he became involved in politics. Lodge served one term in the state legislature, two terms in the House of Representatives, before being elected to the Senate in 1893, a position he retained for the rest of his life. A Republican from the beginning, Lodge began to emerge as a party leader in the Senate during Roosevelt's presidency. He reached the pinnacle of his Senate leadership during and immediately after World War I. As chairman of the Senate Foreign Relations Committee, he played the key role in the Senate's rejection of membership in the League of Nations and failure to ratify the Treaty of Versailles. He emerged as a champion of American independence in world affairs.

the Treaty of Versailles. Instead, Congress eventually ended the war by joint resolution.

Critics of the American failure to join the League claimed over the years that this contributed to the impotence of that organizaton and set the stage for World War II. Of course, it is not possible to rerun the events of history under circumstances different from those that prevailed, but there is no good reason to believe that American participation would have made much difference. The League was a paper tiger, in any case. It was based upon the faulty premise of a commonality that did not exist. It was the injustice of the treaties, the sundering of Europe, and the rise of totalitarianism and spread of socialism that set the stage for World War II. Nor is it descriptively correct to label the United States isolationist in the 1920s. The United States did continue to pursue an independent course in world affairs, but that involved much cooperation as it had always done.

Chapter 9
Bolshevism and the Spread of Totalitarianism

. . . In order to achieve its emancipation, the proletariat must overthrow the bourgeoisie, conquer political power and establish its revolutionary dictatorship.

Now . . . the transition from capitalist society . . . to a Communist society is impossible without a "political transition period," and the state in this period can only be the revolutionary dictatorship of the proletariat.

—V. I. ("Nicolai") Lenin, 1918

National Socialism as a matter of principle must lay claim to the right to force its principles on the whole German nation. . . . It must determine and reorder the life of a people. . . .

—Adolf Hitler, 1925

The Fascist State is a will expressing power and empire. The Roman tradition here becomes an idea of force. . . . For Fascism, the tendency to empire . . . is a manifestation of vitality. . . . Peoples who rise, or who suddenly flourish again, are imperialistic; peoples who die are peoples who abdicate.

—Benito Mussolini

Chronology

1917—Bolshevik Revolution.

1918–1920—Civil War in Russia.

1919—Beginning of Palmer Raids.

1920—American Civil Liberties Union formed.

1921—New Economic Policy (NEP) in Soviet Union.

1922—Fascist "March on Rome."

1923—Mussolini consolidates power in Italy.

1925—Publication of *Mein Kampf*.

1927—Sacco and Vanzetti executed.

1928—Stalin's First Five-Year Plan.

1933—Hitler becomes Chancellor of Germany.

In November of 1917 what was almost certainly the most momentous event of the 20th century occurred. The Bolsheviks (soon to be called Communists) displaced what remained of the government of the Russian empire. They siezed power over the state, brought off a *coup d'état*. The Bolshevik Revolution had begun. It was an event of such cataclysmic importance that it has been difficult ever since to get it into perspective. Communism, the most radical of the socialisms, had attained political power. Before that time, Communism had been only an ideology, one among many, about which professional revolutionaries and intellectuals wrangled. It was the brainchild of an outcast, Karl Marx, who was a disgruntled ideologue, and most of his disciples were usually treated as the enemies of the government in the countries in which they resided. Outspoken advocates of communist revolution were usually outlaws and often enough driven into exile, as Marx had been.

Power in the hands of Communists transformed both Communism and its role in the world. What had been only a potential threat became an actual menace. Now Communism had a power base, a homeland, a center for its operations. It gave Communists the opportunity not only to put their theories into practice in Russia but also to spread them around the world. Moscow became the seat of the Communist International (the Comintern) which proceeded both to propagandize and do espionage work for the Soviet Union in other countries but also to bolster Communist parties, spread subversion, and bring about revolution in other countries. In short, Russia became the center from which a world revolution was supposed to spread.

But the significance of the Bolshevik Revolution went beyond even the tremendous impact that communism has had on countries and international relations in the 20th century. It marked the onset and became the model in many ways for the spread of totalitarianism in this century. As suggested earlier, total war helped to set the stage for totalitarianism by extending the control of government over the lives of a people. Total war, however, was limited largely to war efforts; when the war ended, or shortly thereafter, controls were usually relaxed or removed. Communism in Russia totalized the power of the state on a permanent basis. Other countries not under the sway of communism imitated this totalization of the power of the state. Most notably, totalitarianism came to Fascist Italy in the 1920s and Nazi Germany in the 1930s. To a less dramatic extent, the governments of many other countries increased the role of government in the lives of their citizens, though not always in direct imitation of the Bolsheviks. Of course, the Bolsheviks intended to be a model for communist revolutions in other lands (and they usually have been). As Lenin said on the fourth anniversary of the Bolshevik Revolution:

This victory *is not yet the final victory*. We have made a start. When, at what date and time, and the proletarians of which nation will complete this process is not a matter of importance. The important thing is that the ice has been broken; the road is open and the path has been blazed.[204]

Lenin was speaking of communist revolutions, of course, not totalitarianism, but it happens, and not accidentally, that the one has usually followed the other. There are several features common to totalitarianism of whatever variety, and the Bolsheviks provided a model. First, there is single party rule. All other parties are banished, and only the one party is allowed to propose candidates for office. Second, all power is concentrated in one

Nicolai Lenin (family name, Vladimir Ilyich Ulyanov) (1870–1924)

Lenin founded the Bolshevik Party, engineered the Bolshevik Revolution in Russia, and organized the Communist International. He was born in provincial Russia, the son of a schoolmaster, and received his university training in law. While he was at the university, he was drawn into Marxist circles and before long he was involved in revolutionary activities. After a brief period of law practice, Lenin became a full-time writer, Marxist theorizer, and party organizer. Since revolutionary activities were usually illegal, he spent much time in hiding, in prison, and in exile in the years before World War I, much of it outside Russia. The Bolsheviks were originally a splinter off the Social Democrat (Marxian) party, but after they seized power in Russia they became *the* Communist Party. Lenin was in Switzerland in the early years of World War I, but after the abdication of Czar Nicholas II, he returned to Russia and gained control of the revolutionary movement. Lenin established the pattern for 20th century violent revolution by which a minority usurps control of the political machinery of a country.

national government; any local or provincial governments that survive lose all independence of action. Third, all power is vested in a single person, a dictator, though he may have a variety of titles. Fourth, the government not only exercises unlimited control over the economy but also over whatever aspects of the lives it judges necessary to its purposes. Thus, it controls the press and other means of communication, regiments the lives of the people, has secret police (more precisely, "special police"), often has concentration camps, political prisoners, and the like.

Communism in Russia

Contrary to a widespread impression, the Bolsheviks did not overthrow the autocratic czar. That was done much earlier in the year by what was then called the Provisional Government. The Provisional Government was the successor government to that of Czar Nicholas II. Its claim to legitimacy rested on the fact that it was formed from the Duma, the Russian representative assembly. At the outset, Prince Lvov was chosen to head the government, but it was generally believed that his was only a temporary government which would rule only until a constituent assembly had been called and a constitution had been provided. This was never done during the period from March to November of 1917, in which the Provisional Government technically ruled. Meanwhile, political power was shifting away from this government toward the Soviets (councils) which had been formed widely to take charge locally in the anarchic situation which prevailed from March onward. These were not primarily Bolshevik nor even necessarily Communist organizations at the outset, but their thrust was in the direction of social revolution. Alexander Kerensky took a leading role in the government in May, and in July became prime minister. Since he had a base in both the Provisional Government and the Soviets, it looked for a time that he might be able to pull together the discordant elements in Russia.

While the Provisional Government had a socialist cast to it, the Bolsheviks had no part in the formation of it or membership in it. Nor is it true, as is sometimes implied, that Nicholas II was a tyrant. True, the czars usually ruled autocratically, and Nicholas I (1825–1855) did qualify rather well as a tyrant, but the Romanov regimes which followed were generally less repressive, and Nicholas II (1894–1917) moved cautiously in the direction of constitutional monarchy. Indeed, the constitution adopted in 1906 indicated that he was to share the powers of governing with the elected Duma. Nicholas was in many ways an exemplary monarch. He loved the German princess whom he married, Alix of Hesse-Darmstadt, well, if not always wisely and was a beloved father and devoted to his four daughters and only son by her. He liked hunting especially, though he also appears to have enjoyed in general the trappings of royalty in the last halcyon days of monarchy. If he was not himself a man of great vision, he used two vigorous and far-seeing ministers, Sergei Witte and Piotr Stolypin, to good effect. These men set the stage for industrial progress by encouraging private investment, and Stolypin, before his assassination in 1911, did much to encourage the development of independent farming. (So heady was Stolypin's success that some of the socialists began to despair of appealing effectively to the peasants.) Even though industrialization was proceeding apace in the years before World War I, Russia was still far behind the countries of Western Europe, and the army was hardly equipped to fight a modern war or make a sustained effort to provide the suplies.

None of the above is meant to suggest that Nicholas II could not be autocratic. He was a proud and unrepentant autocrat, proclaimed his autocracy, and appears to have been determined to preserve and pass on his powers undiminished to his frail and sickly son. Nor was he above meddling with the makeup of the Duma, and he freely exercised the power to adjourn or dismiss it. But it was neither the vigorous nor arbitrary use of his power that cost him his throne and, ultimately, his head. The truth is that the basis of his authority had eroded until there came a point when he could no longer command the obedience of his subjects.

The stage was set for this by the ineffective ministers whom he appointed in the years just before and during the early years of the war. The truth was that he was too greatly influenced by his wife in making these appointments, and she, poor woman, was under the influence of a strange and evil man, Grigori Rasputin. It came about in this way. The Crown Prince, Alexis, was afflicted with hemophilia (uncontrolled bleeding). The Czar and Czarina, as well as their daughters, lived in constant fear that the boy would bump or bruise himself so as to set off another bout with the affliction. It happened often enough, and the suffering was such that it was all the family could do to bear it. Physicians could do little to help the boy but try to keep him comfortable until the bleeding stopped. Rasputin, on the other hand, was able, probably by hypnotism, to stop the bleeding sometimes, and this earned him the gratitude of the Czarina. Rasputin used his influence at court to obtain ministerial appointments for men poorly qualified for the jobs.

Nor did it help the Czarina's reputation to be associated with a character such as Rasputin. It was bad enough that she was German in background, once Russia went to war against Germany. But the gossip and tales about her, almost certainly unfounded, helped to undermine the authority. Moreover, it was true that Rasputin had considerable influence over the Czarina, and through her, the Czar.

Another element in the erosion of authority was that of the intellectuals, or intelligentsia as they were then called. These had given rise to revolutionary organizations of one kind or another which became increasingly important from the early 20th century onward. There was the Socialist Revolutionary Party, which contained a considerable number of anarchists, some of whom were responsible for the fairly numerous assassination attempts in the late 19th and early 20th century. There were the Constitutional Democrats who were reformers more than revolutionaries. There was a Labor Group Party which sought to gain control of the industrial workers. Above all, there was the Russian Social Democratic Workers' Party, the Marxist party. It was not a large party, and it was further handicapped by division into two factions: the Mensheviks (minority) and the Bolsheviks (majority). Actually, the Bolsheviks were not the larger of the two factions, but they had taken the name because they had once won one party vote. The Bolsheviks were the more violent and revolutionary of the two, and Lenin was their acknowledged leader. The revolutionary parties had one common purpose: their opposition to the government of the czar. They propagandized, campaigned (when they could), and attempted in whatever ways they could to undermine its authority.

Nor did this change much when the Czar abdicated in March, 1917 and the provisional government took over. Indeed, there were more radicals and revolutionaries to contend with than ever. The provisional government released all the political prisoners, thus setting free those most committed to violent revolution. Not only that but in April, 1917 the man who had taken the name Nicolai Lenin arrived in the country at Petrograd. He had been in exile, along with some of his comrades, but was given safe passage in a sealed railway passenger car through Germany by the German government. Undoubtedly, the German government hoped he would gain power in and take Russia out of the war, which is precisely what happened. The man known to history as Leon Trotsky (born Lev Davidovich Bronstein) arrived in Petrograd shortly after Lenin. He had been in the United States when the provisional government took control in Russia, but he returned to his native land as quickly as he could, aided by gifts from American friends. Lenin and Trotsky were the prime movers of the Bolshevik Revolution.

Another man in Petrograd during this fateful period and who was a prominent Bolshevik was Joseph Stalin (a pseudonym also). That Lenin, Trotsky, and Stalin all adopted pseudonyms was symptomatic both of their attitude toward tradition and the style of their revolutionary lives. By adopting new names they cut themselves off from families and ancestors. Moreover, they were, in effect, outlaws during their czarist days; Stalin even robbed government transports carrying treasure. They were reckoned, rightly, to be dangerous and desperate men.

With their main leaders present in Russia in the spring and summer of 1917, the Bolsheviks worked ever more vigorously to undermine the provisional government and seize power themselves. They promised the factories and mines to the industrial workers, land to the peasants, and an end to what they termed an imperialist war to people generally, and especially to the soldiers. Lenin was like a man possessed almost from the time he returned to Russia. Indeed, he may have been obsessed with a revolutionary vision for years, but the obsession appeared now to have him in its control. If an artist had been assigned the task of painting a portrait of a man possessed, he would have done well to choose Lenin as his model. Lenin looked the part with his wide forehead, large head, and penetrating ideas. He was an ideologue who believed he was now on the brink of turning his idea into reality. As the weakness of the provisional government became more apparent in the summer and fall of 1917, he became more and more determined to take over the government. An uprising in July had failed, and Lenin had to go into hiding. When General Kornilov tried to take control, he, too, was turned back, but this only confirmed Lenin in his belief that the Bolsheviks must act swiftly before a military takeover did occur.

Karl Marx to the contrary notwithstanding, Lenin had become convinced that world revolution was at hand as World War I ground toward the end. Marx might not have disagreed with that, but he certainly had never supposed that it would begin in Russia. It was supposed to occur in the most industrialized countries, and Russia was hardly that. Lenin managed to get around this ideological difficulty by maintaining that the revolution in Russia would be the onset of an imminent worldwide revolution. Imperialism was supposed to be the final stage of capitalism. World War I was the last imperial thrust of a capitalism now suffering its death agony. With the tide of history rolling shoreward to bring revolution, why might it not come to Russia first? If it did, Lenin was Russian, and he had so placed himself that his could be the decisive blow for world revolution.

At any rate, in the fall of 1917 Lenin became more and more impatient for a thrust by the Bolsheviks. While he was still in hiding, he wrote:

> Comrades! Our revolution is passing through a critical time. This crisis coincides with the great crisis of a growing worldwide socialist revolution and of a struggle against world imperialism. The responsible leaders of our party are confronted with a gigantic task; if they do not carry it out, it will mean a total collapse of the internationalist proletarian movement. The situation is such that delay truly means death.[205]

Then, on the eve of the coup, Lenin wrote: "Comrades: As I write these lines . . . , the situation is impossibly critical. . . . We cannot wait! We may lose everything!!"[206]

On the next day (in November, 1917 by our calendar), the Bolsheviks struck in the capital city of Petrograd. They gained control over all the points of power in the city. The climactic event of the *coup* was the storming of the Winter Palace, the headquarters of the Provisional Government. The cabinet was in session even as the Bolsheviks fought their way through the labyrinth of corridors and rooms to where the cabinet was meeting. A guard entered the chamber where the cabinet was sitting:

Kishkin, the Governor-General, did not seem to know whether the Palace had actually been occupied. "It is taken," the cadet replied. "They have taken all the entrances. Everyone has surrendered. Only this room is being guarded. What does the Provisional Government order?"

"Tell them," said Kishkin, "that we don't want bloodshed, that we yield to force, that we surrender."[207]

So it was that the Provisional Government fell with hardly a whimper.

In the next several weeks, the Bolsheviks consolidated their control. Prime Minister Kerensky had escaped before the Winter Palace was taken. He sought to gather an army to retake the capital. He could muster only seven hundred soldiers from the once vast armies of Russia, and this force was repulsed by the Bolsheviks a few days after the *coup* had taken place. Moscow fell to the Bolsheviks with no greater struggle than the one at Petrograd. The Soviets gained control at other places, and the Bolsheviks took measures to exert control over them.

The culminating acts of the Bolshevik seizure of power came with the dissolution of the Constituent Assembly, which attempted to convene in January, 1918. Elections for the assembly had been held late in 1917. Although the Bolsheviks held the centers of power, their candidates received less than one-fourth of the total vote cast. The Socialist Revolutionary Party received more votes than any other party, but they did not have a majority. The question then became whether or not the Bolsheviks would permit the Constituent Assembly to meet and do business. On the day when the first session was to be held the Bolsheviks called out large numbers of soldiers and sailors loyal to them to surround, guard and control the Tauride Palace, where the meeting took place. Even before the delegates assembled a crowd gathered outside the palace; Bolshevik forces fired into the crowd killing several people. When the delegates began to come into the building, armed soldiers and sailors guarded the entrance, examined the credentials of the delegates, and made intimidating comments about whether it would be more desirable to shoot, hang, or bayonet them. In keeping with Russian tradition, the oldest delegate, Sergey Shvetsov, tried to open the meeting. "Suddenly there was an uproar. Everyone was shouting at once, the guards were hammering their rifle butts on the floor, the Bolshevik deputies were pounding their fists on the desks and stamping their feet, while Bolshevik soldiers in the public galleries coolly aimed their rifles at the unfortunate Shvetsov."[208] Another man rudely took over for the Bolsheviks, and a little organizational work was begun. The Bolsheviks quickly wearied of the game, however, turned out the lights, and thus ended the business of the Constituent Assembly.

Two tactics enabled the Bolsheviks to install their own revolutionary government. One was their willingness, even eagerness, to resort to intimidation, terror, and violence. The chaotic situation in Russia set the stage for a takeover by those most willing to use force, and to use it ruthlessly. The Bolshevik leaders—Lenin, Trotsky, and Stalin, who was not so prominent at this time—were men of that ilk. In effect, they were gangsters, gangsters under the influence of an ideology which justified the use of whatever means it took to get their way. They were not petty gangsters, bent on simple thievery; they were international gangsters, set on taking not only the property but also the ways of living of all peoples under their control. The other tactic was the use of the leverage principle in exercising power. The Bolsheviks were a minor party at the time they took over the government, and communist parties are always a minority of the total adult population in every land. Yet they are adept at acting so as to gain the leverage position in any group or organization. They started out by claiming they were a majority among Marxists (Bolshevik means majority). Theirs eventually became the party line for the whole world.

The Soviets were not initially Bolshevik organizations, but they co-opted them. The Bolsheviks adopted the slogan, ''All power to the Soviets!'' Having thrust them into power in this fashion, the Bolsheviks then placed their own people in crucial points of power. Their levers in factories, on large organizations, in the army, and so on, were commissars, who often exercised much more power than appointed or chosen heads of organizations. The combination of ruthless violence and leverage made the Bolsheviks irresistible.

A great deal of confusion existed in the Soviet Union, as the new empire came to be called, during 1918, and indeed all the way down to 1921. In the early stages of the revolution, workers often seized factories and tried to run them; peasants seized large farms and took whatever they could; all property was fair game for a time. On top of this came the civil war between the Reds and Whites, as it was called, and there were contending military forces advancing and retreating over much of the remains of the Russian Empire, 1918–1921. But the Bolsheviks asserted their authority where and when they could, and the outlines of their brutal regime began to take shape. They drove all other parties and all opposition out of the government. One-party rule was established wherever the authority of the Bolsheviks extended.

Lenin emerged almost immediately as a throughgoing dictator, the first of the 20th century, and perhaps the first totalitarian dictator ever. Marx had spoken, of course, of the ''dictatorship of the proletariat,'' and Lenin claimed the authority of the party for his rule. The theory for the concentration of all power was called ''Democratic Centralism.'' The meaning should be clear from this description: ''The party is in a position in which the strictest centralism and the most stringent discipline are absolute necessities. All decisions of higher headquarters are absolutely binding for the lower.''[209]

Lenin's dictatorship was usually exercised directly, personally, and often in the crudest fashion. Much of it was done by telephone, for the desk in his office was covered with the instruments. To get the tenor of his dictation, here are two messages Lenin sent in August, 1918, as civil war was getting underway. "It is necessary to organize an intensive guard of picked reliable men to conduct a merciless mass terror against kulaks, priests and White Guards. . . ." And again, "You must mobilize all forces . . . , introduce immediately mass terror, shoot and deport hundreds of prostitutes. . . . Do not hesitate for a moment. You must act promptly: mass searches for hidden arms; mass deportations of Mensheviks and security risks."[210] Nor did he stop at known enemies; his wrath could be turned upon Bolsheviks as well. He wrote to one group, "I warn you that I shall have the chairmen of the . . . executive committees, the Cheka [Soviet secret police] and the members of the executive committee arrested for this and see that they are shot."[211] Fortunately for them, Lenin neglected to follow through with his threat.

Not all the violence and terror was initiated by Lenin, of course. A local Soviet ordered the execution of Czar Nicholas and his family. They had been in custody since the abdication, and had been sent to eastern locations as the revolution spread. The whole family, the remaining servants, and even their little dog, were murdered in the most brutal manner imaginable. They were herded into a single room and executed gangland fashion. When the murderers thought that everyone was dead, the Crown Prince Alexis, that sickly and afflicted boy, "feebly moved his hand to clutch his father's coat. Savagely, one of the executioners kicked the Tsarevich in the head with his heavy boot. Yurovsky stepped up and fired two shots into the boy's ear. Just at that moment Anastasia . . . regained consciousness and screamed. With bayonets and rifle butts, the entire band turned on her. In a moment, she too lay still."[212] The bodies were wrapped in sheets and taken to another location. There they were dismembered with saws and axes, and their bones dissolved with acid. What remained was thrown down a mine shaft. The Presidium of the Soviet Union gave its approval to this ghoulish and brutal undertaking after the fact.

All these things were done in the name of a revolution which was now imposed from above. The old that the Bolsheviks destroyed they quickly replaced with arbitrary organizations. The old state structure was destroyed, but a new and more autocratic one replaced it, under the theoretical control of the monolithic Communist Party, with all popular limitations on government removed, and with a new secret police to impose the will of the dictator. The old army was hardly demobilized before a new one was built, under the leadership of Leon Trotsky. The Provisional Government had relaxed military authority, abolished the death penalty for desertion, and initially Lenin had the men elect their officers. Now, all this was reversed: the death penalty restored, election of officers abandoned, and compulsory military training established. All foreign alliances were broken, and in its place came the Communist International to foment revolution around the world. The workers did not run the factories for long; the government nationalized the industries, brought back the old mangers to run them, and commissars kept a watchful eye over all. Indeed, all productive property either became government property or under government control. At this point, the peasants had hold of the land, but the government claimed most of their produce.

The social revolution proceeded apace. The Bolsheviks wasted no time in making their assault on the family and religion. In a pamphlet on the family, Alexandra Kollontai, a leading Bolshevik, had this to say:

> *The family ceases to be necessary.* It is not necessary to the state because domestic economy is no longer advantageous to the state, it needlessly distracts women workers from more useful productive labor. It is not necessary to members of the family themselves because the other task of the family—the bringing up of children—is gradually taken over by society.[213]

Lenin did not go so far. Instead, he acted to remove the public and religious supports of the family. A new marriage code required civil registration of marriages and made religious ceremonies of no account at law. Divorce was made available on demand by either or both parties. Illegitimate children were given the same status as legitimate children at law. Both sexes were declared to be equal. (Thereafter, women did heavy work as often as men, but if they were married they usually had to do the housework as well.) Abortion was legalized in 1920 "for so long as the moral survivals of the past and economic conditions of the present compel some women to resort to this operation."[214]

The Bolsheviks (or Communists, as they were now being called) believed that religion was simply a mechanism by which the ruling class controlled the ruled. They were determined, then, to loosen its hold on the people and destroy it, or otherwise make it an instrument of communism. The Communist Party announced in 1919 that it was

> guided by the conviction that the realization of planned order and consciousness . . . can only bring with it a complete dying out of religious prejudices. The party aims at a complete destruction of the link between the exploiting classes and the organization of religious propaganda by assisting the effective liberation of the toiling masses from religious prejudices and by organizing the broadest propaganda in favour of scientific enlightenment and against religion.[215]

But the attack on religion was hardly restricted to propaganda. Church and state were declared to be separate. Church property was confiscated on a huge scale. Church activity in the schools was banned. There was wide-spread persecution of priests or any who attempted to teach religion, and most churches and seminaries were taken over for secular uses. Perhaps the greatest symbolic event in the assault upon Christianity was the movement of the capital from Petrograd to Moscow and locating it in the ancient walled city, the Kremlin. Up until the 18th century, the Kremlin had been the governmental and religious center of Russia. Peter the Great had moved the capital to St. Petersburg, which much later became Petrograd. The government buildings in the Kremlin deteriorated after that, but the great cathedrals and other religious shrines were maintained. When the Communists moved their headquarters into the Kremlin, it signified the replacement of Eastern Orthodox Christianity with a new religion, atheistic communism. The cathedrals and monasteries became museums, for the most part, and the Kremlin became the fearful symbol of communist power.

By 1921, the Russia that had been was virtually in ruins. The old order had been almost completely destyroyed, but the bright utopia foretold by communist prophets had not emerged. Much damage had undoubtedly occurred during the Russian engagement in World War I as well as in the civil war between the Reds and Whites. But much more of the devastation and disruption should be charged to the revolutionary effort to wipe out the institutions of the past and impose a new order. In 1921 industrial production was only about thirteen percent of what it had been before World War I. Seventy-four million tons of grain had been harvested in 1916 compared with only 30 million tons in 1919. Indeed, the Ukraine had long been a grain surplus area; that was no more. The Bolsheviks had almost destroyed the value of the money by drastic increases of the supply (inflation). Famine conditions existed in many areas. Some of the larger cities were very nearly depopulated as people fled the cities which could not be supplied. The population of Moscow had been about 2 million in 1917, but it had fallen to 800,000 by 1920. The population of Petrograd had been 2,416,000 in 1916; it dropped to 722,000 by 1920. The situation was desperate.

In March, 1921, Lenin inaugurated a new program, called a New Economic Policy (NEP). It was a tactical retreat at the economic level from the headlong rush into communism, into the nationalization of industry, government control of all trade, the attempt to abandon the use of money, and the confiscation of farm produce. Lenin declared that the Revolution had "tried to take the citadel of capitalism by a frontal attack," and the effort had failed.[216] Communism must now retreat in order to go forward again at a later date. The smaller industrial plants were returned to their former owners or to private ownership; trade was opened up to private traders, and shortly most retail trade was being conducted by private entrepreneurs; money was restored to serve as a medium of exchange; and farmers were only to be taxed and allowed to sell what remained on the market. The restoration of a measure of economic freedom enabled Russia to make at least a partial recovery between 1921–1928.

Reaction in the United States

The Bolshevik Revolution sent shock waves of fear throughout much of a Western Civilization badly wounded and riven already by a world war. Well it might, for communism was a root and branch assault on that civilization: on Christianity and all other traditional religions, on private property, on the family, and on all the institutions of a civilization. It would have been disturbing enough if it had been clearly confined to a single country, but that was by no means the case. Lenin had proclaimed a coming world revolution, and communism claimed to be international in purpose. The Communist International (Third International) was organized in 1919 with its headquarters in Moscow. Even before that event, communist revolution was spreading to other countries. Finland had declared independence of Russia, which the Bolsheviks accepted, but Soviet Russia supported a Finnish Socialist Workers' Party. It seized power in early 1918, but was driven out by a combination of German and local military forces.

It looked for a brief period as if Germany might do a replay of the Bolshevik Revolution, hard on its heels, in November and December of 1918. The Kaiser abdicated in November, and Germany had a large party, the Social Democrats, who were Marxist in coloration. The main body of them, however, were much more inclined to the gradualist rather than revolutionary approach to socialism. Even so, there was support for the Soviet approach, and the first government formed by Friedrich Ebert styled its members commissars. Much more menacing than this was a group known as the Spartacists, who formed the "Communist party of Germany" and were prepared to use force to take over the government. The government used irregular troops to overwhelm them in the second week of January, 1919, and their leaders, Karl Liebknecht and Rosa Luxemburg, were captured and shot. Independent of these developments, a Soviet-type government was formed in Bavaria, the second largest state in Germmany, under the leadership of Kurt Eisner. Eisner was shot and killed by a student who opposed the revolution, but the Soviet-style revolution proceeded without its leader. Forces from the central government were sent to Munich in April, and they crushed the revolution. It was then replaced by a regularly chosen government.

Hungary was the scene of yet another Soviet-style coup. Bela Kun led this takeover of the government in Budapest in March of 1919. He attempted to get a full-fledged revolution underway seizing the banks, productive industry, and productive property generally. However, his revolution was short-lived, for Rumania invaded Hungary and further despoiled the country. Native Hungarians put down the revolution once the Supreme Allied Council persuaded the Rumanians to withdraw.

This volatile European situation, aggravated by the organization of the Communist International, provided the backdrop for some vigorous governmental action to nip in the bud any revolutionary attempts in the United States. Whether there was any considerable danger of revolution in the United States in 1919 or shortly thereafter, or even whether any such threat was necessary to justify the actions taken by state and federal governments, should remain an open question. History books have generally pooh-poohed the idea that there was any real threat of revolution. Their argument usually is that the number of radicals in the country bent upon revolution was too small to have accomplished anything much. That argument would be more convincing were it not for the fact that communist revolution had just been accomplished in Russia by a *coup d'état* wrought by a minority of the Communists. The degree of disorder and public agitation or confusion is probably much more significant than the number of radicals. But even if revolution was unlikely, it does not follow that radicals should be permitted to foment dissension and disorder until revolution is imminent. Threats to the peace may provide occasion for government action even when the government is not about to be overthrown.

In any case, there was radical activity in the United States in 1919, some of it quite disturbing to the peace and safety of Americans. In the midst of these, in the wake of the formation of the Communist International, a Communist Party of America was organized September 1, 1919. At about the same time a Communist Labor Party was organized. By the end of the year, the Communist Party was estimated to have a membership between 30–60,000, the Communist Labor Party between 10–30,000. In addition, there was a regular Socialist Party, which disavowed violent action, with 39,000 members, and a much larger following in national elections. In addition, labor unions were growing in strength, and some of them, most notably, the Industrial Workers of the World, were revolution-minded.

One of the disturbances of 1919 was the large number of strikes. In the course of the year, there were more than 2,600 strikes involving some 4 million workers. Beginning late in 1918, there were in succession strikes of clothing workers in New York and Chicago, textile workers in New England and New Jersey, a general strike in Seattle, telephone operators in New England, the longshoremen of New York, and switchmen in Chicago rail yards. The Boston police strike was probably the most astounding, for that time. No one would have thought of such a thing! When the police went on strike, the police commissioner fired the strikers. Calvin Coolidge was governor of Masachusetts, and he sent in troops to maintain order and backed the commissioner. "There is no right to strike against the public safety, anywhere, anytime," Coolidge wrote to Gompers, who protested the firings.

An extensive effort was made to organize the steelworkers by the American Federation of Labor. William Z. Foster, who would later emerge as a leader of the Communist Party, played a leading role in the organization effort. United States Steel refused to meet union demands, and hundreds of thousands of steel workers went out on strike. There was widespread violence before the strike was brought to a close. John L. Lewis led the United Mine Workers out on strike late in 1919. Attorney General A. Mitchell Palmer declared that "Evidence obtained at the time of this strike showed active participation therein of the Communist Party of America, urging the workers to rise up against the Government of the United States."[217] Injunctions brought an end to the coal strike.

Perhaps the most disturbing events of 1919 were the bombings that were either attempted or occurred. The general strike by the Industrial Workers of the World in Seattle occurred in February. Mayor Ole Hanson denounced the strike as the work of Bolsheviks and other radicals. At any rate, a large bomb was discovered in his mail on April 28. But those who sent the bombs were not all that selective. The next day, the maid of Senator Thomas W. Hardwick of Georgia got her hands blown off when she attempted to open a package addressed to him. An investigation in the New York Post Office turned up 16 bomb packages, and 20 others were discovered in the mails at other places. They were addressed to such people as Attorney General Palmer, Justice Oliver Wendell Holmes, J.P. Morgan, and John D. Rockefeller. Later on in the spring Palmer's home was destroyed by a bomb, as were those of two judges. (In terms of actual damage, the worst episode did not take place until 1920. A wagonload of explosives was detonated in front of the New York offices of J.P. Morgan and Company, killing 38 people, injuring 200 others, and damaging property worth more than $2 million.)

In August, 1919, Attorney General Palmer organized a General Intelligence Division in the Justice Department and brought in J. Edgar Hoover to direct its activities in gathering information about radicals and their organizations. Both this agency and similar state organizations carried out raids from time to time. When the Justice Department was involved, they are usually referred to as the Palmer Raids. The first of these occurred in early November, 1919, when 250 members of the Union of Russian Workers were rounded up. Some of them were aliens and were recommended for deportation. In December, 249 aliens were loaded on an army transport and shipped back to Russia. In early January, 1920, Palmer's department rounded up several thousand members of the Communist parties, and a goodly portion of those who were aliens were deported. Those who were citizens were sometimes turned over to state authorities for prosecution under criminal syndicalist laws, which many states had.

This crackdown had the salutary effect of quieting the open agitation for revolution. It also served notice on those intent on spreading disorder that they were not welcome in the United States. At the time, Palmer's tough action brought him widespread acclaim, and it gave him a good start toward nomination as the Democratic candidate for President in 1920. However, opposition to him had mounted within the Democratic Party by convention time to the extent that his bid for the nomination failed. After all, the Democrats had drawn a large number of collectivist reformers into their ranks, and these might be expected to be sympathetic with the radicals.

It is well to note in connection with the crackdown on revolutionaries of the appearance of a tactic that has been often used since by Communists, their sympathizers and fellow-travelers. It is the device of taking attention away from Communist methods and violence by focusing attention on real or imagined wrongs done by those who oppose them. To put it more bluntly, it is the device of turning revolutionaries into the victims and their prosecuters into aggressors. This is accomplished by downplaying the purposes and

J. Edgar Hoover (1895–1972)

Courtesy FBI

Hoover was long-time head of the Federal Bureau of Investigation (FBI); beginning in 1924, he served under Presidents stretching all the way from Calvin Coolidge to Richard Nixon. Under his leadership the FBI became an efficient and effective organization, and some of its activities became well known in the 1930s through his magazine articles. Hoover was born in Washington, D.C., worked during the day and went to school at night to get his law degree from George Washington University, and went to work in the Justice Department in 1919. There, he became an assistant to Attorney General A. Mitchell Palmer and aided him in collecting the information which resulted in the Palmer Raids on radical organizations. He became an expert over the years on Communist subversive tactics, and wrote two books on the subject, including *Masters of Deceit* (published in 1958). Although the FBI remained an investigative agency mainly, Hoover made enemies, particularly among those sympathetic with Communist activities, enemies who became very vocal after his death.

methods of revolutionaries and focusing upon the allegedly unsavory tactics of those who act to contain and restrain them. Revolutionaries are portrayed as innocent advocates of unpopular ideas, beset by heavy-handed Yahoos. For example, an historian says of those deported that "most of them were anarchists, including Emma Goldman and Alexander Berkman, and many of them were philosophical anarchists who had no intention of ever using violence." By contrast, "Palmer invaded private homes, union headquarters, and meeting halls. People were held incommunicado, denied counsel, and subjected to kangaroo trials. . . . Not for at least half a century, perhaps at no time in our history, had there been such a wholesale violation of civil liberties."[218] It is easy to see from such descriptions who the good guys and bad guys were; they make good drama but distorted history.

The American Civil Liberties Union was organized under that imposing title in 1920. Under the relentless pressure of this organization, "civil liberty" took on a new meaning: it came to mean especially those liberties belonging to minorities. The ACLU acted mainly by providing attorneys to defend those accused of violating laws, especially laws aimed to restrain radical activities. Their lawyers have often been at the forefront both in getting legislative enactments nullified and in getting courts to become active formulators of rules restraining those who would enforce the law. Roger N. Baldwin, who served for many years as director of the ACLU, was pro-Soviet in posture, and many of the governing board members had an assortment of Communist associations. The first *Annual Report* of the ACLU declared that one of its two aims was to "second the demand for 'rights' of those minorities and individuals attacked by the forces of reaction. The demand for 'rights' is couched usually in an appeal to free speech traditions and constitutional guarantees. . . ."[219] In large, the ACLU has adopted the mantle of constitutional rectitude to defend those engaged in undermining it.

Perhaps the best way to see how the defenders of revolutionaries shift the focus from the perpetrators to their accusers is to examine a celebrated cause of the 1920s—the Sacco-Vanzetti trial. The paymaster for a South Braintree, Masachusetts shoe factory was robbed and killed April 15, 1920. Nicola Sacco and Bartolomeo Vanzetti were charged with the crime, arrested, indicted, tried, found guilty by a jury, sentenced to death by electrocution, and after all appeals had been exhausted were finally executed in 1927. Except for the length of time between conviction and execution, which was unusually long at that time, there was little in this that would make them go down in history. After all, hundreds of murders are committed in any given year in the United States, and many of those convicted have been executed over the years without being mentioned in histories. What made this one different was the agitation made about it by revolutionaries and their sympathizers.

It happened that Sacco and Vanzetti were foreign-born anarchistic revolutionaries. That was irrelevant, of course; they were neither charged with nor convicted of being those things. The only issue before the court was whether or not they had committed a robbery and murder. Of these offenses they were duly convicted and for them they were executed. But neither Sacco and Vanzetti nor their defenders would have it so; they were the victims and America was the villain. When he came before the judge for sentencing Sacco said: "I know the sentence will be between two classes, the oppressed class and the rich class. . . ." Vanzetti said, "I am suffering because I am a radical and indeed I am a radical; I have suffered because I was an Italian, and indeed I am an Italian. . . ."[220] A great hullabaloo was raised about it in this country and in Europe, and many histories still treat the case as if somehow Sacco and Vanzetti were the victims. No mention is made of even the name of the man they robbed and killed.

The Permanent Revolution in Russia

The United States did not accord diplomatic recognition to the Soviet Union until 1933. There were many good reasons for not doing so, but perhaps the best was the Communists were usurpers of political power and did not have a legitimate claim to govern. But there were other reasons of great weight. The Soviet rulers did not acknowledge the international obligations of Russia formulated in the past; indeed, they disavowed them, whether they were debts or treaty obligations. They were bent on undermining legitimate governments around the world and were hardly fit candidates for membership in the community of nations. In sum, the Soviet Union was a hostile force in the world, to say nothing of what the rulers were doing to their own people. Some further observations about developments in the Soviet Union and the system that took shape there are necessary to complete the background story for its impact on American history.

After Lenin's death in 1924, a struggle went on for several years for a successor. Although there were others who sought to direct the future course of the Soviet Union, the main contestants were Leon Trotsky and Joseph Stalin. Trotsky had been much more prominent during the Bolshevik Revolution and its aftermath than anyone except Lenin. That undoubtedly earned him the resentment of other members of the Politburo. His advocacy of pushing for worldwide revolution and doubts that Communism could succeed in a hostile world did not increase his following among those in power either. On the other hand, Lenin had written some caustic things about Stalin in his will. "Comrade Stalin," he wrote, "has concentrated an enormous power in his hands; and I am not sure that he always knows how to use that power with sufficient caution."[221] As a matter of fact, Lenin's critique of Stalin turned out to be one of the greatest understatements ever made, rather like charging Jack-the-Ripper with being careless with knives, but it did not stay for long Stalin's quest for dictatorial power. Stalin maintained that the Soviet Union should press forward toward communism—establish socialism in one country, if necessary—whether or not world revolution proceeded apace. In any case, Stalin won the contest: Trotsky was stripped of party membership and exiled, and by 1928 Stalin had thoroughly concentrated all power in his hands.

As soon as he had done so, Stalin forged ahead vigorously with his Five-Year Plans. He abandoned the New Economic Policy in 1928 and pressed toward industrialization and forced collectivization of agriculture. Small businessmen had their property taken from them; they became outcasts; trade once again became a monopoly of the state; and millions of small farmers (kulaks) were driven from their farms. Wholesale persecution of all those who had acquired small holdings followed, and one of the most

Joseph Stalin
(born Dzhugashvili)
(1879–1953)

Stalin was a Bolshevik agitator and organizer, party leader, and dictator of the Soviet Union from the late 1920s to 1953. He initiated the Five-Year Plans for forced collectivization, ordered the infamous purge trials of the 1930s, developed a vast slave labor camp system (the Gulag Archipelago), and peopled it with millions of his countrymen. He was born in the province of Georgia in the Russian Empire, attended a theological seminary, and was headed toward becoming a priest. However, he became involved with socialist groups and Marxist ideology and was expelled from seminary shortly before he would have graduated. Thereafter, he pursued the peculiar gangster-like life of so many revolutionaries in the years before World War I: in and out of jail, being deported and escaping from exile, organizing revolutionary groups, publishing ideological materials, and the like. Stalin became a follower of Lenin, and after the Bolshevik Revolution became a commissar. In the 1920s, he was secretary general of the Communist Party, and from this power position, he propelled himself to the head of the government after Lenin's death.

brutal—if not *the* most brutal—regimes in history was established under Stalin. The revolution became permanent in the sense that it was an ongoing and continuous thing.

Stalin completed the edifice of what should be called the Communist façade, the false front presented to the rest of the world. The façade has two main purposes: to enable the Soviet Union to operate in a world where most countries are not communist; to give the impression that communism is a success and attract followers. The façade appears in every arena. The vast formal governmental structure is a façade. Several constitutions have been put into effect, yet none of them serve to limit and restrain government or describe the real source and concentration of power. The elections are a façade, for the Party selects all the candidates for office, and there is no choice by the electorate. (Massive efforts are made to get people to vote, though their votes have only propagandic significance.) The vast parliamentary structure is of no account, for all power is concentrated in the Politburo, and usually in the hands of a single person. The proclaimed equality is a façade, for party members, the leaders, and people who serve some purpose, are highly privileged in the Soviet Union. Visitors see model factories, model farms, model prisons, and so on, which bear little relation to the situation generally. The Russian Orthodox Church is a façade, controlled by the government and used for its purposes. Statistics of production are a façade, bearing only a tangential relation to actual production. Even the diplomatic offices in foreign countries are largely covers for secret police and spying activities. People who have had a need or wish to be taken in by the façade have been obliged by the Soviet deception. Indeed, it is difficult for people to believe that so massive a deception could be carried on, but it has.

Behind the false front, maintaining each Communist regime in power, is what is best understood as Terror, an arbitrarily imposed terror. This terror is carried out by the "Organs," as the Russians call them, the secret police who have been called by several initials, Cheka, MVD, NKVD, KGB, and so on, but all relentless imposers of the terror. The degree and extent of the terror has varied from time, though Stalin imposed an almost continuous terror with intensity during his rule from 1928–1953. Though all Soviet citizens may live in greater or lesser dread of the terror, most never experience it in its direst form. That is reserved for those who enter the prison and slave labor camp system of the "Organs."

Ordinarily, the first step toward the terror occurs when a person is taken into custody by the secret police. It can happen at any time and any place. Alexander Dolgun, an American who spent eight years in Soviet prison camps, was walking down a street in Moscow in the middle of the day when he was taken. Most likely, no charge would be made at the time, and since the people most thoroughly terrorized were called political prisoners, the person most likely would be neither aware of nor have committed any crime. The second step is to be taken to a prison nearby to be interrogated. The purpose of the interrogation is to extract a *satisfactory* confession from the prisoner. He will be interrogated for as short or as long a time as is needed to get the desired confession, or until he goes insane or dies from the tortures inflicted upon him. The usual method of getting a prisoner to confess is to put him on the conveyor, as it is called. The conveyor is a system of extended interrogation carried on by relays of fresh interrogators, usually at night, broken by interludes of "rest" during the day in which the prisoner is not allowed to lie down or sleep. One careful student of the process describes it this way:

> Interrogation usually took place at night and with the accused just aroused—often only fifteen minutes after going to sleep. The glaring lights at the interrogation had a disorienting effect. There was a continual emphasis on the absolute powerlessness of the victim. The interrogators—or so it usually seemed—could go on indefinitely.[222]

Other tortures might accompany the interrogation. They could be simple or exquisite, as simple as feeding a prisoner salt fish and allowing him no water for a day, or as exquisite as placing him in a cold room with water covering the floor and no place to sit. One man tells how his mother was tortured: "They beat her with truncheons, trying to get her to incriminate me. They pushed needles under her fingernails. . . . After a very short period of this she went quite insane and without sentencing her, they put her in a prison insane asylum in Ryazan."[223]

Once a confession had been extracted, the next step was to sentence the prisoner. He could be sentenced either after trial or by the secret police. If a trial were held, it was only for show, since there was never any question that the prisoner was guilty. He could be sentenced either to be shot, or to a fate worse than death, to be sent to a Gulag—a slave labor camp. If he were to be shot, the sentence was carried out summarily, without ceremony, as lore would have it, by being shot in the back of the neck with a pistol.

Sentences to slave labor camps might vary from 5 to 25 years, say, though length was not so important, since sentences could be extended by the "Organs," and the chances of surviving even shorter sentences were not good. Millions, perhaps tens of millions, were sent to slave labor camps during Stalin's rule. Some of the most horrible stories have to do with what happened during the period of transport to the camps, whether to far off Siberia or elsewhere. Many died during the period of transportation. Nor did matters improve, except by comparison with the transport or interrogation, once they reached the primitive camps. There they were subject to life in horrid barracks thickly infested with cockroaches, fed minimal food, wore such rags as they had or could somehow obtain, and put to work for long hours in forests, mines, or whatever work they were assigned. They were stripped of all human dignity and continually made to feel they were worthless.

It was on this base of terror that the Soviet regime rested. None dared ordinarily to question it, defy it, or organize against it. The terror might descend at any moment, and for any or no reason. In a sense, the whole Russian Empire became a prison under communism. The borders are guarded, not to keep people out, which is no problem, but to keep the population inside. The people who try to escape without permission are subject to be shot, and permission is difficult to get—may be denied for years or forever. But there are much more horrid prisons within the greater prison, as a lesson and example to those who complain.

Fascism in Italy

Another totalitarian system made its rude appearance in Italy, beginning in the fall of 1922. On October 27, Benito Mussolini's Blackshirts began their famous March on Rome. At Rome, King Victor Emmanuel was induced to name Mussolini as his prime minister and so, with that much of legality behind him, he began his move to become dictator in what he meant to be an all-powerful state. The disorder which had preceded his rise to power prepared the way for it, however. Although Italy had been on the winning side in World War I, Italian armies did not fare well during the war, and Italy carried little weight in the ensuing peace conference. On top of that, a succession of weak governments attempted to govern in the immediate postwar years. In late 1919, workers and peasants began Soviet-style efforts to take over factories and farms. Workers camped in factories, tried to run them, and peasants created a considerable disturbance in the countryside.

In contrast to the American government when confronted with radical disturbances, the Italian government did not act resolutely. Indeed, it behaved much more like the Provisional Government did earlier in Russia. As one European historian put it, "When the workers occupied the factories, the government . . . delayed action and finally negotiated a settlement. To help the agricultural workers it approved their seizure of unoccupied land but objected when the workers seized other uncultivated land as well."[224] In the absence of a firm assertion of governmental authority, assorted gangs took to the streets in paramilitary uniforms, red shirts, blue shirts, black shirts. The Fascist Blackshirts, under Mussolini, were probably the toughest and most violent of these. They took on the Communists and any other gang that stood in their way. In 1920 and 1921, the Fascists spread terror, particularly among socialists and communists, and in the battles that took place hundreds were killed. In 1922, unionists and the Socialist Party called a general strike. It was broken by armed Fascists. In the midst of all this, the government "temporized, negotiated . . . , and did not protect the citizens against violations of civil rights."[225] In view of the fact that the Fascists were already ruling the streets in many places, it may have seemed a logical next step to permit them to have the governmental machinery as well.

Mussolini brought revolution to Italy and inaugurated a totalitarian regime. During the years from 1922–1926, he established himself as the absolute dictator of the country. He accomplished this by the device of a minority party, the Fascist Party. Over the years, the Grand Council of the Fascist Party came to dominate the government. There had been only a few Fascists in the Italian Parliament when he became prime minister, but this was overcome in an ensuing election. Afterward, Mussolini ruled increasingly by decree, gained control of press and radio, took away the independence of the courts, and asserted control over the economy. Various sectors of the economy were organized into syndicates, and these were under Mussolini's authority. Any who opposed the regime were persecuted.

Although the Fascist revolution followed much of the pattern of the Bolshevik Revolution, it was not technically either a socialist or communist revolution. This was so despite the fact that Mussolini was steeped in socialist thought and had been active in socialist revolutionary circles before World War I. Moreover, his organization of the economy into syndicates may have been inspired by syndicalism, a variety of socialism especially prominent in France. Although he started out as a teacher in the schools, he was soon drawn into the propaganda and newspaper work of the socialists. During the years from around 1905 to 1915, he was entangled in pro-socialist, atheistic, and anticlerical work, including the writing of some novels. He broke with the Socialist Party during World War I because of its opposition to the war. When he organized the Fascists, he became bitterly anti-communist, anti-socialist, anti-democratic, and aggressively nationalistic. He had also favored republican government earlier, but as he began to contemplate the necessities of coming to power, he renounced his republicanism and put behind him his formal opposition to the Catholic Church or to religion.

Even so, Italian Fascism was a species of collectivism. It sought a collectivist unity just as Communism does, treated the Italian people as a potentially unified collective, and concentrated all the power of this assumed collective in the state. Communism, however, turns this power mainly, if not exclusively on the people within the state; by contrast, Fascism sought to turn the power on other peoples and other nations. Mussolini glorified war, advocated territorial expansion, and proposed to restore the glory that was Rome. "Fascism is a doctrine," Mussolini said, "which most adequately represents . . . a people like the Italian people, which is rising again after many centuries of abandonment of foreign servitude."[226] Its future lay with empire, he claimed. As for war, he said: "War alone brings all human energies to their highest tension and sets a seal of nobility on the peoples who have the virtue to face it." There was more than a little boast and bombast to Mussolini's rhetoric. He was much more cautious in action than his language suggests, and the war machine he tried to build was less than overwhelming, but he did concentrate power in his hands and enunciate a version of collectivized state which still haunts.

Nazism in Germany

In January, 1933, Adolf Hitler took the oath of office as Chancellor, and thus began the Nazi revolution in Germany. The development of that revolution falls beyond the chronological scope of this volume, but a summary treatment of it is necessary to round out the story of the spread of totalitarianism. Moreover, the stage for this development was definitely set by events in the 1920s. While Nazism was Hitler's own particular brew, it bears more than a family resemblance to Italian Fascism, and owed much to the Bolshevik pattern.

Revolution was several times aborted in Germany in the 1920s, despite the fact that Germany looked to be a better candidate for it than Italy. The Treaty of Versailles had aroused seething resentment in many Germans. The abdication of Kaiser Wilhelm had removed the personal focus of unity for the nation. The Weimar Republic which replaced monarchy hardly commanded the allegiance of most Germans, and the governments of the 1920s had rough going to restrain the partisan armies and multiplicity of parties in the countries. But a Soviet style revolution was nipped in the bud in 1919; the Kapp *Putsch* in 1920 failed; and the Munich *Putsch*, instigated by Hitler in 1923 also failed. Even the destruction of the currency by a monumental inflation in 1923 did not bring down the republic. Indeed, from the mid to late 1920s, republican institutions appeared to be working fairly well, and a measure of stability prevailed. It was, however, the quiet before the storm.

The economic depression, which spread over Europe following the stock market crash in the United States, hit Germany especially hard. As unemployment rose the more radical parties gained in their following, and the partisan armies found it easier to increase their numbers. The Social Democrats, a nonrevolutionary socialist party, lost much of their following, and it became increasingly difficult for any government to command a majority in the ruling house of the German parliament. Hitler's Nazi Party gained national following slowly in the late 1920s. It got a sufficient vote to name 12 delegates to the main house of parliament—12 out of 491! In the election in 1930, however, the Nazis got the second largest number of votes, but they still had only 107 out of a total of 577 delegates.

The elections in 1932 were crucial if the Nazis were to come to power legally. In the first election of that year, the Nazis got the largest vote of any party, but they still fell short of a majority. Their vote, combined with that of the communists, however, could have provided a majority of the delegates. There was no likelihood of that however, for despite the fact that both parties were revolutionary in intent, they were mortal enemies. They could only combine to bring governments down, not to form one. This they proceeded to do with alacrity as soon as the *Reichstag* met. The Communists proposed a no confidence vote, and it carried 512 to 42. The new elections, also held in 1932, hardly changed anything: the Communists gained a few delegates, the Nazis lost a few. The president, General von Hindenburg, tried one last time to form a government without the Nazis. It was short lived, and so it was that he turned to Hitler.

On the face of it, Hitler came to power perfectly legally, if the "Storm

Adolf Hitler
(1889–1945)

With a member of the Hitler Youth, 1936

Hitler was the founder of the Nazi Party, dictator of Germany from 1933–1945, and served, in effect, as supreme commander of German armed forces during World War II. He was born in Branau, Austria, was the son of a shoemaker who became a minor public servant, and received only a minimal formal education. He aspired to be an artist or an architect but did not impress anyone with his talents for these undertakings. In 1912, Hitler moved to Munich, which remained his home base until he became Chancellor in 1933. He was in the German army during World War I, and shortly afterward he became engrossed in revolutionary politics. His peculiar brand of rabble-rousing politics was learned by speaking in beer halls in Munich in the early 1920s. After the abortive attempt to seize the government reins in Munich in 1923, he was sentenced to prison and kept there for about a year. Much of his prison time was spent in writing a book, *Mein Kampf* (My Battle), in which he set forth his historical prejudices, racial theories, and nationalistic ambitions. Once in power, Hitler did not wait long to crack down on Jews and other groups whom he despised, to build up the military forces, and begin the expansionist policies which set off World War II.

Troopers,'' the SA, his private army, be ignored. Actually, however, Hitler had only attained quite limited power as head of the government. What followed that was almost entirely extralegal or illegal until only the semblance of legality remained. But legality meant nothing to Hitler, once he could ignore it. He was a ruffian, a hoodlum, a gangster, as were Mussolini, Stalin, and, for that matter, Lenin. He moved quickly over the next year or so to consolidate his power. He outlawed the Communists, crushed the Social Democrats, made all other parties illegal, broke the power of the unions, and concentrated all power in his own hands. He made himself Führer, i.e., leader, and instituted "Heil Hitler" (from "hail Caesar," no doubt) as the universal greeting for Germans. (Old General Hindenburg refused to address him otherwise than as Herr [mister] Hitler.)

The Storm Troopers instituted a reign of terror from 1933–1934. Hitler's gangsterism may be best illustrated by "The Night of the Long Knives," when he wiped out the leaders of his own Storm Troopers, as well as some other enemies (June 30–July 1, 1934). They were murdered, sometimes in their own homes, in a manner associated with gangland massacres. It is generally believed that several hundred were killed, but the exact number has never been determined. Hitler then proceeded to extend his arbitrary power over all aspects of the lives of the German people.

Nazism was a species of collectivism also. Indeed, Hitler did not even disavow socialism, as Mussolini had done. The full name of the Nazi Party was National *Socialist* German Workers Party. In form the Nazis showed their debts both to the Bolsheviks and the Italian Fascists. The enemy, for Hitler, was not the bourgeosie of the Communists but rather the Jews and what he thought of as ideologized Jews, the Marxists. Unlike Mussolini, Hitler was not bent on restoring the glory that was Rome's but rather to fulfill the long frustrated destiny of the Germans. In any case, the Nazis showed by their practices that they were collectivists—the mass meetings, the raised hand salute in unison, the cries of "Sieg Heil," the multitude of swastika-adorned flags, and the highly emotional speeches of the leaders. These and other such activities were aimed at arousing a single emotion which all would share, the forging of a unity, a collective through shared common experience. So, too, was the appeal to German nationality, to blood and soil, to the master race, to a common destiny. War and military action was glorified by the Nazis, as it was by the Fascists, and Hitler was expansionist and empire-minded as well. If the property of the Germans was not confiscated (that of the Jews was eventually) immediately, the government gained effective control over it.

The world that Woodrow Wilson had sought to make safe for democracy was becoming increasingly less safe for people, much less democratic. By the early 1930s it was beginning to appear that dictatorship and totalitarianism was the wave of the future, as the leaders themselves were proclaiming.

Chapter 10

The 1920s in America

America's present need is not heroics, but healing; not nostrums, but normalcy; not revolution, but restoration; not agitation, but adjustment; not surgery, but serenity. . . .

The world needs to be reminded that all human ills are not curable by legislation, and that quantity of statutory enactment and excess of government offer no substitute for quality of citizenship.

—Warren G. Harding, 1920

The successful business man among us . . . enjoys the public respect and adulation that elsewhere bathe only bishops and generals. . . . He is treated with dignity in the newspapers. . . . His opinion is sought upon all public questions . . . In the . . . wineshops he receives the attention that, in old Vienna, used to be given to Beethoven.

—H. L. Mencken, 1927

As a matter of policy nothing brings home to a man the feeling that he has a personal interest in seeing the Government revenues are not squandered . . . , as the fact that he contributes a direct tax, no matter how small, to his Government.

—Andrew W. Mellon, 1922

Chronology

1920, November 2—Election of Harding.
KDKA of Pittsburgh makes commercial radio broadcast.

1921—Brief economic depression.

1922—Publication of *Babbitt* by Sinclair Lewis.

1923—Death of President Harding.

1924—

February—Begin revelation of Harding "Scandals."
May—Immigration Quota Act.

1925—Scopes Trial in Dayton, Tennessee.

1926—Publication of Hemingway's *The Sun Also Rises*.

1927—Lindbergh's solo flight across the Atlantic.

1928—Election of Hoover.

1929—St. Valentine's Day Massacre.

The United States appeared remote from the World War I-ravaged Europe in the 1920s, remote, too, from the spreading totalitarianism once the disorder which preceded this political disease had been nipped in the bud in 1919 and 1920. Indeed, the 1920s in America was in many respects like a calm between two massive ocean swells—the calm between the great reformist surge before and after World War I and during the Great Depression of the 1930s, That is not to say that there were not striking events, disturbances, and important changes during the 1920s. Indeed, the decade was chock-full of events and developments which caught the eyes of reporters at the time and have been chronicled by historians since. It was an era of national prohibition, bootleggers, and both organized and disorganized crime, of female emancipation, short skirts, unrestrained dances such as the Charleston, when radio first began to provide a mass medium of communication, when baseball emerged fully as the national pastime and Babe Ruth was the slugging popular hero, of popular fads which swept across the land, when the automobile became widely known and courting made its shift from the parlor to the family car, when Charles A. Lindbergh made his solo flight in "The Spirit of St. Louis" across the Atlantic and became a national hero, of land and building booms, of "bears" and "bulls" on the stock market, of popular evangelists such as Billy Sunday and of the sex gospel according to Sigmund Freud, of intellectual alienation, of unbridled enthusiasm for a stock market on which stocks rose higher and higher and some proclaimed that what goes up doesn't necessarily have to come down.

That is, however, to overstate both the contrasts of the era and the extent of the change. It focuses, also, too much on the young and new and not nearly enough on that which endured and had yet been little touched by modern technology. Many farmers who took their first ride in someone else's automobile in the 1920s still went places in buggies or wagons as a rule. Though the refrigerator did begin to become a fairly common household possession for those who had electricity, and houses in cities and towns commonly had running water and indoor plumbing, many millions of Americans still drew or pumped their water from wells and made do with more primitive facilities. Some still lived in hand-hewn log cabins, though they were now becoming scarce. Nor did most Americans abandon the old ways overnight or become worldly irreligious people in imitation of some latest fashion. The attachment to the United States Constitution as it was written still widely prevailed, even in the courts, and the voters elected Presidents who affirmed the virtue of hard work, thrift, and service to others. Neighborliness and helping of others in need was very much alive, especially in rural and small town America.

Indeed, the writing of history in 20th-century America has been far too much influenced by journalism. Journalism focuses upon the unique, the different, even the singular, the abnormal, and that which is reckoned to be newsworthy. This often results in a quite distorted picture of what was actually going on at the time. For no period is this more likely to be the case than the 1920s, when the most popular and probably most influential account of the decade was written by journalist Frederick Lewis Allen, though he was not primarily a newspaperman. The matter has been further complicated by the fact that so many of the intellectuals, who had a considerable impact on forming opinion, were alienated from mainstream America in the 1920s (even more so than usual). If they did not hate America, they certainly took a jaundiced view of what was happening in the country. Their views and their rejection has very much colored historical accounts, nowhere more than in the accounts of politics and the economy.

For example, a recent book on the Harding years, begins with these words in the "Preface":

> The decade of the 1920s offers the American historian an excellent opportunity for . . . reevaluation and reinterpretation. Too long has this period been viewed simply as a deplorable interim between the Progressive Era and the New Deal. Too frequently has it been the subject of superficial judgments and cliche-ridden condemnation. Although exciting nostalgia, the frivolity and the ballyhoo of the twenties have normally been used to prove the decade's utter bankruptcy, and this shallow image of the period has remained to the present day.[228]

And a biographer of Warren G. Harding has observed about the tarnished reputation of his subject that "For the most part his prevailing image has been formed from the journalistic impressions of William Allen White, Mark Sullivan, and Samuel Hopkins Adams, and so thoroughly accepted by scholars that it has hardly been worth while to pursue the image further. Here was a puppet [they imply], a handsome straw man with a rhetorical voice and empty head, taken from a small Ohio town by a set of curious chances to the United States Senate, and finally propelled into the presidency by a cabal of reactionary senators and the oil interests."[229] That these are grotesque distortions should—but probably do not—go without saying.

For these reasons, it may help to get the other developments into better perspective by examining first the mood of the intellectuals, who contributed so much to the distortions.

The Alienation of the Intellectuals

Many, if not most, of the most prominent intellectuals in America in the 1920s were alienated from their fellow Americans. They rejected an American culture which they despised and denounced, the prevailing political, religious, economic, and social patterns of the American people. Beyond that, many went on to extend their hatred to the Western Civilization from which America had sprung. "Never in all history," as one literary critic said, "did a literary generation so revile its country. . . . Fundamentally, of course, they were in their different ways all enemies of the conventional middle-class order, enemies of convention and Puritanism, members of the 'civilized minority,' rebels against all that conspired to keep down the values of art and thought."[230] They not only debunked the past, but all who dwelled therein. They had come out of World War I, as F. Scott Fitzgerald said, "to find all gods dead, all wars fought, all faiths in man shaken. . . ."[231].

Portrait by Luis Quintanilla

Ernest Hemingway (1899–1961)

Hemingway was an American novelist and short story writer. He was born in Illinois, attended public school, and became a reporter after high school. During World War I, he served with an ambulance unit attached to the Italian army and was severely wounded in 1918. After the war, he became a reporter once again and became a foreign correspondent in Paris in 1921. Hemingway was eventually the best known and most successful of the writers who became expatriates in Europe in the 1920s. He learned the terse style of writing as a newspaperman which became his hallmark as a short-story writer and novelist. There was at least some autobiographical content to his early novels. Those of the 1920s told of Americans in Europe; and those of the 1930s indicated his socialist leanings, and the most famous, *For Whom the Bell Tolls*, dealt with the Spanish Civil War. A recurring theme in his works is that of the individual trying to rise above the obstacles that he encounters.

Some of the alienated, especially literary people, became voluntary exiles from America. Paris was the chosen place for budding authors because Paris was an artistic center, where art and innovation were supposed to be appreciated. Thither came Ernest Hemingway, F. Scott Fitzgerald, Ford Madox Ford, and others. They gathered at the salon of Gertrude Stein or Sylvia Beach's bookstore, Shakespeare and Company. In Paris, they talked art and literature, and wrote novels or poetry which depicted their world weariness and disillusion. Perhaps the best-known novels to come out of this experience was Fitzgerald's *This Side of Paradise* and Hemingway's *The Sun Also Rises*. Others came to Paris only briefly, if at all, but went to other countries to settle. For example, T.S. Eliot, whose poem, *The Waste Land*, which became the spiritual guide for those whom Gertrude Stein referred to as the "Lost Generation," settled in England. Sherwood Anderson spent only about a year in Europe, and Ezra Pound, an influential poet, settled in Italy. These were all more or less expatriates from the United States.

But while the expatriates expressed their alienation in an extreme form, they neither started the assault on things American nor carried out the most vigorous criticism. The spirit of alienation was early expressed by Sherwood Anderson, whose most enduring work, *Winesburg, Ohio*, was published in 1919. Sinclair Lewis got the whole thing under way with the publication of a novel, *Main Street*, in 1920. It depicted the life in small town America as dreary, the towns as ugly, and the people as prejudiced and vulgar. The book was a best seller and had sold 390,000 copies within two years. He followed it with *Babbitt*, a businessman, a hustler, a back slapper, and a paragon of what he no doubt thought of as middle-class vices. Lewis described his notion of the ordinary businessman this way: He "votes the Republican ticket straight, he hates all labor unionism, he belongs to the Masons and the Presbyterian Church, his favorite author is Zane Grey. . . . He is a bagman. He is a pedlar. He is a shopkeeper. He is a camp-follower. He is a bag of aggressive wind."[232]

It was H. L. Mencken, however, who set the pace for criticism of things American. He did so in essays usually, appearing sometimes in little magazines which he edited: *The American Mercury* and *Smart Set*, on which George Jean Nathan served as co-editor. Mencken deplored the prevailing conformity in America, declaring that in "no other country in the world is there so short a way with dissenters; in none other is it socially so costly to heed the inner voice and to be one's own man."[233] Americans seem to have a positive love of ugliness, he proclaimed. "Their towns are bedaubed with chromatic eyesores and made hideous with flashing lights; their countryside is polluted; their newspapers and magazines become mere advertising sheets; idiotic slogans and apothegms are invented to enchant them. . . ."[234] Mencken loathed democracy in general and American democracy in particular. American democracy, he claimed, oppresses the individual by making myriad laws to protect him from himself: prohibition to keep him from drowning himself in drink, censorship to stay his urges for pornography and Communist literature, and laws governing the transport of women over state lines lest the irrepressible brute come out and drag some helpless maiden away. "Democracy," Mencken said, "is also a form of religion. It is the worship of jackals by jackasses."[235] As for religion itself, "Save in a few large cities, every American community lies under a sacerdotal despotism . . . , a despotism exercised by a body of ignorant, superstitious, self-seeking and thoroughly dishonest men."[236]

Mencken's arrogance, iconoclasm, and irreverence sometimes brought forth righteous indignation worthy of him. One woman wrote, "The exile of Henry Mencken among us ignorant, naive Americans is a tragedy of modern letters. Self-condemned to this unhappy existence by his own decision, and not by our insistence, he continues to afford us the unparalleled spectacle of his supreme condescension."[237]

Mencken wrote with broad strokes, bringing almost everything about the America of the 1920s under condemnation. Others were somewhat more selective. The business motif of the period brought out their ire most commonly. James Truslow Adams, for example, wrote of America in the 1920s as *Our Business Civilization*. "America already has," he said, "probably the lowest grade mental life of any of the great nations."[238] This

Sinclair Lewis (1885–1951)

Sinclair Lewis

Lewis was an American journalist, satirist, and novelist. He gained fame as a novelist with the publication of *Main Street* in 1920, and added to it with *Babbitt* in 1922. Although Lewis did not belong to that clique of writers who left the United States for Paris in the 1920s, he was one of them in spirit with his critical attitude toward American life. His talent ran to satire and exaggeration, however, rather than to what are usually thought of as serious novels. He satirized the medical profession in *Arrowsmith*, evangelists in *Elmer Gantry*, and wrote 22 novels in all, as well as many stories for popular magazines. He was born in Minnesota, graduated from Yale, and served his literary apprenticeship as a reporter. His characters were more successful as stereotypes than as fully developed individuals.

he ascribed to the focus on material well-being and the thirst for man-ufactured products. Writing in 1931, Frederick Lewis Allen declared that "the typical American of the old stock had never had more than a half-hearted enthusiasm for the rights of the minority; bred in a pioneer tradition, he had been accustomed to set his community in order by the first means that came to hand—a sumptuary law, a vigilance committee, or if necessary a shotgun."[239] George F. Nieberg, in an article in *The Forum*, also in 1931, held "that it is impossible" for "the typical American citizen . . . to live like a civilized man, as it is impossible for him to die like one." More, "his blind unwavering faith in 'success' stories, patent medicines, political platforms, his bootleggers' word of honor, and his boss's stupidity borders upon fanatical fervor."

Katherine F. Gerould may have topped them all in the denunciation of Americans, in an article in *Harper's*, when she explained the alleged popularity of the gangster, Al Capone: "It is not because Capone is different that he takes the imagination: it is because he is so gorgeously and typically American. . . . Of course he was born in this country: could anyone but a native American have adopted so whole-heartedly American principles of action? An immigrant would have taken years to assimilate our ideals; whereas Capone was born to them. . . . There are analogies for Al Capone among the American immortals."[240] In a more general vein, Henry S. Canby calls attention to an aspect of the writing of the major novelists of the 1920s: to the "dogged discontent of Ernest Hemingway, the mystic morbid discontent of William Faulkner, the strong lyric discontent of Willa Cather, the sharp scoffing discontent of Sinclair Lewis. . . ."[241]

Undoubtedly, the above views of America were simplistic, hardly imbued with the great traditions that had informed America, were completely out of sympathy with the Judeo-Christian heritage, were more than a little cock-eyed, however sincerely they may have been written. But right, wrong, or off center, the continued assault on America and its antecedent civilization had an impact. It filtered into the minds of a generation of intellectuals and set the more earnest among them on the quest for a faith. Whittaker Chambers, who went to Columbia University as a student in 1920, went on to join the Communist Party, to become deeply involved in subversive activities as a Communist agent, and after World War II, confessed to his betrayal of his country, has recounted how his student days prepared the way for his later behavior.

Chambers says that when he came to the campus at Columbia, there were no warning signs "that the path was to lead me toward Communism." Indeed, "No member of the Columbia faculty ever consciously guided me toward Communism." Instead, "It was liberalism [the 20th century variety] I was about to encounter . . . , liberalism (both in the honest meaning of that word and in its current sense as a cover-name for socialism) that . . . was about to work on my immature and patchwork beliefs."[242] It was

to cut away what he had of religious beliefs or faith in God, turn his mind
into a vacuum in which there were no certainties, give him a skeptical
attitude toward his culture and civilization, and leave him without rudder or
guide for life. Chambers was primarily interested in literature at the time, or
at least studying it, and most likely the continuing assault on things
American in contemporary writing had its impact. In any case, as he says,
"Columbia did not teach me Communism. It taught me despair. . . . It was
a feeling of despair, not always explicit and seldom definite, but running
like a wistful theme through any view of life that was not merely practically
ambitious. It was the sense of historical sundown, the sense that man had
reached one of the great jumping-off places—or what was worse, a place
where it was impossible to jump because it was the end."[243]

Then, as Chambers says, "Into this vacuum, sprang something which
was waiting just around the corner—something what at first I had no way of
identifying, but which I presently learned was Marxism." In Communism,
Whittaker Chambers found a faith to replace the one he had lost, a hope to
lead him out of despair, and new certainties in a vision of history according
to Marx. In fact, he had found a new religion. As Benjamin Gitlow, who
was himself one until he saw the error of that path, said of American
Communists:

> The Russian Revolution meant . . . a communism that fitted into a
> spiritual vacuum and replaced for them the hold that religion had on
> the spiritual yearnings of ordinary human beings. Communists, to be
> understood, must be taken as human beings to whom commu-
> nism . . . , is a religion to which they adhere fanatically like dogmatic
> religious zealots. But the communist, unlike a religious person, bases
> his conduct on the abnegation of religious influences on life. In the
> communist there is substituted the complete submission of the in-
> dividual to the materialistic, anti-religious philosophy and to the power
> of the Communist party over his life.[244]

Most Americans, whether intellectuals or not, did not become Communists, either in the 1920s or afterward. Some did; most did not. However,
a goodly number of intellectuals were increasingly attracted toward the
Communist experiment in Russia from the late 1920s onward through the
1930s. They shifted from the hopelessness of the alleged Lost Generation
toward a hope in the possibilities of social reconstruction. After Stalin
launched his first Five-Year Plan in 1928, intellectuals were drawn toward
the idea of a planned economy, not necessarily to full-fledged communism
but to the application of the idea in their own lands. Even those who had
never lost hope in the gradual route to socialism through piece-meal reform,
got new hope, amidst their discouragement with prospects for reform in the
1920s, from what was going on in Russia. According to one historian,

leaders in social thought came "to regard the Soviet Union as a model of the experimental method in social practice. The whole conception of a 'social experiment,' the whole notion of planned human intervention into social processes to raise the welfare of the people, had become linked in the minds of America's intellectual and social leaders with the practice of the Soviet Union."[245] He attributed this attitude largely to the reports of intellectuals who traveled to the Soviet Union in the 1920s and early 1930s and published glowing reports about what was going on there.

A careful student of the influence of communism on Americans held that "The fact is that American liberals were . . . dazzled by the idea of 'planning'. . . . Nearly every college professor, poet, social worker, engineer or schoolboy who returned from Russia brought [reports] . . . to swell the shiny mountain of self–deception. The more articulate wrote books."[246]

Among the travelers to the Soviet Union during this period were John Dewey, Rexford G. Tugwell, Paul Douglas, Stuart Chase, Jane Addams, Robert M. La Follette, Maxwell S. Stewart, George Soule, and Edmund Wilson. Of the considerable published material to come out of these trips, the following is a sampling: John Dewey, *Impressions of Soviet Russia*, Sherwood Eddy, *The Challenge of Russia*, George S. Counts, *The Soviet Challenge to America*, Charles A. Beard, "The Rationality of a Planned Economy" (not from one of the travelers), Rexford G. Tugwell, "The Principle of Planning and the Institution of Laissez-Faire," and Maxwell S. Stewart, "Where Everyone Has a Job."

The impact of the Soviet experiment on American thinkers may come out more clearly from a few quotations. The New York *Times* declared that Stalin's first Five-Year Plan was the "most extraordinary enterprise in the economic history of the world."[247] Stuart Chase proclaimed that it was "exciting, stimulating, challenging."[248] John Dewey said of the Soviet undertaking, "In some respects, it is already a searching spiritual challenge as it is an economic challenge to coordinate and plan."[249] "Why," asked Stuart Chase, "should Russians have all the fun in remaking a world?"[250] George Soule said, "We could not assimilate the hard dogmas . . . of Marxism . . . , but we were irresistibly attracted by the idea of planned use of modern industrial technique."

These enthusiasms were bred out of what had to be superficial understandings of people favorably inclined to put the best face on what they saw and heard. Of course, they went only where the Communist leaders wanted them to go and usually saw only what they were supposed to see. Not only were they shielded from the totalitarian practices, but neither they nor people in general had yet been apprised fully of the terrorism on which compliance with the system is based. The slave labor camps were not on their itinerary, nor was the persecution of kulaks and proprietors of small businesses yet a matter of common knowledge.

At any rate, they popularized the notion of a planned economy in what were often ecstatic terms, and the above views provided a part of the backdrop for the New Deal ventures in planning. But these attitudes of intellectuals were told at this point to make it clear why the commonly published views of the 1920s in America were so distorted. Academic intellectuals, who despised Harding and Coolidge and have identified with the alienation of the intellectuals, have generally written the histories. Reformers were disgruntled that they could not continue the Progressive thrust, and those who did not agree with them had somehow to be discredited. Hence, the exaggerations and distortions that have been set forth as history about the 1920s.

Republicans in Power

The Republicans completed the return to control of the government in 1920 that had begun in the Congressional elections two years before. Warren G. Harding won a landslide victory over the Democratic candidate for President, James M. Cox. The Republicans now had overwhelming majorities in both houses of Congress. Viewed from a broad perspective, they were continuing a dominance which had begun during the Civil War and would not definitively come to an end until 1932. It was a Republican Party, too, which by 1920 had been largely purged of the reform impetus which had been in it before the war. There were still some Progressives from the Midwest and West in Congress who were elected as Republicans, but they had now become a small dissident minority.

1. The Harding Administration

Warren G. Harding was a handsome, genial, and kindly man who had gained prominence in state politics in Ohio, now beginning to replace Virginia as the mother of Presidents. His loyal support of the unpopular President Taft in 1912 brought him into national politics and started him on the way to the presidency in 1920. Harding was neither innovator nor reformer; rather, he sought to be a harmonizer, one who unified and drew people together. He had said during the campaign that America needed to return to "normalcy," by which he meant not only peace after the late war but also an end to those disturbances which come from attempting to make drastic changes by legislation. In his inaugural address, Harding said: "Our supreme task is the resumption of our onward normal way. Reconstruction, readjustment, restoration—all these must follow. I would like to hasten them." His harmonizing inclination appears, too, in this admonition in the address: "The supreme inspiration is the commonweal. . . . My most reverent prayer for America is for industrial peace, with its rewards, widely and generally distributed, amid the inspirations of equal opportunity."[251]

Warren G. Harding
(1865–1923)

Courtesy Library of Congress

Harding was the 29th President of the United States. He was born in Ohio, attended Ohio Central College, taught school for a year, and went into newspaper work. In 1884, he purchased a newspaper and made it the leading paper in Marion, Ohio. Had he not become involved in Republican politics, Harding might well have finished his career as a small-town editorial writer and publisher. It was the sort of work he liked best. But he became involved in Ohio politics as a Republican in 1900, and thereafter rose by stages to the highest office in the land. He served first in the Ohio senate, then as lieutenant governor, but failed in his one attempt to become governor. In 1914, Harding was elected to the United States Senate, and before his first term expired he was elected President. His executive experience had been quite limited in scale, and that made the presidency more of a trial to him than it might otherwise have been.

In the selection of a cabinet, Harding chose some men who were already well known, and others from his own circle of acquaintances, as Presidents frequently do. He named Charles E. Hughes as Secretary of State. Hughes had been the Republican candidate for President in 1916, was believed to be more of a Progressive than not, and was generally well liked in reformist circles. Herbert Hoover became Secretary of Commerce and elevated that office to greater prominence than it has generally enjoyed. Hoover had voted for Theodore Roosevelt in 1912, acquired a reputation as a humanitarian in his efforts for Belgian relief in World War I, served as Wilson's Food Administrator, but appeared more conservative than not in the 1920s. Andrew Mellon, an industrialist, was the choice for Secretary of the Treasury, and he continued in that post for the succeeding two Presidents. Harry M. Daugherty, an aspiring political figure from Ohio, was Attorney General. Daugherty was plagued by controversy and criticism, some of it engineered by senatorial Progressives, and was eventually hounded out of office after Harding's death. Harding did not live to regret the appointment of Albert B. Fall as Secretary of the Interior, but had he lived he might have regretted, for Fall was eventually convicted of taking bribes.

It fell to Harding's lot to appoint four justices of the Supreme Court, which must have been a record for a man who lived to serve only two-and-a-half years in the presidency. He appointed William Howard Taft as Chief Justice, and George Sutherland, Pierce Butler, and E. T. Sanford as associate justices. These new appointees, along with two earlier appointees, James McReynolds and Willis Van Devanter provided an assured majority for conservative principles generally, for they were all men in the American judicial tradition, respectful of precedent and toward the Constitution itself. Taft had observed just before going on the Supreme Court that it was important that it should be "a bulwark to enforce the guarantee that no man shall be deprived of his property without due process of law." They probably agreed with President Coolidge, too, when he declared that the pressing question "is whether America will allow itself to be degraded into a communistic and socialistic state, or whether it will remain American."[252] Holmes, Brandeis, and after his appointment in 1925, Justice Harlan F. Stone, were usually the dissenters during the decade. Their dissents were more often quoted in the following liberal years than the majority opinions.

True to his promise, Harding did proceed to restore some measure of normality to American public life. Although he had not been an all-out opponent of membership in the League of Nations when he was in the Senate, he did not propose to revive the notion once he was in the White House. The League was no longer an issue, he thought, and other than professing belief in some sort of undefined association of nations, he maintained that the United States ought to follow its traditional independent course in world affairs. "Confident of our ability to work out our own destiny and jealously guarding our right to do so, we seek no part in directing the destinies of the Old World," Harding said. "We do not mean to be entangled. We will accept no responsibility except as our own conscience and judgment may determine."[253] Secretary of State Hughes worked out treaties with the defeated nations along the lines of the Congressional Resolution ending World War I.

That is not to suggest that the United States isolated itself from Europe or the rest of the world in the 1920s, as was often alleged. On the contrary, both the Harding and Coolidge administration were often much involved in international matters. The United States hosted the Washington Naval Conference of naval powers in 1921. The representatives of the countries agreed to reduce their efforts at shipbuilding and that in total tonnage of capital ships they would observe a ratio expressed in this way: Great Britain 5; United States 5; Japan 3; France 1.7; and Italy 1.7. This agreement did not extend to warships smaller than battleships and dreadnoughts, but some agreement was reached on these at the London Naval Conference in 1928, in which the United States also participated. Ill feelings on the part of

Colombia were finally soothed by a payment of indemnities by the United States to that country for the loss of Panama. Harding worked earnestly to bring the United States into the World Court, whether for good or ill, and progress was made in that direction. So far as the League of Nations was concerned, Americans attended numerous League-sponsored conferences during the 1920s.

On the other hand, the United States did take two important measures to insulate itself in some degree from the world at large. One was the Fordney-McCumber Tariff of 1922. The Republicans had a long history of favoring a protective tariff, and this act was highly protectionist in character. Indeed, it was generally the highest tariff that had been enacted to

Charles Evans Hughes (1862–1948)

Courtesy Library of Congress

Hughes was a lawyer, jurist, and Republican politician. He was born in New York state, graduated from Brown University, and took his law degree at Columbia. In addition to practicing law over a period of more than two decades, he lectured on the law at universities. In 1906, Hughes was elected governor of New York and re-elected after that for another two-year term. Although he was a Republican, he was very much a reformer with progressive tendencies at that time. Taft appointed him to the Supreme Court as an associate justice in 1910, but in 1916 he resigned to make an unsuccessful run for the presidency as the Republican nominee. Harding appointed him Secretary of State in 1921. He tended to take a middle of the road position between the reform and conservative position from this time forward. For example, he favored joining the League of Nations with reservations and favored the United States joining the World Court. In 1925, he resigned from the State Department to resume the practice of law. Hughes served briefly as a judge on the Permanent Court of International Justice until Hoover appointed him Chief Justice of the Supreme Court in 1930.

that time. The rates were especially high on dyes, chemicals, chinaware and imitation jewelry, and wool and sugar, among other farm products, were protected. This tariff posed special problems for America's allies during World War I, who had heavy war debts. Despite protests from the countries involved, the United States insisted throughout the 1920s that payments should be made on the debts. Yet the main means for doing so was by their selling more to the United States than they bought. The Fordney-McCumber Tariff made that more difficult to do. The act did contain a provision which permitted some flexibility in its administration. A Tariff Commission had been authorized in 1916, and by this new provision the President could raise or lower particular rates up to 50 percent on recommendation of the commission. With only a few exceptions, this provision was used by presidents in the 1920s to raise rates.

The other insulating measure was the establishing of highly restrictive immigration quotas. Concern about immigration had been increasing since the 1890s, even as the tide of immigrants from southern and eastern Europe mounted. Labor unions had long been opposed to the importing of immigrant labor, though the more radical unions especially did not take that position in the 20th century. There was concern in some quarters that the very religious and cultural character of the population of the United States would be changed by the New Immigration if it were not halted. The influx of radicals added to this worry, especially after the Bolshevik Revolution and the postwar thrust to spread revolution. Communists were led almost exclusively by the foreign born in this country. A revived Ku Klux Klan gave added impetus to attempts at staunching the influx of immigrants. The Klan was especially strong in the South and Midwest, wielded great influence on political parties, mainly the Democratic Party, and was anti-Catholic, anti-Jewish, suspicious of foreigners in general, and opposed to revolutionists.

The initial approach toward immigration restriction (except for Orientals, who were already virtually excluded) was the literacy test. Earlier attempts by Congress to impose a literacy test on prospective immigrants were turned back by presidential vetos. However, Congress overrode a veto by President Wilson in 1917, and the literacy test began to be used. Even so, immigrants from Europe began pouring in again after World War I. An emergency measure was passed in 1921 establishing quotas, but the provisions of this act were refined and a much more definitive National Origins Act was passed in 1924. The immigrants from a country in any given year were to be restricted to 2 percent of the residents who had come from that country based on the 1890 census. In 1927, the total immigration per year was to be restricted to 150,000, and the number who could come in from any one country was restricted to the proportion of those in the United States from that nation in 1920 to the total population of the country. This formula favored northern Europeans over those from southern and eastern Europe.

Andrew W. Mellon (1855–1937)

Courtesy National Gallery of Art. Gift of Ailsa Mellon Bruce

Mellon was a banker, an industrialist, and Secretary of the Treasury from 1921–1932, serving under three Republican Presidents. His appointment has often been taken as symbolic of the pro-business posture of the Harding and Coolidge administrations, and there is no doubt that he was a leader in the administrations in which he served. Mellon was born in Pittsburgh, studied at what became the University of Pittsburgh, and entered his father's banking business. He dealt successfully with many of the fiscal problems confronting the United States after World War I. At the Treasury he worked to reduce the debt, to reduce taxes, and to encourage private investment, which he held was essential to prosperity. His efforts to get foreign countries to make regular payments on their debts were less successful. In 1932 he left the Treasury to become American ambassador to England.

For example, one calculation indicated that 65,721 persons could immigrate to the United States from Great Britain and Ireland in a year, but only 5,802 from Italy. Other American countries were not subject to these restrictions.

The Harding administration tried to provide a favorable atmosphere for capital accumulation, investment, and production in the country. One of Secretary of the Treasury Mellon's high priorities was to reduce the high wartime tax level. He argued that "High rates tend to destroy individual initiative and seriously impede the development of productive business. Taxpayers subject to the higher rates," he said, "are withdrawing their capital from productive business and investing it instead in tax exempt securities. . . . The result is to stop business transactions . . . and to discourage men of wealth from taking risks. . . ."[254] He managed to get the excess profits tax removed in 1921, but was less successful in getting other rates reduced. The maximum income surtax was reduced from 65 to 50 percent, though Mellon had recommended 40 percent. The tax on corporation income was even raised slightly. Mellon had to wait until 1924 to get something more in accord with what he wanted. While much of the government regulatory machinery remained in place, Harding generally appointed men to boards and commissions who were understanding of the need for capital investment and profit. The government practiced economy rigorously and reduced expenditures over what they had been earlier.

By the beginning of spring in 1923 the Harding efforts at calming the waters and restoring "normalcy" were apparently bearing fruit. Harding had come to office in the midst of a postwar business and agricultural depression. The credit expansion that had fueled the glow of wartime prosperity, the huge orders from Europe for war materials and food, were winding down. For the year and a half before Harding had come to office, President Wilson had been at best a part-time President, and much of the time he had been so incapacitated that he could not make public appearances or see hardly anyone. Radical disturbances and widespread strikes had further disturbed the country. So many constitutional and legal changes had been made during Wilson's eight years that the country was still struggling to absorb them.

Harding must have been a welcome relief from the dour and now truculent Wilson. It was good to have a vigorous and outgoing man in the White House, and one clearly intent on smoothing rather than ruffling feathers. Two major strikes in 1922 did disturb the tranquility of some regions, at least, if not the whole country. The shopmen went on a prolonged strike against the railroads, and a large portion of the coal miners went on strike. The President had only limited constitutional authority to become involved in labor disputes except in cases of interference with interstate commerce or, in cases of disorder, when called upon by the states to send troops. However, railroads were not only generally engaged in interstate commerce but also the federal government had claimed a leading role by establishing a Railway Labor Board. In any case, Harding, true to the general tenor of his administration, used his office to promote peaceful settlements between the unions and management. When this failed, he admonished the companies to proceed with those who would work in the coal mines, urged the state governments to use their power to protect those who wanted to work, and promised Federal troops on call from the states. When neither negotiation nor protection of workers brought an end to the strikes, Attorney General Daugherty went into court in Illinois and got a sweeping injunction against striking rail workers. Before the end of 1922, both rail and coal strikes had substantially ended.

By the spring of 1923, these difficulties were in the past. Readjustments to the postwar deflation had been made; business had recovered, and if farmers had not regained their wartime prosperity, prosperity was becoming general once again. Harding had two years experience as President, and he was generally popular. He liked the pomp, ceremony, and prominence of the presidency from the beginning, but he had been almost overwhelmed by the workload of the office. His prior administrative experience had been quite limited, and he was not used to the continual claims on his time, the making of hard decisions of such import, nor the need for so much firmness in asserting his authority. But during the second year he became more assertive and firmer and was coming much closer to taking the work in his stride.

In March of 1923, Attorney General Daugherty announced that Harding would be a candidate for reelection the next year. The announcement was generally well received; his renomination appeared to be certain; only La Follette was even reckoned to oppose him, and the chances looked good that he would be reelected.

However, Harding complained of tiredness regularly and needed rest continually. He was known to be developing high blood pressure, and in view of his death later in the year, heart trouble may have been a major source of his tiredness. In any case, a cross country train trip and voyage to Alaska was planned for the summer. It would take him away from the strains of Washington, allow him to mend political fences by a series of addresses along the way, and would give him an on the spot opportunity to come to some sort of conclusion for reorganization of departmental control of relations with the territory of Alaska.

The speaking trip across America was a success. The crowds were enthusiastic; Harding was an accomplished orator; and he presented a convincing picture of the achievements and goals of his administration. He got sick, however, on the return trip from Alaska, and by the time he reached San Francisco his condition was critical. He died in San Francisco of what the physicians described as apoplexy—either a stroke or heart attack, or both. Harding was at the peak of his popularity, and the country was shocked and saddened at his sudden death. As the train carrying his body made its way on the long journey from San Francisco to Washington, crowds gathered along the tracks or the stations to view the coffin through the window of his train and to pay an often tearful last farewell to a generally beloved man. The crowds were so great at Chicago that the train could only move at a snail's pace in and out of the station. After the body had lain in state in the White House, it had once again to be loaded on the train for return to burial in his hometown of Marion, Ohio.

Secretary of State Hughes wrote to a friend shortly after Harding's death: "I cannot bring myself to speak of the tragic experience through which we have been; I cannot realize that our beloved Chief is no longer with us." Herbert Hoover told a gathering of engineers: "When he came into responsibility as President he faced unprecedented problems of domestic rehabilitation. It was a time when war-stirred emotions had created bitter prejudices and conflict in thought. Kindly and genial, but inflexible in his devotion to duty, he was strong in his determination to restore confidence and secure progress. All this he accomplished through patient conciliation and friendly good will for he felt deeply that hard driving might open unhealable breaches among our people. We have all benefited by the success of his efforts.''[255]

2. Scandals

But high reputation and public expressions of admiration were short lived for Warren G. Harding. The political buzzards were gathering even before his death, and they succeeded in blackening his reputation and obscuring his achievements by the time they had done with picking at what remained. If Harding had lived to serve for two terms, it is quite possible that his achievements might have so overshadowed any revelations about the deeds or misdeeds of some of those under him that he would have been accounted one of the more able Presidents of the United States. As it was, his death only a little more than midway through his only term opened the way for Congressional committees to have a field day with exposes about some doings during that brief period.

There were three scandals, of sorts, which were brought into the limelight after Harding's death: some profiteering in the Veteran's Bureau, the one called the Teapot Dome Affair, and the selling of influence by people more or less associated with Attorney General Daugherty. Of the three principals in these affairs, two were no longer associated with the government at the time of Harding's death, and the third had committed suicide earlier in the year following a confrontation with Harding.

The first of these affairs to come to light had to do with misdeeds in the Veteran's Bureau, headed by Charles Forbes. Harding had appointed Forbes to this post, though others, including Attorney General Daugherty, were not enthusiastic about it. But Forbes was a highly decorated veteran of World War I and had some experience which helped to qualify him for the job. Rumors of improper behavior in the Bureau were brought to Harding's attention in 1922, and he asked Daugherty to investigate quietly. The Attorney General reported that Forbes was involved in crooked deals, such as selling government-owned hospital supplies far below cost and making undercover deals with contractors. Harding dealt with Forbes in his own way. He called him in, denounced him and probably his ancestors, and told him to get out of town, if not out of the country. Forbes booked passage to Europe and submitted his resignation An associate of Forbes committed suicide shortly afterward.

In the light of revelations in a Congressional investigation after the death of Harding, the situation at the Veteran's Bureau might better have been handled differently. If Daugherty had sufficient evidence of fraud and bribery at the time, he might have sought an indictment of Forbes by a grand jury. At any rate, the investigation begun in late 1923 revealed that there had been extensive wrongdoing in the Veteran's Bureau, and Forbes and the alien property custodian were convicted and sentenced to Federal prison.

Harding, or Daugherty, may have made an error of judgment, or tried to dispose of the affair too hastily.

The Teapot Dome Affair, as it came to be called, was limited to the taking of a bribe by one government official, so far as any wrongdoing was concerned. It was blown up to broader scandalous proportions by conservationists and Progressives who did not approve the policies of the Harding administration. The facts are reasonably clear. Oil reserves at Teapot Dome in Wyoming and Elk Hills in California were set aside for future use by the Navy during the Taft and Wilson administrations. This was more a reflex of the Progressive drive to have the government hold on to mineral resources than anything else. These reserves were under the control of the Department of the Navy until 1921. In that year, by agreement between Secretary of the Interior Albert B. Fall, and Naval Secretary Edwin L. Denby, Harding moved the reserves from Navy to Interior. It was within Harding's authority to do this, and it fitted a pattern of what he worked to do: to reorganize departments so as to remove duplication of activities. Subsequently, Fall managed to lease Teapot Dome to Harry Sinclair and Elk Hills to Edward Doheny, both private oil operators. This was done without fanfare, though Harding was informed. The main reason given for this action was that the oil might be drained away by oil developers on the periphery of the reserves, and the government would lose some of the reserve, at least, without compensation. Shortly after the letting of the last of these leases, Fall resigned from his cabinet position and retired to private life. At the time, there was no hint of any wrongdoing or scandal. However, during the following year or so, observers noted that Fall, who was supposed to be having financial difficulties, was spending rather freely.

Senator Thomas Walsh headed the committee which began a vigorous investigation into Teapot Dome and other oil land deals in the fall of 1923. The committee eventually focused on the question of whether or not Fall had been bribed to deliver the leases. In the investigations, it came out that Fall had indeed received sums of money from the oil men. He was eventually convicted of accepting bribes and sentenced to prison. Sinclair and Doheny were not convicted for bribing, though they were tried, but the oil leases were revoked. Although Denby was not implicated in the bribery at all, he was hounded out of office under Coolidge, who had kept Harding's cabinet.

The other scandal involved people who had been associated with Attorney General Daugherty, and a determined effort was made against Daugherty, led by Senator Burton K. Wheeler. Daugherty had been the closest of all the cabinet members to Harding, was his confidant, and most frequent adviser. Both men were from Ohio, and Harding had come to depend on him. Daugherty had aroused the wrath of the more vigorous supporters of labor unions in Congress in 1922 by the sweeping injunction he obtained against the railway strikers. An attempt was made to impeach him then, but it never got off the ground. However, as a result of the Congressional investigation following Harding's death, Coolidge was finally persuaded to remove him from his cabinet post.

There were several in the "Ohio gang" of influence peddlers who gathered in Washington after the election of Harding, but Jess Smith was the one with the most prominent connections. Smith was close to Daugherty, operated out of the Justice Department at times, and played poker from time to time with the President. Indeed, he had been on the original list to accompany Harding—be among the entourage—on the ill-fated Alaskan trip. Harding, however, had got word of the possibly illegal activities in which Smith was involved, and asked Daugherty to get him out of Washington and back to Ohio. Daugherty did, but Smith returned to Washington shortly afterward. He went to see Harding and apparently came away from the interview in despair. In any case, Smith committed suicide in the wake of his visit with the President.

The Congressional investigations that occurred after both Smith's and the President's death revealed that there had been large-scale illegal activities conducted by Smith and others, such as the selling of permits to obtain large supplies of liquor (during Prohibition) and providing assorted government favors and access to those in government in return for fees. Although Daugherty was tried on charges of involvement in these crimes, he was not convicted. Over the years, he continued to maintain his innocence, and so far as it was ever proved, he was. He was, however, hounded from public office by investigations, but there remained suspicions that he had tried to cover up wrongdoing in which he was involved in one way or another.

After all this furor, the worst that could be said about President Harding was that he used bad judgment in one or two (among numerous) appointments and in selecting one or more of his friends. That his reputation should have been so badly tarnished by these wayward events does not speak well for historians who have generally downgraded his achievements and cast doubt upon his character and beliefs. He deserved better. It should be kept in mind, too, that revelations of corruption have followed both the Civil War and World War II, as well as World War I. Vastly expanded government increases the opportunity for the selling of government favors and places unusual burdens on those who have to make the appointments to the enlarged number of posts. The national prohibition on alcoholic beverages, while much of the demand for these drinks continued, led to widespread corruption of law enforcement officers. The alienation of the intellectuals from Harding's policies contributed to the impact of the revelations. Progressives were at the forefront in the making of the exposés. Only in recent years have major biographies appeared which have begun the difficult task of restoring Harding's reputation.

3. The Coolidge Administration

Republicans, and perhaps the country, was fortunate in the man who succeeded Harding to the presidency. Calvin Coolidge was a man with high moral standards and unquestioned public probity. While Harding's public statements were soothing and usually politic, the thread of principle that ran through his policies was often difficult to locate. Aside from his peaceful intentions, neither his foreign nor domestic policies had the bite of principles. Although Harding's administration is often classified as conservative, its mood was somewhat more progressive than that might suggest. By contrast, Coolidge was a man of clear-cut principle, and his principles were undoubtedly conservative. He believed most firmly in honesty, hard work, thrift, sacrifice, and service. He defended the economic system based on private profit (counterbalanced quite often by losses), repudiated socialism, and championed those sturdy virtues upon which American success had been built. In general, Coolidge did not think that government should intervene in the economy or lives of the people. "If the Federal Government should go out of existence," he said, "the common run of people would not detect the difference in the affairs of their daily life for a considerable length of time." Moreover, "The Government can do more to remedy the economic ills of the people by a system of rigid economy in public expenditure than can be accomplished through any other action."[256]

Calvin Coolidge (1872–1933)

Courtesy Library of Congress

Coolidge was born in Vermont, graduated from Amherst, and studied law with a law firm. Before long, he became involved in local politics in Massachusetts. He rose slowly but surely toward the top position in state politics: city solicitor in Northampton in 1900, clerk of the courts in 1904, elected to the state legislature in 1907, became mayor of Northampton in 1910, to the state senate afterward, became lieutenant governor of Massachusetts in 1916, and governor of the state in 1918. He came to national attention in the last position for his firm stand during the Boston police strike. With that base, he was nominated as the Republican candidate for Vice-President in 1920, elected along with Harding, and upon Harding's death in 1923, Coolidge became President. He always seemed to gain popularity in office, and this happened also in the presidency, to which he was elected to a term on his own in 1924.

Personally, the contrast between Harding and Coolidge could hardly have been greater. Harding was a tall, handsome man, outgoing, liked crowds and ceremony, a golfer and card player, and sensitive to the moods of those around him. Coolidge was short, wizened, taciturn, cryptic, preferred a nap to either company or vigorous exercise, sober, and not given to gaming. His dry wit and cryptic remarks were legendary, and he fancied his reputation for being a man of few words. A woman once approached him at a gathering who said that she had a bet with a friend that she could get him to say more than two words. "You lose," he said, and closed his mouth firmly.

For all the contrasts between the two men, the Coolidge administration was in many respects a continuation of Harding's. As already noted, he continued with Harding's cabinet, though Denby and Daugherty were later dropped. The coolness toward membership in the League of Nations was, if anything, intensified under Coolidge, but the basic policies on the tariff and other issues remained very much the same. Coolidge weathered the revelations in Congress smoothly, was not stampeded into any drastic action, and was not himself even remotely connected with any wrongdoing. His reputation for honesty was so unassailable that there was little electoral impact from the scandals.

Coolidge won the election in 1924 handily. The Democrats were so deeply split between William McAdoo and Alfred ("Al") Smith that it took over a hundred ballots to choose a candidate. McAdoo had greater support than Smith, a Roman Catholic and opponent of prohibition, but neither could get the necessary two-thirds needed at that time for nomination. A compromise candidate, John W. Davis of West Virginia was finally nominated as the Democratic candidate for President. Davis did not succeed very well in uniting the Democrats, nor did they adopt a platform crusading for reform, as they had done in some earlier elections. The election was thrown further out of kilter by the organization of an important third party, the Progressive Party. Its convention nominated Robert M. La Follette as its presidential candidate, and he was endorsed also by the Socialist and Farmer Labor parties. Its radicalism was apparent in the platform, which called for such things as government ownership of railroads and water power resources. Coolidge got 382 electoral votes to 136 for Davis, and 13 for La Follette. Both houses of Congress remained under Republican control.

True to his beliefs, Coolidge led an administration which practiced economy in government. For the last time in American history (to this date), significant reductions were made in the national debt. As a result of deficit spending during the war, the government had a large debt of $24 billion going into the 1920s. By 1930, the debt had been reduced to about $16 billion. This was accomplished by keeping spending well below government revenues. At the same time, however, taxes (except for the tariff) were significantly reduced. The surtax on personal income was reduced from a top rate of 40 percent to 20 percent by the Revenue Act of 1926. Estate taxes were similarly reduced, and gift taxes were abolished. Moreover, despite several rounds of tax reduction, revenues continued to provide a surplus. As President Coolidge said in 1928:

> Four times we have made a drastic revision of our internal revenue system, abolishing many taxes and substantially reducing almost all others. Each time the resulting stimulation to business has so increased taxable incomes and profits that a surplus has been produced.[257]

Coolidge did not ordinarily push for legislative enactments, and he certainly had no huge reform program. In the main, he worked to reduce the role of government in the economy. In one case of this, Coolidge's effort was a continuation from the Harding administration and overlapped into Hoover's early years. It was the issue of what to do with the nitrate plants and hydroelectric dam at Muscle Shoals, Alabama. Construction on these was begun during World War I, to provide nitrogen for munitions, but the dam was not completed until 1925. (It was named Wilson Dam, for Woodrow Wilson.) Once the war was over, the main use for the plants would be to make nitrates for fertilizer and for the dam to make and sell electricity. Since such activity by government would be socialistic, Harding moved to sell the operation to private investors. The only bidder was automaker Henry Ford, but Congress blocked the sale, spurred by the public power enthusiast, Senator George W. Norris of Nebraska. Norris had a vision of using these facilities as the base for a vast government power and reclamation project, and he labored throughout the 1920s to get support for such activities. In 1928, he got a measure through Congress for government operation of the project, but Coolidge killed it with a pocket veto. He got it through again in 1931, only to have it turned back by a ringing veto from Herbert Hoover. Hoover said, in part: ''I am firmly opposed to the Government entering into any business the major purpose of which is competition with our citizens. . . . There are many localities where the Federal Government is justified in the construction of great dams . . . where navigation [and] flood control . . . are of dominant importance . . . , But for the Federal Government deliberately to go out to build up and expand . . . a power and manufacturing business is to break down the initiative and enterprise of the people; it is destruction of equality of opportunity of our people; it is the negation of the ideals upon which our civilization has been based.''[258] That finished this plan until the advent of the New Deal.

The great white hope of farmer organizations in the 1920s was the McNary-Haugen bill. This bill was first brought up in 1924, was in that and ensuing sessions defeated in one or both houses of Congress, until it finally passed in 1927, only to be vetoed by Coolidge. It passed Congress once again in 1928, and Coolidge's veto stuck this time. The measure's significance is somewhat limited, since it never became law, but it was a forerunner of acts passed under the New Deal and a symbol of the continuing collectivist thrust of these years.

The drop in farm prices following World War I, and the declining foreign demand, set the stage for efforts to get the government to intervene on behalf of farmers. Actually, farm acreage and production had been greatly expanded under the spur of European demand during the war. That, plus machinery, fertilizers, and improved seed, enabled farmers to produce more of certain basic products than could be sold at a profit by many of the producers. There was little more reason for farmers to continue to produce at that level than there was for tank manufacturers to continue the high level of wartime production. Nor has there ever been much evidence that government intervention could do anything but aggravate the problem. The Intermediate Credit Act passed in 1922 might temporarily relieve the financial situation of some farmers, but its long-term impact would be to increase production and further lower prices. The Fordney-McCumber Tariff could not protect farmers from world market prices, when they sold on foreign markets.

The McNary-Haugen bill was so complex in its arrangement and so abstrusely phrased that President Coolidge lamented that it would take a book to analyze and expose all its weaknesses. Put very simply, it provided for a Federal Farm Board whose task was to stabilize the prices to farmers of cotton, wheat, corn, rice, tobacco, swine, and such other products as Congress might from time to time add to the list. The board was to aid private and cooperative organizations to buy American agricultural goods and hold them off the market so as to drive the price above the market. Losses for those crops that had to be sold at world prices were to be made up by an equalization fee on those having to do with the crops. Coolidge's vetoes covered an assortment of objections, ranging from the socialistic character of the undertaking to the dangers of retaliation from dumping on the world market to tampering with the market to the likelihood that it would encourage production of surpluses to its unfairness in taxing some for the benefit of others to its unconstitutionality. He was most likely right on all counts, and his 1928 veto stuck.

The Republicans were not entirely consistent in the 1920s, however, in their public posture of opposition to government intervention in the economy or neutrality toward those who clamored for government aid. Coolidge tended to be pro-business in his attitude. "The business of America," he said, "is business." While the protective tariff might be supposed to aid farmers and wage workers as well as businesses (whatever its impact on everyone as consumers), there is reason to doubt that it did. It did, however, protect the chemical industry from foreign competition, as it did some other industries. The government offered subsidies for merchant shipping throughout the twenties, and as commercial flying got underway on some scale, the Post Office subsidized the budding airlines. On the whole, though, there was not much added by Republicans to interventions that were already in place.

Monetarism and Prosperity

The 1920s were the culmination, at least temporarily, of a long span of industrial growth going back at least to the 1840s. During no single period, however, had the growth been so spectacular in providing consumer products. By the 1920s, the United States had clearly emerged as the leading industrial and agricultural nation in the world. It had become also the leading creditor nation, as investments and loans in other countries, particularly in Europe, greatly exceeded those from other nations to the United States. Not only were there large European debts of nations left over from the war but also now a large increase in private lending. The period from 1922–1929 was one of great growth and widespread prosperity in the United States.

Much of this prosperity could be attributed to investment in the development of old and new industries. One industry that grew and expanded by leaps and bounds in the 1920s was that concerned with the production of automobiles, trucks, and busses. Motor vehicle registration had increased from 1¼ million vehicles in 1913 to over 26½ million in 1929. Most of this growth was in the 1920s; indeed, registration of autos and trucks nearly tripled between 1920–1929. Ford completely dominated the market of low-cost vehicles for the first half of the decade. Henry Ford concentrated almost his whole attention on producing the model "T" and reducing the price to the level where almost every family could own an automobile. It was a basic car, no frills, one color—black—, bare and spare, and cranked with a hand crank. He finally brought the price of the model "T" touring car down to its lowest point of $290 in 1924. In the early years, there had been hundreds of automakers, but by the late twenties Ford, General Motors, and Chrysler dominated the field. Although General Motors still lagged behind Ford in total sales, it was forging ahead with its full line of cars ranging from the economical Chevrolet to the luxurious Cadillac. Annual production of cars had reached almost 5 million in 1929.

The automobile and truck spawned a variety of support industries and businesses. By 1929 there were over 50,000 garages and slightly more filling stations. The oil industry burgeoned with the demand for gasoline, and production of this fuel quadrupled during the decade. Steel, copper, glass, and textile industries were expanded to fill the demand for the materials and outfitting of motor vehicles. Trucks began to supplement the railroad as freight carriers. Many new highways were built during the 1920s; most of them were now being paved for the use of motor vehicles, and long-distance highways bore numbers as "U.S. Highways," built by states with subsidies from federal government.

The broadcasting and radio manufacturing and sales industry was developed for the first time in the 1920s. Commercial scheduled broadcasting began with station KDKA in Pittsburgh in 1920. By 1927 there were 700 broadcasting stations in the country, and two radio networks were formed or being formed, NBC and CBS. The making and selling of radio sets became big business, as all sorts of radios were turned out ranging from small table models to large and expensive consoles. Advertising, which had long been the staple of newspapers and magazines gained a new medium with radio, and was now a large-scale industry. Phonographs and records, which had been around for some time, sold well also. They were usually powered by a spring, which was hand cranked. Player pianos were a fad of the 1920s and 1930s; the music was recorded on paper with punched holes and could be played on a piano.

Other more mundane appliances, such as electric refrigerators, vacuum cleaners, stoves, washing machines, and irons did a thriving sales business in the 1920s. Appliances, automobiles, homes, and other goods were increasingly being sold on installment—"easy payment"—plans. Indeed, buying on "credit" became a way of life for many people, and while credit was hardly a new invention, new patterns of credit attuned to weekly and monthly payments of wage workers were regularized.

The motion picture industry came into its own in the 1920s, and by the end of the decade virtually every town in the country had a theater, and cities had large numbers of them, often built to palatial standards. By 1930, weekly attendance at these "picture shows" averaged over 100 million people. Movies had appeared in the decade before World War I, but these were only short films. In 1915, however, D.W. Griffith demonstrated the possibilities of full-length drama in "The Birth of a Nation." Thereafter, full-length features, starring such idols as Rudolph Valentino, Clara Bow, and Charlie Chaplin, became the order of the day. They were all silent films until near the close of the decade.

The construction of housing and building was another greatly expanded industry during the 1920s. Housing starts rose from 405,000 in 1919 to 937,000 in 1925. Though production tailed off after that, it was still much higher than it had been before the war. In addition, numerous public and private buildings were built, ranging from post offices to such skyscrapers as the 77-floor Chrysler building and the Empire State building with 102 stories. Real estate booms were also fostered by new selling techniques.

The chemical industry surged after World War I, sparked by two developments. One was the government seizing of German patents during the war; the Germans had been leaders in this field, but America now forged ahead. The other was the tariff which protected the American manufacturers. Chemicals had become a $4 billion industry by 1929, and numerous products were produced such as cosmetics, perfumes, soaps, rayon, and an assortment of petroleum goods.

Much of the prosperity of the 1920s had a solid base in increasing production, rising incomes, and generally stable prices. Many consumer goods which had started out as luxuries came to be thought of as necessities (electrical appliances, for example). Government had helped to create conditions for business prosperity by reducing taxes and thus left people with more money for investment. In general, too, government removed or did not place additional obstacles in the way of productive activity. The budget was in balance throughout the decade, and the surplus of revenue was used to make considerable strides in retiring the national debt. After 1925, there was a increasing sense that the key to ever increasing prosperity had been discovered. The stock market went from bull to bull market until stock prices reached dizzying heights in late 1928 and through the middle of 1929. An ever larger number of Americans were investing in common stocks, so that the number of stockholders increased from 12 to 18 million between 1920 and 1928. While there are always naysayers, there was much opinion that stocks were going higher and higher and prosperity would reach to everyone. The Republican nominee for President in 1928, Herbert Hoover, declared that "We in America today are nearer to the final triumph over poverty than ever before in the history of any land. The poorhouse is vanishing from among us. We have not yet reached the goal, but given a chance to go forward with the policies of the last eight years, we shall soon . . . be in sight of the day when poverty will be banished from this nation."[259]

But there was a large apple of discord in this visionary Garden of Eden. Much industrial expansion and consumer spending was not soundly based. The glow of prosperity in the 1920s was in considerable measure based on an inflationary credit expansion. Many investors, many companies, and many families were spending what they had not yet produced. The apple of discord was monetarism, the belief that prosperity depends upon the quantity of money in circulation, and, in the 1920s, that largely meant the quantity of credit available. The main engine of this credit was the Federal Reserve System, as its policies were reflected through the banks. It was this credit that fostered real estate booms, much of the construction activity, and a considerable portion of the consumer spending.

A New Economics was on the way toward replacing classical economics. This New Economics was a compound of Marxism, gradualist socialism, Populism, Progressivism, political opportunism, a grotesque mis-understanding of the role of money, and more than a little moonshine. A primary tenet of this New Economics is that the problem of production has been solved. Looked at from that angle, the problem has become one of overproduction or, in another formulation, a problem of distribution. This notion goes back at least to Karl Marx and Friedrich Engels in *The Communist Manifesto*. They referred to crises caused by "the epidemic of over-production." The solution to this "problem" of overproducton, as far as most American thinkers were concerned, was the promotion of increased consumption. Simon N. Patten, an American economist, of sorts, declared in 1893: "The essence of social progress lies not in the increase of material wealth but in a rise of the margin of consumption."[260] Stuart Chase, an economic writer of the 1920s and 1930s, held that the United States reached a condition of abundance in 1902. "Abundance," he said, "is self-defined, and means an economic condition where an abundance of material goods can be produced for the entire population of a given community."[261] More specifically, he described the problem and pointed to the solution this way:

> In respect to the whole body of finished goods, it is not so much *overproduction as underconsumption* which is the appalling fact. As a nation we can make more than we can buy back. Save in certain categories, there is a vast and tragic shortage of the goods necessary to maintain a comfortable standard of living. Millions of tons of additional material could be marketed if purchasing power were available. Alas, purchasing power is not available.[262]

The New Economics based on this tenet has also been called the Economics of Consumption.

In the lingo of these economists, what is needed is to increase the demand for goods. The supply can be readily filled, if the goods are not already lying around unsold, if only the demand were sufficient. The main approach to this alleged problem in the 1920s was monetary, to increase demand by increasing money or credit. The Federal Reserve system did just that for most of the 1920s. It followed a number of policies to increase credit both for foreign and domestic lending. The Annual Report of the Federal Reserve in 1923 proclaimed its purpose as expanding credit:

> The Federal Reserve banks are the . . . source to which the member banks turn when the demands of the business community have outrun their own unaided resources. The Federal Reserve supplies the needed additions to credit in times of business expansion and takes up the slack in times of business recession.

Calculations by economist Murray Rothbard indicate that the total money supply in the United States increased from $45.3 billion in June, 1921 to $73.26 billion in June, 1929. As he says, "Over the entire period of the boom, we find that the money supply increased by $28.0 billion, a 61.8 percent increase over the eight-year period. This is an averge annual increase of 7.7 percent, a very sizeable degree of inflation." Since the currency in circulation was not increased, as Rothbard points out, so that "the entire monetary expansion took place in . . . credit expansion."[263]

The Federal Reserve accomplished this credit expansion in a variety of ways, such as a politically motivated low discount rate, fostering low interest rates, and making money available to foreign buyers of American goods. This credit expansion provided the monetary demand for American goods both at home and abroad. It fueled the credit for installment buying, for business expansion, for construction, and for stock buying on margin, which was rampant by 1929. It also made many of the private foreign loans possible, which made many more exports possible in view of the fact that exports generally exceeded imports.

The basic flaw in monetarism is this. Money, as such, is not really demand, though it appears to serve that function when it is exchanged for goods. Money is a *medium* of exchange, a medium through which exchanges are made. Ultimately, as Say's Law made clear in the early 19th century, all exchanges are of goods for goods. What may confuse us is that in a money economy (an economy in which goods are ordinarily priced in terms of and paid for by money), an intermediate step occurs in which money is exchanged for goods and that money is later exchanged for other goods.

When a credit expansion occurs, an imbalance in trade results. The imbalance is that the goods for which the goods are ultimately to be exchanged have not yet been produced (and, for that matter, may never be). Suppose, for example, that I buy a refrigerator on the installment plan, a purchase made possible by credit expansion. If enough people do that over a given short period, sellers and producers of refrigerators will register these purchases as a rise in demand. Appliance stores will stock more refrigerators and manufacturers may gear up to build larger numbers of this good. Prosperity appears to have arrived. But there is a flaw in it; there is a trade imbalance. Instead of buying other such items, I must work to produce the goods or provide the services to pay back the loan (and so must many others). Meanwhile, trade slows; stores are overstocked with goods; orders fall off, and factories are left with unused capacity. The only way to keep this thing going is by another credit expansion, then another, and so on and on and up and up. Eventually, something may topple the mountain of credit; indeed, something almost certainly will.

Of such credit expansions, the Austrian economist, Ludwig von Mises, had this to say: "There is no means of avoiding the final collapse of a boom brought about by credit expansion. The alternative is only whether the crisis should come sooner as a result of a voluntary abandonment of further credit expansion, or later as a final and total catastrophe of the currency system involved."[264] A temporary voluntary abandonment of further credit expansion did bring on the collapse associated with the Great Depression, but that will be taken up later in its place. The important point here is that the stage was being set in the 1920s for this collapse, set by a continual and mounting credit expansion under the influence of monetarism. The expansion was carried out by the Federal Reserve system working through banks and other credit institutions.

Symptoms of Moral Decline

There were some other events and developments of the 1920s which need to be noticed before taking leave of the period. In one way or another, they may be seen as symptoms of moral decline, some subtly and others more dramatically so. The trend toward credit living may be a symptom of moral decline, an attempt to consume what you have not produced. At most times, of course, there are those who live beyond their means, but this does not necessarily become a matter of public morality. There is greed involved in all cases, but it becomes institutionalized greed when government organs foster an ongoing credit expansion. But there were other symptoms in the 1920s.

One of the symptoms was the decline of the influence of the family in the bringing up of children. There were several sources of this declining influence. One was the separation of much of the family during a goodly portion of the day. As more and more men (and sometimes women as well) worked away from families in factory, mine, and office, they were separated from them during most of the waking hours. Compulsory school attendance took children away from the homes during longer and longer portions of the year, as the school year was extended. The automobile provided a means for young people to escape quickly from the watchful eyes of parents or people in the local community. The radio initially provided family entertainment and may even have enlivened family life, but movies provided a largely alien influence to that of the family. National radio networks and Hollywood-made movies were nationwide in scope and only limitedly subject to local and family influence. The emancipation of women, signalled by the 19th Amendment and ratified in the 1920s by "flappers", and shortened hemlines, was registered by increasingly common divorces.

National prohibition of alcohol, authorized by the 19th Amendment and enacted by the Volstead Act, may have appeared to many of those who favored it as a highly moral undertaking. It was not. It was an attempt to take the selling and consumption of alcohol entirely out of the moral realm, to make it a crime and forbidden. It did not succeed. The Volstead Act was almost certainly greeted by the most extensive evasion of any law in American history. Drunkenness remained a moral problem, and drinking may have been as widespread as ever. Criminality, however, became commonplace; scoff-laws abounded; bootleggers abounded, and organized crime found its greatest opportunity in providing the forbidden beverage. Al Capone built an underworld empire in Chicago, based on the sale of illegal beverages. The first Prohibition Commissioner had proclaimed: "We shall see that [liquor] is not manufactured, nor sold, nor given away, nor hauled in anything on the surface of the earth, or under the earth or in the air."[265] Few believed this was possible by 1930, and a great many had become convinced that the game was not worth the candle.

A considerable effort was made in the mid-1920s to bring the question of teaching biological evolution in the schools to a head. The question as raised had both moral and religious overtones. Bluntly put, it was whether man's origins were spiritual or material, whether God had created man in His image or whether man had evolved from lower animals. A great deal hinges undoubtedly upon the answer that is given to the question. Some Christian leaders raised the issue about evolutionary theory being taught in the schools, pointing out that it tended to undermine the Bible account of Creation, and, more broadly, religious faith. Indeed, a crusade got under-way to get state legislatures to forbid the teaching of evolutionary theory, at least in tax-supported schools and colleges. William Jennings Bryan, the orator with Populistic leanings, was prominent in the effort. As Bryan put the question, "Shall teachers paid by taxation be permitted to substitute the unproven hypothesis of scientists for the 'Thus saith the Lord' of the Bible, and so undermine the faith of Christian taxpayers?"[266] Undoubtedly, the question may have gone to the heart of the rightness and practicality of state-run public schools for people of diverse and other beliefs, but it never became an issue of that. The Great Commoner, with his populistic and democratic leanings, was hardly the man to raise it.

There were efforts in several states to get a law against the teaching of evolution passed by the state legislature. The first legislature to do so was Tennessee in 1925. The American Civil Liberties Union went to work right away to get a teacher to violate the law. John T. Scopes, a biology teacher in Dayton, Tennessee obliged, and got himself charged with violating the law. The trial of Scopes in the summer of 1925 drew national attention, as reporters, evangelists, and assorted commentators descended on the town. Indeed, the trial became a circus, with Bryan providing his services to the state for the prosecution, and Clarence Darrow acting in defense. Darrow was a nationally famous (or infamous) lawyer, an agnostic, and frequently involved in unionist and radical cases.

The Scopes case was a simple one at the trial level. Scopes admitted he had broken the law; the prosecution had nothing more to prove, and the defense could hardly avert a guilty verdict. Even so, Darrow attempted to offer expert testimony on evolutionary theory, but the court declined to take up that issue. Whereupon Darrow got Bryan sworn as an expert on the Bible and proceeded to make fun of Bible stories and miraculous events. It was a debacle. Bryan died a few days later, and it is possible that the grilling he took contributed to his demise. Scopes was found guilty and fined. The supreme court of Tennessee removed the fine but upheld the conviction. No further appeals were possible because no penalty or punishment was given.

The issues that did not get adequately raised at the Scopes trial did not disappear, but they were temporarily obscured by the hot air of Darrow, the religious cynic, and the ineptitude of Bryan, who was better at shallow oratory than operating in the deep. The secularization of education has proceeded apace since then.

Notes

1. A. J. P. Taylor, *English History: 1914–1945* (New York: Oxford University Press, 1965), p. 1.

2. Allan Nevins, *The Emergence of Modern America* (New York: Macmillan, 1961), p. 32.

3. Harold U. Faulkner, *American Economic History* (New York: 1954), p. 345.

4. See Thomas C. Cochran, "Did the Civil War Retard Industrialization?" *Views of American Economic Growth: The Agricultural Era*, Thomas C. Cochran and Thomas B. Brewer, eds. (New York: McGraw–Hill, 1966), pp 252–61.

5. Samuel Smiles, *Self-Help* (New York: William L. Allison, n.d., rev. and enl. ed.), p. 21.

6. R. H. Newton, *Social Studies* (New York: 1886), p. 167, as quoted in Ida M. Tarbell, *The Nationalizing of Business* (New York: Macmillan, 1936), p. i.

7. Quoted in T. Harry Williams, Richard N. Current and Frank Freidel, *A History of the United States*, vol. II (New York: Alfred A. Knopf, 1959), p. 158.

8. Quoted in Charles A. Beard and Mary R. Beard, *The Rise of American Civilization* (New York: Macmillan, 1956, 2 vols. in one) vol. II, pp. 134–35.

9. Francis B. Simkins, *A History of the South* (New York: Doubleday, 1954), p. 190.

10. Wilbur J. Cash, *The Mind of the South* (New York: Doubleday, 1954), p. 190.

11. R. R. Palmer and Joel Colton, *A History of the Modern World* (New York: Alfred A. Knopf, 1958), p. 431.

12. Franklin L. van Baumer, ed., *Main Currents of Western Thought* (New York: Alfred A. Knopf, 1967, 2nd rev. ed.), p. 491.

13. Richard L. Schoenwald, ed., *Nineteenth Century Thought: The Discovery of Change* (Englewood Cliffs, N.J.: Prentice–Hall, 1965), p. 151.

14. Baumer, *op. cit.*, p. 505.

15. Quoted in Richard Hofstadter, *Social Darwinism in American Thought* (New York: George Braziller, 1959, rev. ed.), p. 34.

16. Schoenwald, *op. cit.*, p. 121.

17. Quoted in William Irvine, *Apes, Angels and Victorians* (New York: McGraw-Hill, 1955), p. 42.

18. Baumer, *op. cit.*, p. 533.

19. Quoted in Irvine, *op. cit.*, p. 96.

20. Quoted in Henry S. Commager, *The American Mind* (New Haven: Yale University Press, 1954), p. 85.

21. Quoted in Jacques Barzun, *Darwin, Marx, Wagner* (Garden City, N.Y.: Doubleday Anchor Books, 1958, rev. ed.), p. 37.

22. Eugen Weber, ed., *The Western Tradition* (Boston: D. C. Heath, 1959), p. 672.

23. Eugene C. Black, ed., *Posture of Europe* (Homewood, Ill.: The Dorsey Press, 1964), p. 472.

24. Quoted in Morris Hillquit, *Socialism in Theory and Practice* (New York: Macmillan, 1909), p. 63.

25. James H. Robinson, *The New History* (New York: Macmillan, 1912), pp. 17–18.

26. Harry E. Barnes, *The New History and the Social Sciences* (New York: The Century Co., 1925), p. 589.

27. Quoted in Williams, Current and Freidel, *op. cit.*, vol. II, p. 80.

28. Quoted in Malcolm Cowley, "Naturalism in American Literature," *Evolutionary Thought in America*, Stow Persons, ed. (New York: George Braziller, 1956), p. 304.

29. *Ibid*, p. 303.

30. Commager, *op. cit.*, pp. 110–11.

31. Quoted in Cowley, *op. cit.*, p. 315.

32. Herbert Spencer, *Social Statics* (New York: Appleton, 1865), p. 334.

33. Quoted in Hofstadter, *op. cit.*, p. 45.

34. *Ibid.*

35. *Ibid.*, pp. 45–46.

36. *Ibid.*, p. 46.

37. William G. Sumner, "Sociology," *American Thought: Civil War to World War I*, Perry Miller, ed. (New York: Rinehart, 1954), p. 73.

38. William G. Sumner, "The Absurd Effort to Make the World Over," in *Ibid.*, p. 94.

39. *Ibid.*, p. 104.

40. Quoted in Eric F. Goldman, *Rendezvous with Destiny* (New York: Vintage Books, 1956), p. 66.

41. Sumner, "Sociology," Miller, *op. cit.*, p. 82.

42. Quoted in Hofstadter, *op. cit.*, p. 59.

43. Quoted in Commager, *op. cit.*, p. 206.

44. Lester F. Ward, *Dynamic Sociology*, vol. II (New York: D. Appleton and Co., 1920), p. 468.

45. *Ibid.*, vol. I, p. 36.

46. *Ibid.*, p. 37.

47. Lester F. Ward, *Pure Sociology* (New York: Macmillan, 1909, 2nd ed.), pp. 569–70.

48. *Ibid.*, p. 571.

49. Samuel Smiles, *Thrift* (Chicago: Belfords, Clarke and Co., 1879), pp. 20–21.

50. Baumer, *op. cit.*, p. 524.

51. Weber, *op. cit.*, p. 609.

52. Henry George, *Progress and Poverty* (New York: Schalkenbach Foundation, 1955), p. 8.

53. Ray A. Billington, *et. al.*, eds., *The Making of American Democracy*, vol. II (New York: Holt, Rinehart and Winston, 1962 rev. ed.), pp. 99–100.

54. Quoted in Arthur M. Schlesinger, *The Rise of the City* (New York: Macmillan, 1933), p. 65.

55. *Ibid.*, pp. 65–66.

56. Quoted in Samuel E. Morison and Henry S. Commager, *The Growth of the American Republic* (New York: Oxford University Press, 3rd ed. rev., 1942), p. 178.

57. Billington, *op. cit.*, vol. II, p. 57.

58. *Ibid.*, p. 60.

59. Nathaniel Weyl, *The Jew in American Politics* (New Rochelle, N.Y.: Arlington House, 1968), p. 116–7.

60. *Ibid*, pp. 117–118.

61. Z. A. Jordan, ed., *Karl Marx: Economy, Class and Society* (New York: Schribner's, 1971), p. 292.

62. Quoted in David McClellan, *Karl Marx: His Life and Thought* (New York: Harper & Row, 1973), p. 119.

63. Karl Marx and Friedrich Engels, *Selected Works* (New York: International Publishers, 1968), p. 204.

64. Quoted in Erik von Kuehnelt-Leddihn, *Leftism* (New Rochelle, N.Y.: Arlington House, 1974), p. 127.

65. Bertram D. Wolfe, *Marxism* (New York: Dial, 1965), p. 369.

66. Weber, *op. cit.*, pp. 618–19.

67. Schoenwald, *op. cit.*, p. 69.

68. Quoted in F. S. C. Northrup, "Evolution in Its Relation to the Philosophy of Nature and the Philosophy of Culture," Persons, *op. cit.*, p. 68.

69. *Fabian Tract #7.*

70. *Fabian Tract #70.*

71. A.M. McBriar, *Fabian Socialism and English Politics* (Cambridge: Cambridge University Press, 1962), p.95.

72. Quoted in Pittsburgh *Press* (June 19, 1966), sec. I, p. 11.

73. George, *op. cit.*, p. 8.

74. Quoted in Daniel Aaron, *Men of Good Hope* (New York: Oxford University Press, 1951), p. 104.

75. *Ibid.*, p. 132.

76. Edward Bellamy, *Looking Backward, 2000–1887* (Boston: Hougton Mifflin, 1888), p. 56.

77. *Ibid.*, p. 243.

78. Quoted in Morison and Commager, *The Growth of the American Republic*, p. 160.

79. George B. Tindall, ed., *A Populist Reader: Selections from the Works of American Populist Leaders* (New York: Harper & Row, 1966), pp. 114–15.

80. Basil Rauch and Dumas Malone, *Empire for Liberty*, vol. II (New York: Appleton-Century-Crofts, 1960), p. 133.

81. Clarence A. Wiley, *Economics and Politics of the Agricultural Tariff* (New York: H.W. Wilson, 1927), p. 40.

83. Commager, *Documents of American History*, vol. I, p. 579.

84. *Ibid.*, p. 578.

85. *Ibid.*, p. 549.

86. Quoted in Vincent P. De Santis, *et. al.*, *America Past and Present* (Boston: Allyn and Bacon, 1968), vol. II, p. 185.

87. Quoted in Richard Hofstadter, *The Age of Reform: From Bryan to F.D.R.* (New York: Alfred A. Knopf, 1955), p. 64.

88. Commager, *Documents of American History*, vol. I, p. 542.

89. Alfred H. Kelly and Winfred A. Harbison, *The American Constitution* (New York: W.W. Norton, 1955, rev. ed.), p. 516.

90. *Ibid.*, pp. 524–25.

91. *Ibid.*, p. 525.

92. George D. Herron, "Christ and the Social Revolution," *American Issues*, Merle Curti, Willard Thorp and Carlos Baker, eds. (Philadelphia: J.B. Lippincott, 1960), p. 705.

93. Thomas G. Manning, ed., *The Chicago Strike of 1894* (New York: Henry Holt, 1960), p. 34.

94. Foster R. Dulles, *Labor in America* (New York: Thomas Y. Crowell, 1960, 2nd ed.), p. 28.

95. Joseph R. Buchanan, *The Story of a Labor Agitator* (Freeport, N.Y.: Books for Libraries Press, 1971), p. 14.

96. Quoted in Walter G. Merritt, *Destination Unknown* (New York: Prentice-Hall, 1951), p. 151.

97. Commager, *Documents of American History*, vol. I, p. 296.

98. Quoted in Tarbell, *op. cit.*, p. 161.

99. Quoted in Philip Taft, *Organized Labor in American History* (New York: Harper & Row, 1964), p. 154.

100. Manning, *op. cit.*, 58.

101. John D. Hicks, *The Populist Revolt* (Lincoln: University of Nebraska Press, 1961), p. 156.

102. Tindall, *op. cit.*, p. 181.

103. Quoted in Robert F. Durden, *The Climax of Populism* (Lexington: University of Kentucky Press, 1966), p. 149.

104. Hicks, *op. cit.*, p. 160.

105. Tindall, *op. cit.*, p. 161.

106. *Ibid.*, p. 149.

107. *Ibid.*, p. 111.

108. Billington, *op. cit.*, vol. II, pp. 107–08.

109. Charles S. Peirce, "What Pragmatism Is," *Philosophy in the Twentieth Century*, William Barrett, ed. (New York: Random House, 1962), p. 144.

110. William James, "What Pragmatism Means," *Pragmatism and American Culture*, Gail Kennedy, ed. (Boston: D.C. Heath, 1950), p. 22.

111. John Dewey, *Reconstruction in Philosophy* (New York: Henry Holt, 1920), p. 156.

112. James, *op. cit.*, p. 23.

113. Dewey, *op. cit.*, p. 124.

114. Henry D. Aiken, "Introduction," Barrett, *op. cit.*, p. 62.

115. James, *op. cit.*, p. 15.

116. Dewey, *op. cit.*, p. 124.

117. Commager, *The American Mind*, p. 214.

118. Quoted in Lawrence H. Cremin, *The Transformation of the School* (New York: Alfred A. Knopf, 1961), p. 99.

119. Quoted in Edward A. Krug, *The Shaping of the American High School* (New York: Harper & Row, 1964), p. 254.

120. *Ibid.*, p. 123.

121. Cremin, *op. cit.*, p. 220.

122. Joe Park, ed., *Selected Readings in the Philosophy of Education* (New York: Macmillan, 1963), p. 135.

123. John Dewey, *Democracy and Education* (New York: Macmillan, 1963), p. 135.

124. John Dewey, *Problems of Men* (New York: Philosophical Library, 1946), p. 58.

125. Dewey, *Democracy and Education*, p. 101.

126. Quoted in John H. Snow and Paul W. Shafer, *The Turning of the Tides* (New York: Long House, 1956), p. 30.

127. Charles H. Hopkins, *The Rise of the Social Gospel in American Protestantism* (New Haven: Yale University Press, 1940), p. vi.

128. Washington Gladden, *Applied Christianity* (Boston: Houghton Mifflin, 1886), pp. 69–70.

129. Walter Rauschenbusch, *Christianity and the Social Crisis* (New York: Macmillan, 1907), p. 265.

130. George D. Herron, *Between Caesar and Jesus* (New York: Crowell, 1899), pp. 24–25.

131. Gladden, *op. cit.*, pp. 100–01.

132. Richard T. Ely, *Social Aspects of Christianity* (New York: Crowell, 1889), p. 73.

133. Richard H. Quint, *et. al.*, eds., *Main Problems in American History* (Homewood, Ill.: Dorsey, 1964), vol. II, p. 67.

134. Billington, *op. cit.*, vol. II, p. 182.

135. Herbert Croly, *The Promise of American Life*, Cushing Strout, intro. (New York: Capricorn Books, 1964), p. 51.

136. *Ibid.*, p. 5.

137. Walter E. Weyl, *The New Democracy* (New York: Macmillan, 1912), p. 13.

138. Walter Lippmann, *Drift and Mastery*, William E. Leuchtenburg, intro. (Englewood Cliffs, N.J.: Prentice-Hall, 1961), p. 147.

139. *Ibid.*, p. 98.

140. Croly, *op. cit.*, p. 377.

141. Weyl, *op. cit.*, pp. 265–66.

142. *Ibid.*, p. 266.

143. Lippmann, *op. cit.*, p. 49

144. Richard W. Leopold, Arthur S. Link and Stanley Coben, eds., *Problems in American History* (Englewood Cliffs, N.J.: Prentice-Hall, 1966), vol. II, p. 146.

145. Billington, *op. cit.*, vol. II, p. 151.

146. Leopold, Link and Coben, *op. cit.*, pp. 139–40.

147. Richard B. Morris, ed., *Encyclopedia of American History* (New York: Harper & Brothers, 1953), p. 287.

148. Billington, *op. cit.*, vol. II, p. 177.

149. Quoted in John D. Hicks, *The American Nation* (Boston: Houghton Mifflin, 1955 3rd ed.), pp. 294–95.

150. Quoted in C. Vann Woodward, *The Strange Case of Jim Crow* (New York: Oxford University Press, 1957, new and rev. ed.), pp. 18–21.

151. *Ibid.*, pp. 54–55.

152. *Ibid.*, p. 83.

153. Quoted in C. Vann Woodward, *Origins of the New South* (Baton Rouge: Louisiana State University Press, 1951), p. 359.

154. George E. Mowry, *The Era of Theodore Roosevelt* (New York: Harper, 1958), p. 197.

155. See Clarence B. Carson, *The Flight from Reality* (Irvington, N.Y.: The Foundation for Economic Education, 1969), ch. 22.

156. Richard Powers, ed., *Readings in European Civilization since 1500* (Boston: Houghton Mifflin, 1961), pp. 632–33.

157. Richard Hofstadter, *The American Political Tradition* (New York: Vintage Books, 1954), p. 278.

158. Theodore Roosevelt, *The New Nationalism*, William E. Leuchtenburg, ed. (Englewood Cliffs, N.J.: Prentice-Hall, 1961), p. 36.

159. Woodrow Wilson, *The New Freedom*, William E. Leuchtenburg, ed. (Englewood Cliffs, N.J.: Prentice-Hall, 1961), pp. 130, 164.

160. Arthur S.Link, *American Epoch* (New York: Alfred A. Knopf, 1955), p. 96.

161. *Ibid.*, p. 94.

162. Williams, Current and Freidel, *op. cit.*, vol. II, p. 348.

163. Quoted in Morris, *op. cit.*, p. 295.

164. Commager, *Documents of American History*, vol. II, p. 33.

165. *Ibid.*, p. 22.

166. Quoted in Frank N. Magill, ed., *Great Events from History* (Englewood Cliffs, N.J.: Salem Press, 1975), vol. III, p. 1374.

167. Commager, *Documents of American History*, vol. II, pp. 50–51.

168. Quoted in Leuchtenburg, "Introduction," Roosevelt, *The New Nationalism*, p. 6.

169. *Ibid.*, p. 4.

170. Leopold, Link and Coben, *op. cit.*, vol. II, p. 196.

171. *Ibid.*, p. 198.

172. Arthur S. Link, *Woodrow Wilson and the Progressive Era* (New York: Harper & Row, 1954), p. 34.

173. Horace Coon, *Triumph of the Eggheads* (New York: Random House, 1955), p. 87.

174. *Ibid.*, p. 86.

175. Link, *Woodrow Wilson and the Progressive Era*, p. 39.

176. Quoted in *ibid.*, p. 48.

177. Commager, *Documents of American History*, vol. II, p. 99.

178. Link, *Woodrow Wilson and the Progressive Era*, p. 58.

179. *Ibid.*, p. 119.

180. Link, *American Epoch*, p. 161.

181. Eugen Weber, *A Modern History of Europe* (New York: W.W. Norton, 1971), p. 774.

182. Commager, *Documents of American History*, vol. II, p. 96.

183. Quoted in Malone and Rauch, *op. cit.*, vol. II, p. 371.

184. Commager, *Documents of American History*, vol. II, pp. 130–32.

185. *Ibid.*, p. 130.

186. George Dangerfield, *The Strange Death of Liberal England* (New York: Capricorn Books, 1961), pp. 18–19.

187. Taylor, *op. cit.*, p. 73.

188. *Ibid.*, p. 53.

189. Philip Ross, *The Government as a Source of Union Power* (Providence: Brown University Press, 1965), p. 18.

190. George H. Mayer and Walter O. Forster, *The United States and the Twentieth Century* (Boston: Houghton Mifflin, 1958), p. 248.

191. Gilbert C. Fite and Jim E. Reese, *An Economic History of the United States* (Boston: Houghton Mifflin, 1965, 2nd ed.), p. 518.

192. Quoted in Frederick L. Paxon, *American Democracy and the World War*, vol. II (Boston: Houghton Mifflin, 1939), pp. 225–26.

193. John F. Stover, *The Life and Decline of the American Railroad* (New York: Oxford University Press, 1970), p. 175.

194. Sidney L. Miller, *Inland Transportation* (New York: McGraw-Hill, 1933), p. 156.

195. Quoted in Link, *American Epoch*, p. 203.

196. Quoted in Frank P. Chambers, *This Age of Conflict* (New York: Harcourt, Brace and World, 1962, 3rd ed.), p. 109.

197. *Ibid.*, p. 100.

198. Commager, *Documents of American History*, vol. II, p. 126.

199. Quoted in Mayer and Forster, *op. cit.*, p. 263.

200. *Ibid.*, pp. 274–75.

201. *Ibid.*, pp. 304–05.

202. Leopold, Link and Coben, *Problems in American History*, vol. II, p. 235.

203. *Ibid.*, p. 233.

204. Robert C. Tucker, *The Marxian Revolution* (New York: W.W. Norton, 1969), p. 132.

205. Quoted in Robert V. Daniels, *Red October* (New York: Charles Scribner's Sons, 1967), p. 71.

206. *Ibid.*, p. 157.

207. *Ibid.*, p. 196.

208. Robert Payne, *The Life and Death of Lenin* (New York: Simon and Schuster, 1964), p. 431.

209. Quoted in Alfred G. Meyer, *Leninism* (New York: Praeger, 1957), p. 99.

210. Payne, *op. cit.*, p. 482.

211. *Ibid.*, pp. 480–81.

212. Robert K. Massie, *Nicholas and Alexandra* (New York: Dell, 1967), p. 515.

213. Quoted in Edward H. Carr, *Socialism in One Country*, vol. I (New York: Macmillan, 1958), p. 32.

214. *Ibid.*, p. 29.

215. *Ibid.*, p. 38.

216. Quoted in Sidney Harcave, *Russia: A History* (Philadelphia: J.B. Lippincott, 1952), p. 501.

217. Leopold, Link and Coben, *op. cit.*, vol. II, p. 245.

218. William E. Leuchtenburg, *The Perils of Prosperity, 1914–1932* (Chicago: University of Chicago Press, 1958), p. 78.

219. Quoted in William H. McIlhany, II, *The ACLU on Trial* (New Rochelle, N.Y.: Arlington House, 1976), p. 114.

220. Quoted in Williams, Current and Freidel, *op. cit.*, vol. II, p. 418.

221. Quoted in Eugene N. Anderson, *Modern Europe in World Perspective* (New York: Rinehart, 1958), p. 296.

222. Robert Conquest, *The Great Terror* (Toronto: Macmillan, 1968), pp. 140–41.

223. Alexander Dolgun with Patrick Watson, *Alexander Dolgun's Story* (New York: Ballantine, 1976), p. 446.

224. Anderson, *op. cit.*, p. 216.

225. *Ibid.*

226. Benito Mussolini, "The Doctrine of Fascism," *Readings on Fascism and National Socialism* (Denver: Alan Swallow, n.d.), pp. 23–24.

227. *Ibid.*, p. 15.

228. Robert K. Murray, *The Harding Era* (Minneapolis: University of Minnesota Press, 1969), p. 3.

229. Francis Russell, *The Shadow of Blooming Grove: Warren G. Harding in His Time* (New York: McGraw-Hill, 1968), pp. xiv–xv.

230. Alfred Kazin, *On Native Grounds* (Garden City, N.Y.: 1956), p. 149.

231. Quoted in *ibid.*, p. 150.

232. Quoted in Clarence B. Carson, "What is Liberalism?," *The Rockford Papers* (January, 1980), p. 11.

233. H. L. Mencken and George Jean Nathan, *The American Credo* (New York: Alfred A. Knopf, 1921, rev. and enl. ed.), pp. 41–42.

234. *Ibid.*, p. 26.

235. H. L. Mencken, *A Mencken Crestomathy* (New York: Alfred A. Knopf, 1949), p. 621.

236. Mencken and Nathan, *The American Credo*, p. 45.

237. Catherine B. Ely, "The Sorrows of Mencken," *The North American Review*, vol. CCXXV (January, 1928), p. 23.

238. Leopold, Link and Coben, *Problems in American History*, vol. II, p. 258.

239. Frederick L. Allen, *Only Yesterday* (New York: Bantam Books, 1959), p. 160.

240. See Clarence B. Carson, *The Fateful Turn: From Individualism to Collectivism* (Irvington, N.Y.: The Foundation for Economic Education, 1963), pp. 94–99.

241. *Ibid.*, p. 101.

242. Whittaker Chambers, *Cold Friday* (New York: Random House, 1964), pp. 93, 99.

243. *Ibid.*, pp. 93, 138.

244. Benjamin Gitlow, *The Whole of Their Lives* (Boston: Western Islands, 1965, The Americanist Library), p. 97.

245. Lewis S. Feuer, "American Travelers to the Soviet Union 1917–1932: The Formation of a Component of New Deal Ideology," *American Quarterly* (Summer, 1962).

246. Eugene Lyons, *The Red Decade* (New Rochelle, N.Y.: Arlington House, 1970), pp. 103–04.

247. Quoted in Frank A. Warren, III, *Liberals and Communism* (Bloomington: Indiana University Press, 1966), p. 70.

248. *Ibid.*, p. 66.

249. Quoted in Lyons, *op. cit.*, p. 107.

250. Quoted in Warren, *op. cit.*, p. 59.

251. Quoted in Russell, *op. cit.*, pp. 13–14.

252. Kelly and Harbison, *op. cit.*, pp. 681–82.

253. John D. Hicks, *Republican Ascendancy* (New York: Harper & Row, 1960), p. 25.

254. Quoted in Hicks, *The American Nation*, p. 491.

255. Murray, *op. cit.*, p. 459.

256. Quoted in Williams, Current and Freidel, *op. cit.*, vol. II, p. 434.

257. Hicks, *Republican Ascendancy*, p. 107.

258. Commager, *Documents of American History*, vol. II, p. 227.

259. Leopold, Link and Coben, *Problems in American History*, vol. II, pp. 266–67.

260. See Simon N. Patten, *Essays in Economic Theory*, Rexford G. Tugwell, ed. (New York: Alfred A. Knopf, 1924).

261. Quoted in Charles S. Wyand, *The Economics of Consumption* (New York: Macmillan, 1937), p. 54.

262. Stuart Chase, *The Nemesis of American Business* (New York: Macmillan, 1931), p. 78.

263. Quoted in Murray N. Rothbard, *America's Great Depression* (Princeton, N.J.: D. Van Nostrand, 1963), p. 112.

264. Ludwig von Mises, *Human Action* (Chicago: Henry Regnery, 1966, 3rd rev. ed.), p. 572.

265. Quoted in Williams, Current and Freidel, *op. cit.*, vol. II, p. 460.

266. Quoted in Link, *American Epoch*, p. 337.

Glossary

Anarchism—a theory that government is not necessary and should be abolished. It necessarily assumes that men are by nature good, but that they are made evil by a system imposed by the powers that be or enforced by government. Most socialist thought was more or less influenced by the same strain of ideas that went into anarchism, and in the latter part of the 19th century revolutionary socialists were hardly distinguishable from anarchists. Anarchists sometimes went about abolishing government directly by assassinating political officials.

Animalism—the doctrine that man is simply an animal, that he is moved by animal appetites, and that he does not have a spiritual nature. This view was one logical extension of Darwinism, but less strongly stated it appears in much of modern psychology and literature.

Armistice—a ceasing of hostilities during a war prior to the working out of peace treaties. Neither side need have surrendered, though the armistices at the end of World War I were treated as surrenders by the Allies.

Belligerents—the countries who are at war, as distinct from those which are neutral. The term is used in international relations in discussing how those who are at war may treat enemy ships at sea, for example, as opposed to those of neutrals.

Bimetallism—a governmentally established money system in which two different metals, such as gold and silver, are used as money. In such circumstances, governments usually try to set a fixed ratio of exchange between the two metals, for example, 15 ounces of silver for one ounce of gold. Since market price of these metals fluctuates, one of them is usually overvalued in relation to the other. The undervalued metal ceases to circulate, following Gresham's Law.

Bolshevik—in Russian, the majority. Lenin's faction got a majority on one of numerous votes at an international meeting of Marxists. Thereafter, he called his the Bolshevik Party, thus asserting a claim to dominance which had hardly been earned. After the Bolsheviks took over in Russia, they changed the name to the Communist Party.

Brandeis Brief—a presentation by a lawyer which focuses on social circumstances rather than upon the law, upon selected facts rather than logic. Louis D. Brandeis was the first to win a major case by using such a brief.

Central Bank—usually a single national bank which asserts authoritative control over the currency, foreign exchanges, and the like. It is usually more or less under government control. Most major European countries had central banks, but the United States had not had one since the 1830s. The Federal Reserve system provided a central banking system once it was organized.

Collectivism—a system that emphasizes the whole of society as a collective unit rather than the individuals composing it. All socialisms are more or less collectivistic.

Comintern—an abbreviation of the Communist International, organized in the Soviet Union after World War I. It was headquartered in Moscow, controlled by Soviet authorities, aimed to spread Communism around the world both by open and covert means, and usually controlled Communist parties in other countries.

Concentration Camp—a guarded enclosure for holding political prisoners, prisoners of war, and aliens. The phrase picked up harsh overtones because of the harsh treatment of camp inmates by the Nazis. But the Soviet Union has long had the most extensive and brutal camp system, called Gulags in Russia (also known as slave labor camps). Millions of inmates have died over the years as a result of severe working and living conditions.

Conservative Darwinism—the view that man cannot by taking thought change the supposed laws of political, social, and economic development. Any sort of drastic reform was doomed to failure. Society must follow its own evolutionary course.

Constituent Assembly—a gathering of delegates for the purpose of making or altering a constitution. A constituent assembly met in Russia in early 1918, but it was shut down by the Bolsheviks.

Contraband—goods which neutrals cannot ship to belligerents in time of war without having them subject to seizure and confiscation. Arms and ammunition are always considered contraband, but other goods helpful to a war effort may also be included.

Contract Labor—imported workers brought into the United States under work contracts. Unionists particularly opposed this arrangement, for it permitted employers to bring in foreign workers at lower wages than those prevailing in the United States.

Conveyor—a system of interrogation employed by the secret police in the prisons of the Soviet Union in order to get confessions. It involved a variety of deprivations, discomfort, and sometimes torture, but above all, extended periods of questioning by relays of fresh interrogators. The main object is to wear the prisoner down to the point that he will give the desired confession.

Coup d'État—a swift and illegal takeover of a state, usually by force. The Bolsheviks seized power in Russia by a *coup d'état*.

Crop Lien—a pledge of his forthcoming crop by a farmer to get credit. In short, the farmer puts up his crop as security for a loan or extended credit. Critics have charged that merchants and landlords took unjust advantage of tenants by this device, but the system itself was not unjust.

Darwinism—an ideology built on the evolutionary theories of Charles Darwin. In the broadest perspective, Darwinism is the view that all development occurs by a gradual process of evolving, and that in the course of time changes of nature may occur by this process. It is said that Darwin was not much of a Darwinian himself.

Democratic Centralism—a Communist phrase used as a justification for concentration of power and dictatorship.

Dollar Diplomacy—a phrase used mostly by Democrats to attack the foreign policy of President Taft. Taft sometimes used private investors to accomplish programs desired by the government.

Expatriate—a person has been either banished or has voluntarily left his country to take up residence elsewhere. Literary and artistic Americans who left the United States in the 1920s are often referred to as expatriates. In most cases, they did not give up their American citizenship, so theirs was more a matter of attitude than allegiance.

Expeditionary Force—a military force sent on a military expedition to other lands, usually overseas. American forces in Europe in World Wars I and II were described as expeditionary.

Fascism—a totalitarian political system established by Mussolini in Italy in the 1920s. It was collectivist, nationalist, and aggressively expansionist. Like totalitarian systems elsewhere, it had a dictatorship, one-party rule, government control of the economy, and was oppressive.

Fellow-Traveler—a sympathizer with Communism who does not become a party member nor come under party discipline. In short, he is an unorganized traveler on the road to Communism who is quite often useful to Communists in their various undertakings: contributing money to communist causes, joining Communist fronts, and defending the innocence of Communist-controlled organizations.

Flexible Currency—a currency whose amount can be increased or diminished according to need. Those who favor such a currency usually opposed the gold or any fixed standard. Flexible currency is a monetarist notion.

Gradualist Socialism—the movement toward socialism gradually—step by step or in stages. Control over property is often approached indirectly, by regulation, conservation, prescriptions as to use, for example, rather than by outright seizure and confiscation of property. Gradualists suppose that by indirection and step by step the object of socialism will eventually be obtained. It is also known as evolutionary socialism.

Graduated Income Tax—a tax in which the rate increases as income rises. It is also known as a progressive tax. Those with higher incomes not only pay more taxes but also a higher percentage than those with lower incomes.

Grand Army of the Republic—(G.A.R.)—an organization of Union veterans after the Civil War. They were politically quite influential, sought to get benefits for their members, and to never let the nation forget that Confederates had been rebels and traitors.

Insurgents—those involved in an uprising or rebellion. They may be rebels in a civil war, but the term is also used more figuratively to describe any group trying to overturn any established order. For example, Progressives elected to office from around 1906 to 1910 were dubbed Insurgents in the Republican Party because they wanted to replace the Old Guard that was in power.

Insurrection—a rebellion or uprising against the established government.

Interlocking Directorates—occur when one or more directors of a corporation also serve on the boards of other corporations. When key men serve on a number of boards of companies in the same business they might conceivably effectively control an industry. Reformers did not have to have actual wrongdoing to proscribe interlocking directorates where they could.

Irreconcilables—those members of the Senate who would not be reconciled in any way to United States membership in the League of Nations. They joined with either of the other groupings of Senators to vote against joining with or without reservations.

Kulak—a Russian farmer with small landholdings and income. Stalin met resistance from them during the forced collectivization of agriculture in the late 1920s and early 1930s. They were brutally crushed and millions of them died. Kulaks were described in Soviet literature as if they had been wealthy landlords who took advantage of the peasants, when in fact they were the next thing to peasants themselves.

Labor Theory of Value—the theory that all the value in goods is produced by labor. Karl Marx made this the cornerstone of his claim that workers were being exploited (taken advantage of) by their employers. It also provided a sort of theoretical basis for the allegation that the rich were getting richer and the poor poorer.

Missing Link—a convenient notion for evolutionists when they come across species so remote from the one most nearly similar to them. There must be a missing link, or missing links that, if discovered, would make the evolution from one species to another more plausible. Such links are imaginary unless or until they are discovered.

Mobilization—to assemble a military force for action, as in calling up reserves or concentrating forces along the border of another nation. It is ominous when the armies of a country are mobilized and a threat to the peace, for it signals the likelihood that the country is preparing an invasion.

Monetarism—the claim that a certain amount of money is necessary for the effective operation of an economy. Rather than allowing prices to adjust to the money supply, the monetarist seeks to maintain prices at some level by adjusting the money supply. Monetarists usually favor an inflation of the currency.

Monism—the belief that there is only one level or order of reality. Dualism is the counter belief that there are two or more levels of reality. Materialism is a monistic belief, for example, because it holds that all reality is composed of matter. Monism has been widespread in the 19th and 20th centuries.

Natural Selection—the belief that a selective process occurs in nature. Darwin made this central to his explanation of the evolution of species. A related belief is that in the struggle for survival the superior (or fittest) of a species tend to survive. Hence the idea that progress occurs naturally.

New Economic Policy (NEP)—a policy instituted by Lenin in 1921. It restored some measure of freedom to the economy, allowing small traders, manufacturers, and farmers to trade and produce privately.

New Nationalism—a phrase used to describe Theodore Roosevelt's program in the campaign of 1912. It called for the assertion of the power of the national government over the economy. The government was conceived as the collective organ of the people and the President as the leader and spokesman. The idea took hold, but Roosevelt lost in his bid for the presidency.

Panacea—a cure-all for whatever is supposed to ail a society or country. The single tax, for example, was a panacea.

Pragmatism—a philosophy, or substitute for philosophy, which gained sway in the 20th century. The basic idea was that such truth as an idea contained could be measured by the result of putting it to the test of action. Principles, theories, and the wisdom of the past were reckoned to be of no account unless they got the desired results.

Protectorate—a weak country placed under the protection of a strong one. In the settlements after World War I, a number of newly freed colonies were made pro-

tectorates of victorious nations. This was done on the basis that these countries were too unstable or too weak to protect themselves and needed a protector. The condition of a protectorate was expected to be a part way station between colony and independence under international guidance.

Progressivism—an ideology and political movement in the early 20th century. It was an attempt to associate the idea of progress with reform measures in such a way as to make the expanded role of government appear to be progressive.

Provisional Government—a government formed to act in the interval between the fall of a government and the adoption of a new constitution. Russia had a provisional government between the time of the abdication of Czar Nicholas II and the Bolshevik takeover.

Putsch—in German, a small or minor uprising or revolt. By its limited nature, it does not succeed in ruling for more than a brief period, if at all.

Rediscount—to discount a promissory note again. When a loan is made the lender may discount it, that is, take his interest in advance out of the amount of the loan. He may, in turn, sell the note, and it would be discounted once again. Federal Reserve banks are authorized to rediscount certain kinds of notes, thus expanding the loan capacity of banks.

Reform Darwinism—a reform theory built on the view that man has reached a stage in evolution in which he can take over the direction of social development by acting with others collectively. This provided a position within Darwinism for those favoring a gradual or evolutionary movement toward socialism.

Reichstag—the popularly elected branch of the German parliament in the 1920s and early 1930s. Its members were named by parties and seats apportioned upon party vote in general elections. Governments were formed—the chancellor and his cabinet from the Reichstag.

Relativism—the view that the validity of statements is relative to time and place and the outlook of the person who makes it. There are no universal truths, in this view, because everything is always undergoing change.

Rote Learning—a process of learning by memorization and repetition. Progressives in education denounced "rote learning," and sought to replace it with class discussion and activity.

Scientific Socialism—a phrase used by Karl Marx to distinguish the socialism he advanced from other varieties, usually denounced as utopian. Marx claimed that the coming of socialism was inevitable, but that it would come in each country when conditions were right. The science of which he spoke was supposed to be the result of the systematic study of historical trends.

Scientism—an ideology or faith in science itself. Science tends to get "thingified," as if it were something separable from the men and their theories by which scientific positions are formed. Those who accept scientism, whether they are aware of it or not, tend to accept science as ultimate authority and absolute truth.

Secular Humanism—the view that man is wholly human and has only a human destiny. In this view, there is no hereafter for which man should be preparing himself and that such justice as there ever is will be obtained here on earth. Secular humanists work to order society on these premises.

Segregation—to set apart from the rest. It usually refers to racial segregation in American history. Such segregation is ordinarily legally imposed (may be distinguished thereby from social separation) and defines those situations and activities in which those of different races are to be separated from or use different facilities.

Sharecropping—an arrangement by which a landlord provides the land, equipment, and housing for a tenant farmer; the crops the tenant produces are then divided equally between the landlord and tenant. This became a widespread practice in the South after the slaves were freed, though whites as well as Blacks might be sharecroppers.

Single Tax—an idea attributed to Henry George, the author of *Progress and Poverty*. George claimed that the produce of land—that part that does not come by way of labor or capital—belongs to society rather than indvidual owners. He thought that such "unearned income" ought to be taxed for the general welfare, and that the single tax would be sufficient to provide for the expenses of government.

Social Gospel—a movement to use the power of government to make over society in accord with Christian ideals. Most commonly, the social gospel was socialistic in tendency, opposed private ownership of capital, the free market, and favored government regulation and control. It began to have a considerable impact on some of the major denominations by the early 20th century.

Stalwarts—a faction within the Republican Party in the 1870s and 1880s. Stalwarts stood by the party organization and were little interested in creating an appointive civil service.

Subsidiary Coins—metal coins used to facilitate the making of small purchases and change. Nickels and pennies were subsidiary coins in the United States when the basic coins were silver or gold. The larger denominations of silver and gold coins were supposed to have silver or gold content equal to their face value. Subsidiary coins have only their named (or nominal) value.

Summum Bonum—the greatest or highest good. It is best applied to the belief that some one thing is the chief good, and ranks far above all other goods.

Syndicalism—a variety of socialism advanced in France. It was based on trade union dominance of the society.

Sweat Shop—a phrase first applied to a factory or workshop in which workers were paid by the piece for what they produced. Nowadays, it is used to refer to any non-unionized shop, especially those where the pay is low and the work rules are hard on workers.

Totalitarianism—a system in which the government is unrestricted in the use of power and intrudes its power into as many aspects of the lives of the people as it chooses. Examples of totalitarian systems are: the Soviet Union, Communist China, Nazi Germany, and Castro's Cuba.

Trade Union—a union made up of those pursuing a particular trade, such as carpenters, plumbers, and brickmasons. The American Federation of Labor was originally composed mostly of trade unions. The phrase is sometimes used, especially by the British, as a synonym for labor union.

Trust—in common usage, a corporation formed for the purpose of controlling an industry, though the word means basically something held in trust for another. John D. Rockefeller devised an organization which held in trust stock of several corporations, which enabled him to manage a large portion of the oil industry. Thereaf-

ter, the word "trust" came to be applied to all large corporations with control of a large portion of an industry, though they were not technically trusts.

Ultimatum—a final statement of terms by one nation to another by which relations between the two can be maintained. If the other nation should reject those terms, the result would almost certainly be a diplomatic break, if not a declaration of war.

Wall Street—a street in New York City where many banking and investment firms are located. The phrase has long been used as a synonym for the financial dominance of that city and of what socialists like to call finance capitalism.

White Primary—a party primary election in which voting was restricted to whites. The Democratic Party in most Southern states established white primaries in the early 20th century, to keep blacks from voting in what generally came to be the deciding election for state offices.

Suggestions for Additional Reading

The research and writing of history was well on its way to becoming an established academic discipline in the latter part of the 19th century. While many have continued to write history who were untrained in the discipline in the graduate schools of universities, the interpretation of American history has been increasingly dominated by academic historians. As history gained sway in the academies, traditional philosophy lost much of its hold. In its wake come a flood of ideologies which dominated the interpretation of history: Marxism, Darwinism, socialism, Progressivism, and others. If all those which had some influence were listed, it might suggest a greater diversity of interpretation than has generally been the case. In general, however, there have been some dominant strains in the interpretation, most of which are biases, and which readers of these histories need to be aware. History writing becomes increasingly secular in its orientation; those writing from the 1920s onward often had an anti-American bias; the anti-capitalistic mentality, as Ludwig von Mises called it, has been widespread; and those writing about America have most often shared what is now called the liberal outlook. That does not mean that works affected by bias may not be quite valuable, but the reader needs to be aware of that bias so that he may discount it.

The story of American industrial growth in the latter part of the 19th century has been most often distorted by what is described above as the anti-capitalist mentality. A general antidote to this attitude can be found in Friedrich A. Hayek, ed., *Capitalism and the Historians*. The general histories have to be read with care, but there is much to be learned from Allan Nevins, *The Emergence of Modern America*, and, though Ida M. Tarbell is usually identified with the muckrakers in her *History of the Standard Oil Company*, her volume on *The Nationalizing of Business* is generally fair. The works by E. C. Kirkland on the subject, *The Coming of the Industrial Age* and *Industry Comes of Age*, are generally well balanced. Anyone wishing to examine the more vitriolic attacks on businessmen during this period can find them in Matthew Josephson, *The Robber Barons* and Henry D. Lloyd, *Wealth Against Commonwealth*. A good counterpoint to such things can be found in thorough biographies of businessmen or stories of particular businesses, such as, Allan Nevins, *Study in Power: John D. Rockefeller*, in two volumes; Albro Martin, *James J. Hill: The Opening of the Northwest*; and R. W. Fogel, *The Union Pacific Railroad*. For the coming of manufacturing to the South, see C. Vann Woodward, *Origins of the New South*.

Naturalism has most often been dealt with as a literary movement in America, and most histories do not treat the movement whole in this fashion. For a good introduction to the characters involved with the development and spread of Darwinian evolution, see William Irvine, *Apes, Angels and Victorians*. Jacques Barzun provides a more critical view of Darwin's theories in *Darwin, Marx, Wagner*. The impact of Darwinism on America is the theme of Stow Persons, ed., *Evolutionary Thought in America*. Richard Hofstadter focused on the social application, particularly what has come to be called Conservative Darwinism in *Social Darwinism in American Thought*. Primary essays can be found in Perry Miller, ed., *American Thought: Civil War to World War I*.

The New Immigration is described in Oscar Handlin, *The Uprooted*, Peter Roberts, *New Immigration*, and John Higham, *Strangers in the Land*. The radicalism of emancipated Jews is covered by Nathaniel Weyl, *The Jew in American Politics*. For a concise discussion of revolutionary and evolutionary socialism, see Clarence B. Carson, *The World in the Grip of an Idea*, chs. 2 and 3. Bertram D. Wolfe provides an in depth examination of *Marxism*, and David McCord Wright explores his economic and historical fallacies in *The Trouble with Marx*. The movement for reform in America in the late 19th and into the 20th century is described in the following: Eric F. Goldman, *Rendezvous with Destiny*; Richard Hofstadter, *The Age of Reform*; Clarence B. Carson, *The Fateful Turn*; Daniel Aaron, *Men of Good Hope*. For the English Fabians, see A. M. McBriar, *Fabian Socialism and English Politics*. The standard work on Populism has long been John D. Hicks, *The Populist Revolt*. A competent work on labor unions is Philip Taft, *Organized Labor in American History*.

American acquisition of overseas possessions is described in H.W. Morgan, *America's Road to Empire* and J.W. Pratt, *Expansionists of 1898*. Roosevelt's contribution to Progressivism is covered in George E. Mowry, *The Era of Theodore Roosevelt*. An excellent history of the social gospel is Charles H. Hopkins, *The Rise of the Social Gospel in American Protestantism*. Progressive education and its impact on the schools is at the center of Lawrence H. Cremin, *The Transformation of the School* and John H. Snow and Paul W. Shafer, *The Turning of the Tides*. William E. Leuchtenburg's editions of *The New Nationalism* and *The New Freedom* provide primary source material on these subjects. Henry F. Pringle did a thorough biography in *The Life and Times of William Howard Taft*. The beginning of a major change in America in the pre-World War I years is the subject of Henry F. May, *The End of American Innocence*. Arthur S. Link, *Woodrow Wilson and the Progressive Era* and *Wilson: The New Freedom* details the domestic reform and Latin American intervention of the early Wilson presidency.

For America's entry into World War I, see Walter Millis, *Road to War* and Charles C. Tansill, *America Goes to War*. There is a general account of American involvement in the war in Frederick L. Paxson, *American Democracy and the World War* in 2 volumes. Preston W. Slosson focuses more on the home front in *The Great Crusade and After*. The propaganda effort by the United States is described in James R. Mock and Cedric Larson, *Words that Won the War*. On the military side, Edward M. Coffman, *The War to End All Wars: The American Military Experience in World War I*. The industrial effort is treated in Bernard M. Baruch, *American Industry in War*. American involvement in the peace settlements is described in Thomas A. Bailey, *Woodrow Wilson and the Lost Peace* and Herbert C. Hoover, *The Ordeal of Woodrow Wilson*.

The Bolshevik Revolution is studied in Bertram D. Wolfe, *Three Who Made a Revolution*; Edmund Wilson, *To the Finland Station*; Robert C. Tucker, *The Marxian Revolution*; Robert Payne, *The Life and Death of Lenin*. For the general impact of revolution on the people, see Eugene Lyon, *Worker's Paradise Lost*. Robert Conquest, *The Great Terror*, describes the terrorizing of the population. Italian Fascism is the subject of Herman Finer, *Mussolini's Italy* and Herbert W. Schneider, *Making the Fascist State*. Nazi Germany is depicted in a variety of ways in Alan L. Bullock, *Hitler: A Study in Tyranny*; Albert Speer, *Inside the Third Reich*; Stephen H. Roberts, *The House That Hitler Built*; William L. Shirer, *The Rise and Fall of the Third Reich*.

General works on the 1920s, scholarly and otherwise, include: William E. Leuchtenburg, *The Perils of Prosperity*; Frederick L. Allen, *Only Yesterday*; George H. Soule, *Prosperity Decade*; John D. Hicks, *Republican Ascendancy*. For the credit expansion which set the stage for the coming of the depression, see Murray Rothbard, *America's Great Depression*. Benjamin Gitlow provided a revealing account of American Communist activity in the 1920s in *The Whole of Their Lives*. The most balanced account of the Harding presidency to date is Robert K. Murray, *The Harding Era*. On Coolidge, it is D. R. McCoy, *Calvin Coolidge: The Quiet President*.

Index